THE COMFORTER

by Brian J. Bailey

Edited by Paul and Betsy Caram

Printed in the United States of America

Printed by:

Swyers Printing
Four Centre Drive
Quaker Centre
Orchard Park, NY 14127

For further information or
additional copies contact:

Zion Christian Publishers
7436 Starville Road
Marine City, MI 48039

Phone (810) 765-5560
Fax (810) 765-4531

ISBN # 0 - 9643924 - 1 - 0

Dedication

This book is reverentially dedicated to the Holy Trinity, trusting that in some small way it faithfully portrays the life, work and ministry of the blessed Holy Spirit.

In so doing, my prayer is that the Father, the Son, our Lord and Savior Jesus Christ, and the Comforter who is the Holy Spirit, will receive glory.

ACKNOWLEDGMENTS

We wish to extend our thanks to all the following:

To Claudia, Rebeca, and Raquel Molina—for their meticulous attention to detail involved in the final stages of the compilation of this book.

To Brian Alarid—for his diligence behind the computer while he assisted in the editing and formatting of the manuscript of this book.

To Sandra Higman and Joyce Walcott —for transcribing numerous teachings on the Holy Spirit used in the content of this book.

To Mary Humphreys—for her skill in handling the grammar and sentence structure of this book, and her willingness to take time out of her busy schedule.

To Leslie Sigsby, Jessica Sparger, Sharon Miller and Lois Kropf—for their superb "final touches" in the proofreading of this book.

To Pastor Joe Cilluffo—for his beautiful drawing of the front cover.

Table of Contents

PREFACE

We have chosen as the title of our book "The Comforter," because this is the primary ministry of the Holy Spirit. As the Lord Jesus took His last journey upon earth from the upper room to Gethsemane, He said to His disciples, "It is expedient for you that I go away, for if I go not away, the Comforter will not come unto you; but if I depart, I will send him unto you" (Jn. 16:7).

This beloved Comforter is always with us to encourage and strengthen us in our life's journey from earth to heaven. He will guide us into all truth, and He will show us things to come in our lives, as well as those things that will occur among the nations and the Church.

This book is presented with the hope that you will experience and know the Holy Spirit as the one who enables you to be born again, the one who endues you with power from on high when you are baptized with the Holy Spirit, and the one who anoints you for service.

Brian J. Bailey

Part One

THE PERSON OF THE HOLY SPIRIT

The Trinity

A. Seven Aspects of the Person of the Holy Spirit
B. His Membership in the Godhead
C. The Symbols of the Holy Spirit
D. The Names of the Holy Spirit

THE TRINITY

The God of all the universe, the only true God whom we serve, consists of three distinct, separate Persons. These three Persons are God the Father, God the Son (the Lord Jesus Christ), and God the Holy Spirit. Although They are three Persons, we must understand that They are only *one* God, not three gods in one person. The Godhead is revealed as plural in Genesis 1:26, where the Lord said, "Let *us* make man in *our* image." From the very beginning of God's Word, in the first chapter of the Bible, the Lord makes it clear that there are three Persons in the Godhead.

God the Father is called the Ancient of Days (Dan. 7:9,13), and the Majesty on High (Heb. 1:3). He is usually viewed as sitting upon the throne (Dan. 7:9, Rev. 5:6-7). He is the source and origin of everything. Out from Him came two other persons who always existed in Him. The Father has a form and shape like the Son, but He is a spirit (see Jn. 5:37, 4:24). God the Son, the Lord Jesus Christ, is the Jehovah of the Old Testament. He is the One, not God the Father, who appeared to Abraham, Moses, and the other prophets. He looks just like the Father, only younger.

The Lord Jesus could say to Philip in John 14:9, "He that hath seen me hath seen the Father." They look identical to each other. The Son is the "express image of the Father" (Heb. 1:3), but the Father appears a little older. The Son has a tangible, human body, for He is the physical expression of the Godhead, and it is He who rules and administrates His Father's kingdom.

The Holy Spirit is also a Person. He is the third Person of the Trinity. He is a separate being who came out from God, although equal with God (see Jn. 15:26). He is a spirit, but He also has a form like the Father and Son. The Holy Spirit is always referred to in the Scriptures as "He" and not "it." He is not just an influence, but a Person. He carries out the commands of the Father and Son, and His primary purpose is to exalt the Son.

The Father, Son, and Holy Ghost are equal. They are essentially the same in character, and They are unified in vision, thought, and purpose. Philippians 2:6 says of Jesus, "Who, being in the form of God, thought it not robbery to be equal with God." In John 5:17 Jesus said, "My Father worketh hitherto, and I work."

The result of this statement can be seen in verse 18. "Therefore the Jews sought the more to kill him, because he not only had broken the sabbath, but said also that God was his Father, *making himself equal with God*." Thus, the Father and Son are clearly equals.

Just before the Lord Jesus went to the cross, He promised that He would send *another* Comforter in His place, which we know is the blessed Holy Spirit (Jn. 14:16, 16:7). (This word *another* in the Greek literally means "another of the same kind.") Only an equal can be sent in someone's stead. Therefore, we can clearly say from the Scriptures that the Father, Son, and Holy Spirit are equal.

However, there are differing degrees of authority in the Godhead. The Father is supreme. He is the greatest in position and authority. The Son made this very clear in John 14:28, where He said, "My Father is greater [in authority and position] than I." The Son and the Holy Spirit are in submission to the Father's will. Jesus said to His Father, "Not my will, but thine be done." The Son is the heir of all His Father's estate, and the Father has given all things into His hands (see Heb. 1:2, Jn. 3:35, 13:3). His desire is to make us co-heirs with Him.

The Lord Jesus will inherit all the kingdoms of this world (Rev. 11:15). He rules His Father's kingdom with the help of the Holy Spirit. In the Millennium, the Son will physically rule on earth in person. However, He will still be in submission to His Father. First Corinthians 15:28 makes this truth clear: "And when all things shall be subdued unto him, then shall the Son also himself be subject unto him that put all things under him, that God may be all in all." The Holy Spirit, likewise, only does what the Father tells Him to do (Jn. 16:13). The Trinity works together in perfect unison and harmony to run the universe.

The Trinity Revealed in Scripture

The Trinity can be seen in many places in Scripture. We will now look at just a few of them. In the creation, God the Father gave the commandment for the earth to be created and to take its form. He did all this by the Son, who *proclaimed* the words of His Father (Heb. 1:2, Eph. 3:9, Col. 1:16). Yet it was the Holy Spirit who moved upon the face of the earth, and caused everything to come into existence and order (Gen. 1:2-3).

These three members of the Godhead can also be seen in the incarnation of Christ. The Father prepared a human body in the womb of Mary for His Son Jesus through the agency of the Holy Spirit (see Heb. 10:5). Luke 1:32-35 says: "He shall be great, and shall be called the Son of the Highest: and the Lord God shall give unto him the throne of his father David… And the angel said unto [Mary], The Holy Ghost shall come upon thee, and the power of the Highest shall overshadow thee: therefore also that holy thing which shall be born of thee shall be called the Son of God."

Here the Father is spoken of as the *Highest* and also the *Lord God*. Jesus is called the *Son of the Highest*, and the Holy Spirit is referred to as the *Holy Ghost*. Thus, we see clearly in the Holy Scriptures the irrefutable evidence of the three members of the Godhead.

The Father, the Son, and the Holy Spirit are seen again at the baptism of Jesus in the Jordan River. "And Jesus, when he was baptized, went up straightway out of the water: and, lo, the heavens were opened unto him, and he saw the Spirit of God descending like a dove, and lighting upon him: And lo a voice from heaven, saying, This is my beloved Son, in whom I am well pleased" (Mt. 3:16-17). While the Son was standing in the river being baptized, the Holy Spirit came upon Him in the form of a dove, and the Father spoke from heaven saying He was well pleased with His Son.

The Trinity is also depicted in the water baptismal formula given by the Lord Jesus in Matthew 28:19: "Go ye therefore, and teach all nations, baptizing them in the name of the Father, and of the Son, and of the Holy Ghost." Paul made this very clear when he rhetorically asked the Corinthians if he had baptized any of them in his own name (see 1 Cor. 1:12-15). Of course, Paul had not baptized any in his own name! They were all baptized in the name of the Father, the Son, and the Holy Ghost.

The Trinity is revealed through the crucifixion as well. Paul said in Hebrews 9:14, "How much more shall the blood of Christ, who through the eternal Spirit offered himself without spot to God, purge your conscience from dead works to serve the living God?" The Son of God went to the cross in the enabling power of the Holy Spirit that was with Him, offering Himself without spot unto His Father.

The Father raised Christ from the dead through the agency of the Holy Spirit. Romans 8:11 gives us the scriptural evidence of this fact: "But if the Spirit of him that raised up Jesus from the dead dwell in you, he that raised up Christ from the dead shall also quicken your mortal bodies by his Spirit that dwelleth in you." Paul repeats this truth in Romans 6:4: "Therefore we are buried with him by baptism into death: that like as Christ was raised up from the dead by the glory of the Father, even so we also should walk in newness of life." It is this same Spirit that will raise up the saints on resurrection day.

A beautiful portrait of the Trinity is seen at the martyrdom of Stephen. Acts 7:55-56 says of Stephen, "But he, being full of the Holy Ghost, looked up steadfastly into heaven, and saw the glory of God, and Jesus standing on the right hand of God, And said, Behold, I see the heavens opened, and the Son of man standing on the right hand of God." Here Stephen, full of the Holy Spirit, had his eyes opened to see the Son standing at the right hand of the Father. He was waiting to receive him into heaven. Normally, Christ is *seated* at the right hand of God, but here He is *standing* to welcome one of His choice saints.

The three members of the Godhead are also seen in heaven: "And I beheld, and, lo, in the midst of the throne and of the four beasts, and in the midst of the elders, stood a Lamb as it had been slain, having seven horns and seven eyes, which are the seven Spirits of God sent forth into all the earth. And he came and took the book out of the right hand of him that sat upon the throne" (Rev. 5:6-7).

When John the Beloved saw a book in heaven that was sealed, he wept because no man was found worthy to open this book. However, then the Lamb of God, the Lord Jesus, prevailed to open the book and He took the book out of the right hand of God the Father who was sitting upon His throne. The Lamb is revealed as having seven eyes, which are the seven Spirits of God. This is the Holy Spirit that rested on Christ. Thus, the Trinity is clearly revealed in the Scriptures.

The Trinity Revealed in Scripture

1. In creation
2. In the incarnation of Christ
3. In the baptism of Jesus
4. In the baptismal formula
5. In the crucifixion
6. In the resurrection of Jesus and every believer
7. In the martyrdom of Stephen
8. In heaven

In Second Corinthians 13:14 there is an apostolic benediction given by the Apostle Paul that helps us see the Trinity: "The grace of the Lord Jesus Christ, and the love of God, and the communion [or fellowship] of the Holy Ghost, be with you all. Amen."

Paul speaks of the grace of the Lord Jesus Christ, the love of God the Father, and the communion of the Holy Ghost. How can we have communion or fellowship with an influence? Obviously, we cannot. Thus, the Holy Spirit is a person, and He longs for those with whom He can fellowship, and with whom He can share His most intimate feelings and desires.

As we have already mentioned, the Son looks just like the Father. The only difference is that the Father's appearance is a little older. In the same manner, the Holy Spirit also has a form. It would be rare, however, for a person to have a vision of the Holy Spirit, or to actually see Him. Nonetheless, we can fellowship with Him because we were made in His image, and He is God. Psalm 103:13 speaks of God the Father who pities (or fondles and touches) us as a father does His children.

Many years ago, I had a vision of God the Father from the back, and in this vision He was gently touching the children in heaven. At times, we may even feel the hand of the Lord Jesus Christ upon us. I have felt the Lord's hand upon me on a number of occasions. In the same way, we can also feel the Holy Spirit covering us and anointing us, and we can have fellowship with Him. This is a tremendous privilege and honor. Let us not take it lightly.

We should pray to the Holy Spirit just as we pray to God the Father and to the Lord Jesus. Why? Because He is the third

Person of the Godhead. The Holy Spirit must become a reality to us. We need to become dependent upon Him and conscious of His presence at all times. Every born-again, Spirit-filled believer should feel the need to draw closer to the Holy Spirit. In essence, that is the purpose of this book.

A. SEVEN ASPECTS OF THE PERSON OF THE HOLY SPIRIT

The Holy Spirit is not simply a force or an influence, but rather an individual who has all the attributes and qualities associated with a distinct personage. If we are to understand the importance of the third member of the Godhead, we must examine these attributes. Therefore, we are now going to consider seven aspects of the person of the Holy Spirit.

1. He has a mind

The Apostle Paul stated in Romans 8:27 that He who "searches the hearts knows what is *the mind of the Spirit*, because he makes intercession for the saints according to the will of God." From this scripture we understand that the Holy Spirit has a mind. A mind is not associated with an influence. It is one of the key attributes of a person.

The apostles declared in Acts 15:28, "*For it seemed good to the Holy Ghost*, and to us, to lay upon you no greater burden than these necessary things." In this situation in Acts chapter 15, the Holy Spirit was making His mind and thoughts clearly known to the apostles regarding the ordinances the Gentiles should observe. Thus, we have a good example here of the mind of the Spirit.

2. He has a will

When making reference to the distribution of the nine gifts of the Holy Spirit in First Corinthians 12:11, the Apostle Paul says, "But all these [are the work of one and the same Spirit] dividing to every man severally as he *will.*" Therefore, the Holy Spirit also has a will. It is the Holy Spirit who decides which gifts we should have, and He divides several gifts to each believer as He wills.

3. He has feelings

The Holy Spirit also has emotions and feelings. Paul wrote to the Ephesian believers, "And *grieve not the holy Spirit of God*, whereby ye are sealed unto the day of redemption" (Eph. 4:30). Isaiah 63:10 speaks of the rebellious Israelites who *vexed* the Holy Spirit. If we disobey the Lord and do things that are displeasing to Him, we bring grief to the Holy Spirit.

At times we can feel the grief we have caused Him, for the Holy Spirit has the ability to communicate His feelings to our hearts. Also, the Holy Spirit is very compassionate, for He seeks to produce love and all of His other fruits in our lives (see Gal. 5:22-23).

4. He can be lied to

As a person, the Holy Spirit can be lied to. Peter said to Ananias in Acts 5:3, "Why hath Satan filled thine heart *to lie to the Holy Ghost*, and to keep back part of the price of the land?" We cannot lie to an influence; we can only lie to a person. In John 16:7-15, the Holy Spirit is referred to as "He" or "Him" twelve times. He is never referred to as "it" in the original Scriptures.

5. He can be blasphemed

The Lord Jesus declared in Matthew 12:31-32: "All manner of sin and blasphemy shall be forgiven unto men: but the *blasphemy against the Holy Ghost* shall not be forgiven unto men. And whosoever speaketh a word against the Son of man, it shall be forgiven him: but whosoever speaketh against the Holy Ghost, it shall not be forgiven him, neither in this world, neither in the world to come."

In this passage Christ placed the Holy Spirit on the same level as Himself. He said that those who blaspheme the Holy Ghost will not be forgiven. Thus, the Holy Spirit, as a person, can be blasphemed just as the Son of God can be blasphemed. Blasphemy of the Holy Spirit occurs when one attributes the works of the Holy Spirit to the devil, knowing in one's heart that these works are actually of the Holy Spirit.

6. He can speak

The Holy Spirit has the ability to speak; a force or an influence does not. As recorded in Acts chapter 10, Peter received a vision that clearly revealed to him that the Gentiles were accepted by God. As he was meditating upon this vision, he heard someone speak to him: "*The Spirit said unto him*, Behold, three men seek thee. Arise therefore, and get thee down, and go with them, doubting nothing: for I have sent them" (Acts 10:19-20). Speaking is the action of a person. I want to repeat this—the Holy Spirit is not an "it" but a "He."

This truth about the Holy Spirit's ability to speak is also revealed in the book of Revelation. John concluded each message to the seven churches of Asia with this phrase: "He that hath an ear, let him hear *what the Spirit saith* unto the churches" (cf. Rev. 2:7, 2:11, 2:17, 2:29, 3:6, 3:13, 3:22). We can hear the Holy Spirit speaking to us if we have listening ears, and if we have ears that are attentive to Him. Therefore, we need our spiritual ears opened more and more.

7. He can be insulted and quenched

The Holy Spirit can be insulted, just as the Lord Jesus can be insulted. In Hebrews 10:29 we read, "Of how much sorer punishment, suppose ye, shall he be thought worthy, who hath [trampled] under foot the Son of God, and hath counted the blood of the covenant, wherewith he was sanctified, an unholy thing, and hath [insulted] the Spirit of grace?"

The Holy Spirit can be insulted by our actions and words. If we turn back to our old ways after we have known the Lord as our Savior, we insult the Holy Spirit. Furthermore, Paul tells us in First Thessalonians 5:19, "Quench not the Spirit." These seven points of the person of the Holy Spirit offer overwhelming evidence and proof that the Holy Spirit is indeed a person, and not simply an influence.

Seven Aspects of the Person of the Holy Spirit

1. He has a mind
2. He has a will
3. He has feelings
4. He can be lied to
5. He can be blasphemed
6. He can speak
7. He can be insulted and quenched

B. HE IS A MEMBER OF THE GODHEAD

As we said earlier, the Holy Spirit is a member of the Godhead. As such, He has all the qualities and characteristics of the other two members of the Trinity—the Father and the Son. There are many proofs in the Holy Scriptures that the Holy Spirit is a member of the Godhead, but we are only going to look at six of them.

1. He is Eternal

One of the characteristics of the Godhead is that They are eternal (see Psa. 90:2, 1 Tim. 1:17). They had no beginning, and They have no ending. Jesus was, and is, and is to come (Rev. 1:4). In Hebrews 9:14 the Apostle Paul writes, "How much more shall the blood of Christ, who through the *eternal Spirit* offered himself without spot to God, purge your conscience from dead works to serve the living God?"

Therefore, Scripture clearly states that the Holy Spirit is eternal. It is also clear that He has the same characteristics as the other two members of the Godhead.

2. He is Omnipresent

Another attribute of the Godhead is that They are omnipresent. They can be everywhere at once. In Jeremiah 23:24 the Lord asks: "Can any hide himself in secret places that I shall not see him? saith the Lord. Do not I fill heaven and earth? saith the Lord." God fills heaven and earth. Jesus will be seen by everyone around the world at His second coming (Rev.1:7, Mt. 24:30). The Holy Spirit is also omnipresent. He has the ability to be everywhere at the same time.

In Psalm 139:7 King David asks this question: "Whither shall I go from thy spirit? or whither shall I flee from thy presence?" Then he continues: "If I ascend up into heaven, thou art there: if I make my bed in hell, behold, thou art there. If I take the wings of the morning, and dwell in the uttermost parts of the sea; Even there shall thy hand lead me, and thy right hand shall hold me" (Psa. 139:8-10).

God directs the affairs of hell, as well as the affairs of heaven. People who have had visions of hell confirm this. King David was aware that it did not matter where he went because the Holy Spirit is everywhere. He felt the presence of the Holy Spirit with him at all times. Therefore, if we walk in the light, we can be assured that the Holy Spirit will always be with us regardless of where we go.

3. He is Omnipotent

Like the other two members of the Godhead, the Holy Spirit is omnipotent, or all-powerful. The angel of the Lord said to Mary in Luke 1:35, "The Holy Ghost shall come upon thee, and the power of the Highest shall overshadow thee: therefore also that holy thing which shall be born of thee shall be called the Son of God." The Holy Spirit is called "the power of the Highest," for He possesses all power.

The Lord Jesus declared in Matthew 28:18, just before He ascended into heaven, "All power is given unto me in heaven and in earth." From these scriptures we see that Christ was anointed, empowered, and energized by the Holy Spirit during His three and a half year ministry upon earth. All power was given unto Him by the Father, through the agency of the Holy Spirit. Because the Holy Spirit is omnipotent, even as Christ, He is clearly a member of the Godhead. The Lord spoke to Zerubbabel in Zechariah 4:6-7 that it would not be by the force or power of man that he would finish the temple and prevail against the Persian Empire which was hindering him from completing it. Instead, the work of building the temple would be completed by the tremendous power of the Holy Spirit. The Holy Spirit is all powerful! He is able to overcome the hindrances and obstacles of all the nations of the earth.

Many times in Scripture the Lord chides His people for not looking to Him for their deliverance when an opposing army came against them. He rebuked Hezekiah for sending ambassadors to Egypt for help against the Assyrian army that was advancing against Jerusalem (see Isa. 31:1-5, 36:6). It is the power of the omnipotent Holy Spirit that we should trust in at all times!

4. He is Omniscient

Another divine attribute of the Holy Spirit is that He is omniscient, or all-knowing. The Apostle Paul stated in First Corinthians 2:9-11: "As it is written [in Isaiah 64:4], Eye hath not seen, nor ear heard, neither have entered into the heart of man, the things which God hath prepared for them that love him. But God hath revealed them unto us by his Spirit: for the Spirit searcheth all things, yea, the deep things of God. For what man knoweth the things of a man, save the spirit of man which is in him? even so the things of God knoweth no man, but the Spirit of God."

Man is a spirit. He is a spirit living in a physical body. We can only really know a person when we know his spirit. By grace, we are capable of understanding the spirit of others because we are also a spirit. In like manner, the Holy Spirit understands the

Father because the Holy Spirit is divine. The Holy Spirit comprehends all things that pertain to God and man. Therefore, whenever we need to know something, we should ask the Holy Spirit to reveal it to us. One of His ministries is to reveal the things of the Father and Son unto us.

5. The Holy Spirit is Called God and Lord

Through the Scriptures we can see that the Holy Spirit is called God. In the account of Ananias lying to the Holy Ghost, Peter said in Acts 5:3-4: "Ananias, why hath Satan filled thine heart to lie to the *Holy Ghost*,...thou hast not lied unto men, but unto *God*." The Holy Spirit is distinctly called God in this passage.

The Holy Spirit is also called Lord in Second Corinthians 3:16-18: "Nevertheless when [Israel] shall turn to the Lord, the veil shall be taken away. Now the *Lord* is that Spirit: and where the Spirit of the Lord is, there is liberty. But we all, with open face beholding as in a glass the glory of the Lord, are changed into the same image from glory to glory, even as by the Spirit of the Lord." *Lord* is the title of Jesus Christ. Therefore, the Holy Spirit is clearly a member of the Godhead because He is called by the same title as the Son.

6. He is Mentioned as a Member of the Godhead by Christ

The Lord Jesus Christ clearly mentions the Holy Spirit as a member of the Godhead in John 15:26: "But when the Comforter is come, whom I will send unto you from the Father, even the Spirit of truth, which proceedeth from the Father, he shall testify of me." Christ said that He would send someone else to take His place after He left. That replacement was the Holy

Spirit Himself, the third Person of the Trinity (Jn. 16:7). The Holy Spirit came forth from the Father even as the Son.

Six Aspects of the Holy Spirit as a Member of the Godhead

1. He is Eternal
2. He is Omnipresent
3. He is Omnipotent
4. He is Omniscient
5. He is Called God and Lord
6. He is Mentioned as a Member of the Godhead by Christ

C. SYMBOLS OF THE HOLY SPIRIT

The Holy Spirit is represented by many forms and symbols in the Scriptures. He is revealed in the Word of God in a number of different ways, and I would like to consider several of them with you now.

1. The Dove

One of the most common and familiar symbols of the Holy Spirit is the dove. Worldwide, the dove is considered a symbol of peace and the Holy Spirit. When Jesus was baptized, He came up out of the water and "the heavens were opened unto him, and he saw the Spirit of God descending like a dove, and lighting upon him" (Mt. 3:16). John the Baptist testified, "I saw the Spirit descending from heaven like a dove, and it abode upon [Him]" (Jn. 1:32). The dove reveals many of the characteristics of the Holy Spirit. For example, a dove has no gallbladder. Gall, which speaks of bitterness, is not resident within a dove. In the same way, there is no bitterness in the Holy Spirit.

2. Oil

Oil is another symbol of the Holy Spirit. The Lord Jesus was anointed by the Holy Ghost, and since the anointing in the New Testament is by oil, the symbol of the Holy Spirit is also oil. In his sermon to the house of Cornelius, Peter declared that "God anointed Jesus of Nazareth with the Holy Ghost and with power" (Acts 10:38). Christ was anointed by the Holy Spirit.

The Apostle James exhorts the elders of the church to pray for anyone who is sick, "anointing him with oil in the name of the Lord" (Jas. 5:14). Anointing oil was first used by Jacob when he poured oil upon the altar he had erected to the Lord at Bethel (Gen. 28:18-19). As seen in Exodus 30:23-31, the anointing oil was poured over the furniture of the tabernacle and also upon the high priests to consecrate them for service. The Holy Spirit is the One who anoints us as believers.

3. Fire

Another familiar symbol of the Holy Spirit is fire. Hebrews 12:29 says, "For our God is a consuming fire." As seen in Acts 2:3, the first recorded outpouring of the Holy Spirit on the day of Pentecost resulted in cloven tongues like fire coming upon the hundred and twenty assembled in the upper room. "And there appeared unto them cloven tongues like as of fire, and it sat upon each of them."

The disciples were baptized with the Holy Ghost and with fire. This is exactly what John prophesied that the Lord would do: "I indeed baptize you with water unto repentance: but he that cometh after me is mightier than I, whose shoes I am not worthy to bear: he shall baptize you with the Holy Ghost, and with fire" (Mt. 3:11). The baptism of the Holy Spirit is associated not only with the infilling of the Spirit, but also with fire.

I remember my encounter with God when I was baptized in the Holy Ghost in the mountains of England. I had been asking the Lord to baptize me in the Holy Spirit for some time, and I still had not received. Then one time during a holiday period, I went to a seaside resort in England to meet with the Lord. After I had been there for a few days, the Lord told me to take a bus to Dartmoor. So I took my little pocket Bible, and journeyed by bus to the beautiful hills of Dartmoor.

When the bus arrived there, I waited at the bus stop to see where everyone else was going. Then I headed in the opposite direction so that I could be all alone with the Lord. When I found a nice little spot that was secluded and quiet, I began pleading with the Lord again to baptize me in the Holy Ghost. While I was praying, I distinctly heard a voice say to me, "John, John."

I didn't know what to do, so I turned in the pages of my Bible to the gospel of John. My fingers stopped at John 20:22, where it states that the Lord Jesus breathed on His disciples and said, "Receive ye the Holy Ghost." At that moment, something started rolling inside of me, and I began to speak in other tongues. After I was baptized in the Holy Ghost, I could not touch my body for several days because I was extremely hot. It actually felt as if I was literally on fire. Thus, the baptism of the Holy Spirit includes spiritual fire, which is a symbol of the Holy Spirit.

4. Wind

The Holy Spirit is also represented by wind in the Scriptures. On the day of Pentecost, the Holy Spirit filled the place where the disciples were gathered in the form of a mighty wind. Acts 2:2 records this tremendous manifestation of the Holy Spirit: "And suddenly there came a sound from heaven as of a rushing mighty wind, and it filled all the house where they were sitting." In Ezekiel chapter 37 the prophet was commanded to prophesy to the wind, a wind that would breathe upon the slain multitudes. As he prophesied, the winds of the Spirit came and resurrected a whole army.

5. Water

Also associated with the Holy Spirit is water. During the Feast of Tabernacles, Christ stood up in the temple and declared in John 7:37-38: "If any man thirst, let him come unto me, and drink. He that believeth on me, as the scripture hath said, out of his belly shall flow rivers of living water."

Many years after this remarkable speech by Christ when John the Beloved inscribed the words of Jesus in his gospel under the anointing of the Holy Spirit, he interpreted these words of Jesus thusly: "But this spake he of the Spirit, which they that believe on him should receive: for the Holy Ghost was not yet given; because that Jesus was not yet glorified" (Jn. 7:39).

Water is a symbol of the Holy Spirit in the sense that rivers of life should flow out from us after we are baptized in the Holy Ghost. Throughout the canon of Scripture, rain is a constant type of the outpouring of God's Spirit.

6. Light

Another symbol of the Holy Spirit is light. In the holy place of the Tabernacle of Moses, there was a candlestick which had seven candles. This represented the seven Spirits of the Lord. It was this candlestick that gave light to the holy place. Therefore, light is also a type of the Holy Spirit. When we are born-again, light comes into our inner man because of the entrance of the Holy Spirit (2 Cor. 4:6). This light should grow brighter and brighter as we continue to walk with Christ. However, sometimes the light is extinguished when men turn away from God (Rom. 1:21, Mt. 6:22-23).

7. Masculine Pronouns

Throughout Scripture, in both the Old and New Testaments, the Holy Spirit is referred to as a person. Isaiah 40:13 says, "Who hath directed the Spirit of the Lord, or being *his* counsellor hath taught *him*?" In this verse the Divine Spirit is clearly referred to with the masculine pronouns "His" and "Him." The New Testament was written in the Greek language, because throughout the Roman Empire at that time, Greek was the universal language. It was the official language and the language of the common people. The Scriptures from the original Greek help us to understand the person of the Holy Spirit. When the Lord Jesus Christ spoke of the Holy Spirit in John 16:7-8, 13-14, He used the Greek word "ekeinos," which is a masculine pronoun meaning "he." Therefore, the Holy Spirit is like the Father and the Lord Jesus Christ—they all have masculine attributes.

There is a beautiful picture of the Trinity portrayed in the Old Testament through Abraham, his son Isaac, and his servant

Eliezer. Abraham (a type of the Father) had a son of promise, Isaac (a type of Christ), who was the heir of all his possessions. When Abraham was seeking a bride for his son Isaac, he sent Eliezer (a type of the Holy Spirit) to the country of Mesopotamia to choose a bride for Isaac from among his relatives. Today, the Father is selecting a Bride for His Son, the Lord Jesus Christ. The Bride of Christ is, of course, a composite body of faithful believers.

There are qualifications to be a part of the Bride of Christ. Just as Eliezer would not choose just anyone to be the bride of Isaac, so also the Holy Spirit only selects those who have met the qualifications to be the Lord's Bride. Eliezer chose Rebekah because she was industrious and had a servant's heart. She was not only willing to draw water from the well for Eliezer, but also for his camels, which would have taken a very long time. In the same manner, the Holy Spirit is searching the world today for those who will become the Bride of Christ. Through this excellent example in Scripture, we can see that these three godly men clearly reveal that the Trinity is masculine.

Symbols of the Holy Spirit

1. The Dove
2. Oil
3. Fire
4. Wind
5. Water
6. Light
7. Masculine Pronouns

D. THE NAMES OF THE HOLY SPIRIT

One of the primary characteristics of a person is that he or she has a name. This is something every person around the world has in common. The Holy Spirit Himself has many names. These names reveal His character, nature, and ministry. In this section, we are going to consider a few of His principal names that are revealed in the Scriptures.

1. The Spirit of God

One of the names of the Holy Spirit used frequently in the Scriptures is the Spirit of God. He is referred to by this name in the second verse of the Bible in Genesis 1:2: "And the earth was without form, and void; and darkness was upon the face of the deep. And the *Spirit of God* moved upon the face of the waters." He is also called by this name in the New Testament. Paul said to the Corinthian believers, "Know ye not that ye are the temple of God, and that the *Spirit of God* dwelleth in you?" (1 Cor. 3:16).

2. The Spirit of Judgment

Another name of the Holy Spirit is the Spirit of Judgment. The prophet Isaiah declared, "When the Lord shall have washed away the filth of the daughters of Zion, and shall have purged the blood of Jerusalem from the midst thereof by the *spirit of judgment*, and by the spirit of burning" (Isa. 4:4).

As the Spirit of Judgment, the Holy Spirit determines the judgment everyone receives as a punishment for his sins. The Spirit of Judgment brings conviction of sin and convinces men of their needs, but He also gives a door of hope.

3. The Spirit of Burning

The Holy Spirit is also called the Spirit of Burning in Isaiah 4:4: "When the Lord shall have washed away the filth of the daughters of Zion, and shall have purged the blood of Jerusalem from the midst thereof by the spirit of judgment, and by *the spirit of burning*." The Spirit of Burning is the spiritual fire that purifies the Lord's people. If we yield to His dealings in our lives, He will burn up all the dross that is within our hearts (Mt. 3:11-12).

4. The Spirit of Truth

The Spirit of Truth is another title of the Holy Spirit. This is His title in John 14:17. "Even the *Spirit of truth*; whom the world cannot receive, because it seeth him not, neither knoweth him: but ye know him; for he dwelleth with you, and shall be in you." The Lord spoke again of the ministry of the Spirit of Truth in John 16:13, when He said, "He will guide you into all truth: for he shall not speak of himself; but whatsoever he shall hear, that shall he speak: and he will show you things to come." The Holy Spirit is also referred to by this title in John 15:26. The very nature and character of the Holy Spirit is enveloped with truth. Jesus said, "I am...the truth." Truth is a key attribute of the entire Godhead.

5. The Spirit of Life

The Holy Spirit is also called the Spirit of Life. In the last days when the two witnesses come, they will be slain after their three and a half year ministry. When they have lain dead in the streets of Jerusalem for three and a half days, the Spirit of Life will come back into them. It is the Holy Spirit who will revive them and quicken them (Rev. 11:11).

We read the words of the Apostle Paul in Romans 8:2: "For the law of *the Spirit of life* in Christ Jesus hath made me free from the law of sin and death." The Holy Spirit is the One who gives us life, and He gives unto us freedom from sin and death. *Life* is also one of the titles of the Lord Jesus Christ (Jn. 14:6). In Deuteronomy 30:20 we are exhorted to "cleave unto the Lord," for He is our life. Thus, it is the Holy Spirit who imparts true life unto us, and apart from Him we can have no life!

6. The Spirit of Adoption

The Spirit of Adoption is another name of the Holy Spirit. Paul stated in Romans 8:15, "For ye have not received the spirit of bondage again to fear; but ye have received the *Spirit of adoption*, whereby we cry, Abba, Father" (see also Gal. 4:6). The spirit of bondage is from Satan, and it speaks of a habit or sin from which we cannot obtain deliverance. Yet, when we are adopted into the family of God through the Holy Spirit, we are freed from the power of the kingdom of darkness. The Holy Spirit is the Spirit of Adoption.

The adoption ceremony, as practiced in the Roman Empire, was customarily sealed in the presence of seven witnesses. These seven witnesses represent the seven Spirits of God (the Holy Spirit) which bear witness with our spirit that we have been adopted by God. Paul confirmed this in Romans 8:16 when he said, "The Spirit [Himself] beareth witness with our spirit, that we are the children of God."

7. The Holy Spirit of Promise

The Holy Spirit is called the Holy Spirit of Promise in Ephesians 1:13: "In whom ye also trusted, after that ye heard the word of truth, the gospel of your salvation: in whom also after that ye believed, ye were sealed with that *holy Spirit of promise*." God promised that He would send us the Holy Spirit. It is the Holy Spirit who quickens promises to the people of God.

8. The Spirit of Grace

In Hebrews 10:29 the Holy Spirit is called the Spirit of Grace: "Of how much sorer punishment, suppose ye, shall he be thought worthy, who hath [trampled] under foot the Son of God, and hath counted the blood of the covenant, wherewith he was sanctified, an unholy thing, and hath [insulted] the *Spirit of grace*?" The Holy Spirit is the One who imparts the grace of God to us when we are in need of strength (scc Heb. 4:16). Therefore, when a believer grieves the Spirit, he cuts off the flow of grace into his life.

9. The Spirit of Glory

Another name of the Holy Spirit is the Spirit of Glory. Peter encourages us in First Peter 4:14: "If ye be reproached for the name of Christ, happy are ye; for the *spirit of glory* and of God resteth upon you: on their part he is evil spoken of, but on your part he is glorified." This "glory" that enshrouds the saints of God is also a defense against our adversaries (see Isa. 4:5).

10. The Holy Spirit

Finally, the most commonly used name for the third Person of the Trinity is the Holy Spirit. Christ stated in Luke 11:13, "If ye then, being evil, know how to give good gifts unto your children: how much more shall your heavenly Father give the *Holy Spirit* to them that ask him?" King David prayed, "Take not thy

Holy Spirit from me," in Psalm 51:11. The Spirit of God is holy, just as the Father and Son are holy, and He desires to make us holy.

The Names of the Holy Spirit

1. The Spirit of God
2. The Spirit of Judgment
3. The Spirit of Burning
4. The Spirit of Truth
5. The Spirit of Life
6. The Spirit of Adoption
7. The Holy Spirit of Promise
8. The Spirit of Grace
9. The Spirit of Glory
10. The Holy Spirit

In conclusion to Part One, I would just like to say once again that the Holy Spirit is clearly a person. He has all the attributes of a person. Therefore, since we love God the Father and God the Son, let us also come to know intimately and love deeply the third Person of the Trinity, the blessed Holy Spirit!

Part Two

THE MINISTRY OF THE HOLY SPIRIT

In Part Two we are going to consider the different ministries of the Holy Spirit. When man studies theology, he can only do so in a fragmentary way because man cannot totally comprehend an infinite God. This is especially true when we try to analyze the third member of the Godhead, the Holy Spirit. When we make reference to the ministries of the Holy Spirit, we cannot possibly cover every aspect of His ministry and work. Nonetheless, the Scriptures show us a number of clearly delineated titles of the Holy Spirit, which reveal His ministry upon earth among the saints.

1. HE IS THE COMFORTER

Christ revealed one of the ministries of the Holy Spirit when He called Him the Comforter. The Lord said to His disciples in John 14:16-17, "And I will pray the Father, and he shall give you another *Comforter* [of the same kind], that he may abide with you for ever; Even the Spirit of truth; whom the world cannot receive, because it seeth him not, neither knoweth him: but ye know him; for he dwelleth with you, and shall be in you."

One of the primary ministries of the Holy Spirit is that He is the Comforter of the saints. There are, in reality, three Comforters—the Father, Son, and Holy Spirit. A *comforter* means "one who comforts and encourages." The Greek word *parakletos* is translated "comforter." This word has a beautiful connotation from the original language. In New Testament times, it referred to an actual military position in the Roman army. The Roman Empire was renowned for its military greatness and the skill of its highly trained soldiers. Notwithstanding, no matter how good a soldier might have been, there were times when every soldier needed encouragement—especially when he had been marching for hours over rough terrain, and he knew that at the end of that march he would have to meet the enemy. Also, the chances were that he would lose many of his fellow soldiers in battle.

Therefore, to encourage the soldiers in the Roman Empire, the army was ministered to by the *parakletos*. These were men who would walk beside the marching companies. They would shout words of encouragement to the soldiers and sing songs of victory to them as they marched along. They lifted up the arms that were hanging down and they strengthened the knees that were feeble (cf. Heb. 12:12). The *parakletos* (or encouragers) would remind them of past victories and the weaknesses of the enemy. As they spoke to the soldiers of the strength of Rome, they were lifting up their spirits.

Jesus Christ entitled the Holy Spirit the *Parakletos*, or the Comforter. He walks alongside of us through all of life's adverse experiences. Isn't that wonderful to know! Truly, we have no reason to fear, because the Holy Spirit is always there to strengthen us when we feel as if we cannot go on any further. He is always there to remind us of past victories—times when we thought we would lose the battle, and yet we won simply because He was there beside us. The Lord Jesus promised that He would never leave us alone. As we walk on the pathway that He has ordained for our lives, He will cause the Holy Spirit to walk beside us and encourage us. Our Comforter reminds us that the Captain of our salvation has already won the battle and has already overcome the world for us. He encourages us by telling us that we are ordained for victory and that we are more than conquerors through Christ. The Holy Spirit is the One who walks beside us and lifts up our spirits. Be encouraged by this—the blessed Holy Spirit is ever present to comfort us.

2. HE IS THE TEACHER

The Holy Spirit is also the Teacher of the Church. Christ said, "The Comforter, which is the Holy Ghost, whom the Father will send in my name, he shall *teach* you all things, and bring all things to your remembrance, whatsoever I have said unto you" (Jn. 14:26). The Apostle Paul revealed two aspects of the teaching ministry of the Holy Spirit when he said in First Corinthians 2:9-10: "Eye hath not seen, nor ear heard, neither have entered into the heart of man, the things which God hath prepared for them that love him. But God hath *revealed* them unto us by his Spirit: for the Spirit *searcheth* all things, yea, the deep things of God."

The first important aspect of any good teacher is that he must be one who is constantly studying and searching for fresh truth. Likewise, the Holy Spirit is constantly searching out the deep things of God. The Lord is eternal, and He is so vast that there are no boundaries to His knowledge. Paul said in Ephesians 2:7, "That in the ages to come he might show the exceeding riches of his grace in his kindness toward us through Christ Jesus." It will take all of eternity for God to express the riches of His grace to us. One of the things that is quite remarkable about heaven, which many have seen in visions, is that the saints of God are being taught in heaven for all of eternity. Many have seen visions of some of the great men of God from the past teaching congregations in heaven the eternal Word of God. Thus, the truth of God is so immense and great that it will take us all of eternity to comprehend the Lord and His marvelous works. For this reason, the Holy Spirit is constantly searching the *archives* of God, seeking the deep and hidden truths of God and His Word, so that He might reveal them to us.

However, *revealing* is not the end of a teacher's objective and ministry. After teaching his pupils various truths, he then must cause them to understand those truths. It is not sufficient for a teacher just to expound knowledge. He must instill that knowledge into his pupils so that they really comprehend it, and the truth becomes a part of them. Therefore, like many able teachers of old, the Holy Spirit first studies and searches the deep things of God, then He reveals them to us. Finally, He instills and impresses those truths upon the hearts of His pupils—the saints of God.

Three Aspects of a Teacher

1. He Searches
2. He Reveals and Teaches
3. He Reiterates and Instills

As the Teacher of the Church, the Holy Spirit has another mission. Christ said, "*The Holy Ghost...shall bring all things to your remembrance, whatsoever I have said unto you*" (Jn. 14:26). The Spirit brings back to our memory things that we have forgotten from the Word and things that the Lord has spoken to us over the years. When I was nine years old, an angel appeared to me while I was in my father's garden in England.

The angel spoke to me and told me many things that God wanted to do in my life. This made a great impression upon me. However, I did not tell anyone about this angelic visitation, and as the years passed, I forgot about it. Years later, after I had given my life to the Lord, the Holy Spirit reminded me in a very real way of everything that the angel had told me, and it was a source of great encouragement.

The Lord Jesus said in Luke 12:11-12, "And when they bring you unto the synagogues, and unto magistrates, and powers, take ye no thought how or what thing ye shall answer, or what ye shall say: For the Holy Ghost shall teach you in the same hour what ye ought to say." When we are in pressing situations and we do not know what to say, the Holy Spirit will give us the words to speak and He will bring things to our remembrance.

Many times we study the Word of God and then we forget what we learned. Often we can become discouraged by this and think that we are not retaining any knowledge. However, the truth of the matter is that the words of the Lord are spirit and life. When we read the Bible or the Lord speaks to us while we are in prayer, those things go deep down into our spirits. We may forget them with our minds, but they are still in our spirits. At the appropriate time, the Holy Spirit will bring them back to our remembrance. Therefore, study God's Word and know that as you do, seeds of life are being sown into your heart, which for a season are hidden, but in time they will spring forth.

3. HE IS THE SPIRIT OF TRUTH

The Holy Spirit is also called the Spirit of Truth. Christ promised, "When he, the *Spirit of truth*, is come, he will guide you into all truth: for he shall not speak of himself; but whatsoever he shall hear, that shall he speak: and he will show you things to come" (Jn. 16:13). Another aspect of the Holy Spirit's ministry is to guide us into *all* truth. The truth is not just information and knowledge, or merely something that we acquire through study. It is something that comes down into the very core of our being so that we become the embodiment of those teachings. King David said to the Lord in Psalm 51:6, "Behold, thou desirest truth in the inward parts: and in the hidden part thou shalt make me to know wisdom." The Holy Spirit desires to guide us into all truth.

King Solomon possessed tremendous wisdom. Kings and rulers came from countries around the world to hear his wisdom. Yet, Solomon himself did not walk in the truths that he expounded to others. The Holy Spirit does not want His students to be like this. He wants to make sure that we walk in all that He reveals to us. He wants the truth to be in our minds and in our inward parts, and He desires that we walk in the truth (see Psa. 86:11).

The second part of John 16:13 says that the Holy Spirit "shall not speak of Himself." Like any good teacher, the Holy Spirit does not speak of Himself. Instead, He speaks of the One He is seeking to exalt—the Lord Jesus Christ.

"But whatsoever he shall hear, that shall he speak." The Holy Spirit tells us the things He hears the Father and Son say. This is the secret to every great teaching ministry. A true teacher is one who hears from God, and then shares those truths with others (see Mt. 10:27). That is how the Lord Jesus taught, as expressed in Isaiah 50:4: "The Lord God hath given me the tongue of the learned, that I should know how to speak a word in season to him that is weary: he wakeneth morning by morning, he wakeneth mine ear to hear as the learned." Jesus was the greatest teacher of all times because God opened His ear to hear every morning. Not a day passed that Christ was not up early in the morning meeting with His Father and spending time waiting upon Him and listening to Him speak. Because of this relationship with His Father, and because He had a listening ear, Jesus could speak and preach with great authority (see Mt. 7:29).

Another essential ingredient for a teacher is not only to teach, but to respond to the words of God and to be obedient and faithful to the truth (cf. Mt. 5:19). Isaiah 50:5 continues the words of Jesus, "The Lord God hath opened mine ear, and I was not rebellious, neither turned away back." Christ heard from God, and then He responded to what God told Him to do. This is also true of the Holy Spirit. Without this response, no one will succeed as a teacher.

Referring to the Holy Spirit, the last part of John 16:13 says, "He will show you things to come." Throughout the whole of the Church Age, everyone has gravitated to teachings that concern the second coming of Christ. The Lord's return is very important indeed, for more is written in the Scriptures concerning Christ's second coming than His first coming. However, it is more important for us to understand what God is going to do in His Church in the last days than to know all the political events that are going to take place before His return. Ephesians 5:27 tells us that the Lord is coming for a Church without spot or wrinkle. Thus, our primary objective should be to make ourselves ready for His return so that we can have a part in the last day revival.

Not only is the Spirit of Truth going to teach us about the second coming, He is also going to show us things that will come to pass in our personal lives. This aspect of the Holy Spirit's ministry is vital to our spiritual walk; for we are strengthened and encouraged as the Holy Spirit imparts understanding to us and gives us promises. He wants to reveal to us what God has planned for our lives. For when we believe and rejoice in what He says, we can make it through the valleys of life and come to the fulfillment of those promises.

The purpose of the Holy Spirit is also to glorify Christ. This is clearly seen by the words of Jesus in John 16:14: "He shall glorify me: for he shall receive of mine, and shall show it unto you." The Holy Spirit magnifies Christ and reveals Him unto us. At times, He may even give us visions of the Lord. Some of these visions of Christ reveal His life and ministry on earth, and help us understand what He is like.

Then Christ said in John 16:15, "All things that the Father hath are mine: therefore said I, that he shall take of mine, and shall show it unto you." Since Christ is the only begotten Son of God, the Father has entrusted everything into His power. Therefore, when the Holy Spirit takes the things of Jesus and reveals them to us, He is actually taking the things that the Father has given to the Son.

4. HE IS AN UNCTION OR AN ANOINTING

The Holy Spirit is also an unction or an anointing. The Apostle John declared in First John 2:20, "But ye have an unction from the Holy One, and ye know all things." The Holy Spirit is the anointing that abides, as seen in First John 2:27: "But the anointing which ye have received of him abideth in you, and ye need not that any man teach you: but as the same anointing teacheth you of all things, and is truth, and is no lie, and even as it hath taught you, ye shall abide in him."

It is the Holy Spirit who anoints us to understand the Word of God and enables us to discern between the true and the false, and the holy and the profane. The Holy Spirit is the abiding anointing within us that teaches us truth. I have felt the Holy Spirit urge me at times to study certain subjects, but I was not sure at the time why He was doing this. Yet I have found that when I follow His leading, the Word of God is opened up to me in a very beautiful way, and I get fresh insight.

In my personal life, I always try to allow the Holy Spirit to control the subjects and the order of subjects I study. In so doing, the Scriptures come alive, and they are made simple and clear. I would commend this kind of relationship with the Holy Spirit in your ministry and devotional life.

I remember one particular year when I was scheduled to teach a course called "The Life of Christ" at Zion Ministerial Institute, located in the state of New York. I was trying to prepare for the course, but I was having the most difficult time studying. I only had about one more week before classes started, and I just could not discern what was wrong.

Then as I started to pray and circumstances continued to unfold, I began to understand why. With only a few days notice, I was called upon to teach the Holy Spirit class because the scheduled teacher had to cancel unexpectedly. The Spirit of God knew all along that I would have to teach the Holy Spirit class before the Life of Christ class, and that is precisely why I could not get a flow for my Life of Christ course. As I began to study for the Holy Spirit course, it became vividly alive and I began to receive an abundance of fresh thoughts. If we flow with the Holy Spirit, we will find that He will cause us to study those things that will prepare us for every situation we encounter.

5. HE IS THE AUTHOR OF THE SCRIPTURES

Another aspect of the Holy Spirit is that He is the Author of the sacred Scriptures. Every chapter and verse in the Word of God was given through the inspiration of the Holy Ghost. Paul said that "All scripture is given by inspiration of God, and is profitable for doctrine, for reproof, for correction, for instruction in righteousness" (2 Tim. 3:16). The Apostle Peter also confirmed this truth when he declared that "prophecy came not in old time by the will of man: but holy men of God spake *as they were moved by the Holy Ghost*" (2 Pet. 1:21). Truly, the Holy Spirit must be considered the Author of both the Old and New Testaments.

All sixty-six books of the Bible were written by men of God as the Holy Spirit inspired them to write God's message. Therefore, when we seek to rightly interpret God's Word, we must ask the Holy Spirit to reveal to us what He really meant when He moved upon the Bible writers to write what they did. If we neglect this vital key, we will err in our interpretation of the Scriptures.

6. HE IS THE REPROVER

The Holy Spirit also has the ministry of reproving. The last words of Christ while He was upon earth reveal so much about the ministry of the Holy Spirit. One of the most admirable qualities of the Lord is the fact that many of His finest teachings were given as He was on His way to the cross. This speaks volumes about His character. What control of spirit He possessed on the way to Calvary's death! Remember, these messages were not given in a nice, comfortable classroom atmosphere, but as He walked from the upper room to the Garden of Gethsemane.

In John 16:8-11 Jesus spoke on the coming Holy Spirit. "And when he is come, he will reprove the world of sin, and of righteousness, and of judgment: Of sin, because they believe not on me; Of righteousness, because I go to my Father, and ye see me no more; Of judgment, because the prince of this world is judged."

The Holy Spirit is the Reprover. He is the One who convicts people of sin. When we do something that displeases the Lord, we feel such terrible conviction and anguish in our heart. This is the Holy Spirit at work in our lives. It was the Holy Spirit who convicted Paul of his lifestyle that was so contrary to the ways of God (see Acts 9:5). This is the ministry of the Holy Spirit. He not only convicts the saints, but He also convicts sinners of sin, righteousness, and judgment.

The Holy Spirit convicts men of the *sin* of unbelief. People have been hardened by life and they do not believe in the Lord. Disbelief in the Lord is the root sin of mankind. In the last days, the Lord is going to pour the spirit of grace and supplications upon the nation of Israel when the Lord returns. When they embrace their Messiah, they will ask Him why He has nail scars in His hands. He will tell them that He obtained them in the house of His friends. Then all Israel shall mourn and repent for not believing in the Lord Jesus Christ when He came to Israel the first time. This will be national repentance taking place as the result of the conviction of sin by the Holy Spirit (Zech. 12:10-12).

It is the Holy Spirit's prerogative to convict of sin. *We cannot* convict people of sin. Our responsibility is seen in the words of

Paul in Second Timothy 2:24-26: "And the servant of the Lord must not strive; but be gentle unto all men, apt to teach, patient, In meekness instructing those that oppose themselves; if God peradventure will give them repentance to the acknowledging of the truth; And that they may recover themselves out of the snare of the devil, who are taken captive by him at his will." We cannot make people repent of their sins and believe in the Lord. Only the Lord can give repentance and only the Holy Spirit can convict people. Our responsibility is to witness and present the truth to people in a gentle way—not trying to force them to believe. Often, we turn people away from the gospel by trying to do the Holy Spirit's work of convicting them. We should tell people the truth with a loving and understanding spirit, not with condemnation; then leave the rest up to the Holy Spirit and allow Him to convict them of sin.

The Holy Spirit also convicts men of *righteousness*, and of how far they are falling short of it. God has accepted the righteous sacrifice of His Son, and Him alone. Christ is man's only means of pardon, and the only hope he has of becoming righteous. There is no other way. It is the Holy Spirit who convicts people of righteousness. It is the Holy Spirit who makes us aware of our need to be clothed upon with the Lord's righteousness and not our own (see Phil. 3:9).

The Holy Spirit convicts of coming *judgment* because Satan's power was judged on the cross and his doom was sealed there. Not only will Satan suffer the vengeance of eternal fire—so will all those who follow him. Another aspect of the Holy Spirit's mission is to convict people of eternal judgment. It is an interesting fact that as you study the words of the Lord Jesus Christ, you find that He spoke more about judgment and the pangs of eternal torment in hell than He did about the blessings of eternal life and heaven. Ezekiel chapter 31 depicts the end of the proud Assyrians. They were once a mighty empire, but their end will be in the pit of hell. The Holy Spirit seeks to warn everyone about eternal judgment, and seeks to convict them in order to spare them from this terrible fate.

When we preach, we should ask the Holy Spirit to anoint us so that our listeners will be convicted, forsake their old ways, and turn to the Lord with all of their hearts. We need the Reprover to be present when we preach. Otherwise, our words will have no impact upon our audience. It does not matter how eloquent or intelligent we are; unless we are speaking under the anointing of the Holy Spirit, people will not be affected by our words.

7. HE IS THE INTERCESSOR

The Holy Spirit is also the Intercessor. He not only teaches us and guides us into all truth, He also shows us how to pray. He actually prays *through* us. The Apostle Paul makes this very clear in Romans 8:26-27. "Likewise the Spirit also helpeth our infirmities: for we know not what we should pray for as we ought: but the Spirit [Himself] maketh intercession for us with groanings which cannot be uttered. And he that searcheth the hearts knoweth what is the mind of the Spirit, because he maketh intercession for the saints according to the will of God."

Many people pray sincerely for what they believe (or hope) is the will of God, but they pray amiss because of their natural mind and their own personal desires. Regrettably, many young people choose a mate with their natural mind. That is why it is so important to allow the Holy Spirit to pray through us. He knows the mind of God and He knows whom God chose to be our companion before the foundation of the world. We should allow the Holy Spirit to pray through us for everything; as all too frequently we pray for things that are not God's will. Consequently, when we receive them, instead of being blessings, they become burdens and trials for us. This is why we should pray in tongues very much every day, and allow the Holy Spirit to pray through us, remembering that He knows how to pray rightly for our needs.

8. HE REVEALS AND SETS US INTO OUR CALLINGS

Although the originator of our callings is the Lord Jesus (cf. Eph. 4:11), the Holy Spirit is the One responsible for initiating our callings and placing people into ministerial offices in the Church (see Acts 20:28). This is seen very clearly in Acts 13:1-2: "Now there were in the church that was at Antioch certain prophets and teachers; as Barnabas, and Simeon that was called Niger, and Lucius of Cyrene, and Manaen, which had been brought up with Herod the tetrarch, and Saul. As they ministered to the Lord, and fasted, *the Holy Ghost said*, Separate me Barnabas and Saul for *the work whereunto I have called them*."

The Holy Spirit indicated that He had placed a calling and ministry upon Barnabas and Saul. He also indicated when it was the appointed time for them to be separated from that church and be sent forth. Recognizing that it was the Holy Spirit who was speaking, the brethren prayed and laid their hands on them, and sent them forth by the Holy Ghost (Acts 13:4).

This is another aspect of the ministry of the Holy Spirit. He reveals God's call upon our lives; He then indicates when it is God's time to send us forth. During times such as these, the brethren pray for us, and we are sent forth by the power of the

Holy Spirit. It is important to realize that the Holy Spirit controls our destinies. It was the Holy Spirit who called Paul to be a missionary and sent him forth.

9. HE IS THE CO-CREATOR

Now I would like to consider the role of the Holy Spirit in the creation of man and the universe. We often think of the Father and Son as being the Ones who created mankind and this earth, but many of us rarely consider how the Holy Spirit assisted in creation. The Scriptures are very clear that He is the Co-Creator along with the Father and the Son. We are told in Genesis 1:2: "And the earth was without form, and void; and darkness was upon the face of the deep. And the Spirit of God moved upon the face of the waters." Therefore, the Holy Spirit was very active in the creation.

Let us consider for a moment the relationship between the Father, Son, and Holy Spirit. In one sense, the Father is greatest in authority. He is the One who originates all plans and purposes of the Godhead. The Son is the administrator of the Godhead. He administers and rules His Father's kingdom. The Holy Spirit is the third member of the Godhead. He is the One who carries out the plans and purposes of God, and He equips the saints of God to do the will of the Father and Son. These different functions of the Trinity are clearly seen in First Corinthians 12:4-6. "Now there are diversities of gifts, but the same Spirit. And there are differences of administrations, but the same Lord. And there are diversities of operations, but it is the same God which worketh all in all." In verse four we read that the giftings (or equipping) is done by the Holy Spirit. Verse five tells us about the administrative work of the Lord Jesus Christ. And verse six speaks of the operations of God the Father, who originates everything. Therefore, it is clear that the Father orchestrated and organized the creation of this world. The Son administered the creation and spoke it into existence; the Holy Spirit carried out these commands.

We also read in Psalm 104:30 in the NIV, "When you send your Spirit, they are created, and you renew the face of the earth." At the time of the creation, the Spirit of God was sent forth to aid in the work of creation and to renew the face of the earth which had been brought under judgment because of the fall of Satan.

The Holy Spirit also was the Co-Creator of man, as seen by the words of the patriarch in Job 33:4: "The spirit of God hath made me, and the breath of the Almighty hath given me life." Thus, we can see that the Holy Spirit was involved in the fashioning of man.

10. HE IS INVOLVED IN THE SALVATION OF EVERY BELIEVER

When we think of the new birth and salvation of a believer, we can see from the Word of God that the Holy Spirit plays a very important role. The Lord Jesus Christ taught Nicodemus in John 3:5-8: "Except a man be born of water and of the Spirit, he cannot enter into the kingdom of God. That which is born of the flesh is flesh; and that which is born of the Spirit is spirit. Marvel not that I said unto thee, Ye must be born again. The wind bloweth where it listeth, and thou hearest the sound thereof, but canst not tell whence it cometh, and whither it goeth: so is every one that is born of the Spirit." The Lord Jesus is our Savior, but we are born-again *by* an act of the Spirit of God. When we give our hearts to the Lord, the Holy Spirit comes into our hearts and dwells within us.

The Apostle Paul confirms this in Romans 8:16. "The Spirit [Himself] beareth witness with our spirit, that we are the children of God." It is the Holy Spirit who bears witness with our spirit that we are born-again and adopted into the family of God. The Holy Spirit is the One who convicts us while we are yet sinners, and begins to prick our hearts. He begins drawing us to the Fountain of Living Waters, the Lord Jesus Christ. Thus, the Spirit plays a very active role in the salvation of every believer.

11. HE IS OUR SANCTIFIER

The Holy Spirit is also the One who sanctifies us. Paul said in Romans 8:13, "For if ye live after the flesh, ye shall die: but if ye through the Spirit do mortify the deeds of the body, yc shall live." It is through the enabling power of the Holy Spirit that we mortify the deeds of our flesh and we become totally sanctified, thus obtaining eternal life (cf. Col. 3:5). On the other hand, if we allow our flesh to direct us and govern us, we will die spiritually and go to hell.

Many years ago, on the day before I gave my heart to the Lord, I had an awesome experience. During that night, I had two distinct visions. In the first vision, I saw the world. I saw people being born as babies, then growing up and coming to manhood. I saw them living their lives and then dying. Sadly, it seemed as if there was no purpose whatsoever in their lives. Then I had another vision. In the second vision I saw what happens to unredeemed mankind after they die. I saw people literally falling into hell. Hell is a very real place! All these people had been born, they had grown to manhood, they had lived their lives, and finally they had died. Then at the end of their lives they went to hell. I then saw the Lord with His arms stretched forth, pleading with mankind.

The day after I had these two visions, I went to the scientific research laboratory in London, England, where I worked. I wanted desperately to do something that would change this world. With much gusto, I tried to convert a fellow worker to my political party that morning. He patiently listened to me speak, then he said: "I don't know much about your politics, but I do know one thing. God has a plan for your life, and it begins when you receive Jesus Christ as your Savior." To this I replied, "I believe!" At that very moment, the Lord appeared and stood right in front of me, and I was born-again by the Spirit of God. I knew I was born-again, because as I walked down the streets it was as though I was walking on air. I was so joyous. Something had happened to me, and my life was instantly changed!

One does not have to go to a laboratory in England to be saved, nor does one need to have such dramatic visions as I had. However, in order to become born-again, we must be convicted by the Holy Spirit that we are going to hell unless we lay hold of the pardon that is provided by Jesus Christ. Let us remember, however, that the Holy Spirit is not only interested in getting us saved. He also wants us to have complete victory over our sinful flesh! God's ultimate purpose in saving us is that we may become totally free from our old man through the tremendous power of the Holy Spirit.

12. HE IS INVOLVED IN THE RESURRECTION

The Holy Spirit is not only involved in our creation, salvation, and complete sanctification, but He is also responsible for our resurrection. The Apostle Paul declared in Romans 8:11, "But if the Spirit of him that raised up Jesus from the dead dwell in you, he that raised up Christ from the dead shall also quicken your mortal bodies by his Spirit that dwelleth in you." Jesus was raised from the dead by the Holy Spirit. He is also the One who will quicken and raise our mortal bodies on Resurrection Day. Therefore, the Holy Spirit is with us the whole of our lives, and He governs every aspect of our lives!

13. HE LEADS IN WORSHIP

In John chapter 4 the Lord Jesus reveals the heart of the Father. In this passage, He is speaking to the woman at the well who had been married five times and was presently living with someone else. She was looking for satisfaction in human love. The Lord in His graciousness singled out this woman for one of the most remarkable revelations in the whole of God's Word. In His compassion, He saw the reason why she had remarried several times. Deep in her heart there was a longing for satisfaction and fulfillment. Therefore, the Lord made known to her that *the source* of all satisfaction is found only in Him. We are only complete in Christ! When she inquired where she should worship, in Samaria or Jerusalem, the Lord introduced her to a new concept. He wanted her to know that true worship depends more upon the condition of the heart than one's geographical location.

Christ said to her: "The hour cometh, and now is, when the true worshippers shall worship the Father in spirit and in truth: for the Father seeketh such to worship him. God is a Spirit: and they that worship him must worship him in spirit and in truth" (Jn. 4:23-24). It is the Holy Spirit who enables us to worship God in spirit and truth. He is the Spirit of Truth, and He seeks to orchestrate our praise and worship unto Jesus. That is why it is so crucial for us to pray for the anointing of the Holy Spirit to be in our church services and in our personal times of worship.

Let us draw near to the Holy Spirit and experience Him in a new way; for He is the master conductor of worship in heaven and on earth. Therefore, all of our worship services, musicians, and song leaders should be under the control of the Holy Spirit. When this happens, we will see God move *mightily* in our services.

The Ministry of the Holy Spirit

1. He is the Comforter
2. He is the Teacher
3. He is the Spirit of Truth
4. He is an unction or an anointing
5. He is the Author of the Scriptures
6. He is the Reprover
7. He is the Intercessor
8. He reveals and sets us into our callings
9. He is the Co-Creator
10. He is involved in the salvation of every believer
11. He is our Sanctifier
12. He is involved in the resurrection
13. He leads in worship

Part Three

THE SEVEN SPIRITS OF THE LORD

In Part Three we are going to consider the seven Spirits of the Lord. These seven Spirits are an extension of the Holy Spirit. To help illustrate this spiritual truth, we could use the analogy of the human body. As our hands and our fingers are an extension of us, so also are the seven Spirits of the Lord an extension of the person of the Holy Spirit.

The seven Spirits of the Lord are seen symbolically in the book of Revelation as lamps. Revelation 4:5 says, "And out of the throne proceeded lightnings and thunderings and voices: and there were seven lamps of fire burning before the throne, which are the seven Spirits of God." The seven Spirits are represented here by lamps of fire.

In Revelation 5:6 the Apostle John had a revelation and he saw into heaven: "And I beheld, and, lo, in the midst of the throne and of the four beasts, and in the midst of the elders, stood a Lamb as it had been slain, having seven horns and seven eyes, which are the seven Spirits of God sent forth into all the earth." Here the seven Spirits of the Lord are represented by *horns* and *eyes*. Horns speak of power and strength, and eyes are used to record what they have seen.

In Second Chronicles 16:9 we read that "the eyes of the Lord run to and fro throughout the whole earth, to show himself strong in the behalf of them whose heart is perfect toward him." These "eyes" are the seven Spirits of God.

In Revelation 1:4 John wrote to the seven churches in Asia for which he was responsible. His salutation began like this: "Grace be unto you, and peace, from him which is, and which was, and which is to come; and from the seven Spirits which are before his throne."

This is a very interesting statement. John was speaking on behalf of the Holy Spirit. He said, "Grace and peace be unto you ...from the seven Spirits which are before His throne." Because John could speak on their behalf, we know that the seven Spirits are an extension of the Holy Spirit. A person cannot speak on behalf of an influence.

In Revelation 3:1 the seven Spirits are also included in the message to the church of Sardis: "These things saith he that hath the seven Spirits of God, and the seven stars; I know thy works, that thou hast a name that thou livest, and art dead." Through these scriptures we see that John was very intimate with the Holy Spirit. John not only knew the Father and the Son, but he was also very close to the Holy Spirit, and he reveals much of His nature and attributes in his writings.

These seven Spirits are enumerated for us in Isaiah 11:2: "And the spirit of the Lord shall rest upon him, the spirit of wisdom and understanding, the spirit of counsel and might, the spirit of knowledge and of the fear of the Lord." In the Tabernacle of Moses there was a candlestick with three pairs of lamps extending from a center lamp. This center lamp represents the Spirit of the Lord. The others are paired together—wisdom and understanding, counsel and might, knowledge and the fear of the Lord.

The Seven Spirits of the Lord

1. The Spirit of the Lord
2. The Spirit of Wisdom
3. The Spirit of Understanding
4. The Spirit of Counsel
5. The Spirit of Might
6. The Spirit of Knowledge
7. The Spirit of the Fear of the Lord

1. THE SPIRIT OF THE LORD

The function of the first of the seven Spirits, which is the Spirit of the Lord, is seen in Isaiah 61:1: "The spirit of the Lord God is upon me; because the Lord hath anointed me to preach good tidings unto the meek; he hath sent me to bind up the broken-hearted, to proclaim liberty to the captives, and the opening of the prison to them that are bound." The Spirit of the Lord, as we can see in Isaiah 61:1, is the anointing to preach and speak for God.

Isaiah 61:1 is referring to Christ who was anointed by His Father. *Christ* actually means "The Anointed One." His triple name is the Lord Jesus Christ. (Lord means *God*, Jesus means *Savior*, and Christ means the *Anointed One*.) How was He anointed? Peter tells us in Acts 10:38 that "God anointed Jesus of Nazareth with the Holy Ghost and power." More specifically, we are told in Isaiah 61:1 that it was the Spirit of the Lord that anointed Christ to preach (see also Luke 4:18).

When we stand before people to preach the Word of God, we need to feel the Holy Spirit energizing us. I thank God for the Holy Spirit, because without Him I certainly would not be able to preach. It is so very wonderful when you feel that precious anointing coming upon you, and you feel the Spirit of the Lord activating your mind and bringing to your remembrance things that you have heard before.

Although I recommend that all who preach should study diligently for their sermons and use notes when they speak, nevertheless, we must rely upon the Spirit of the Lord to anoint us when we preach. One of the most wonderful experiences in life is to have the anointing of God come upon us and take control of us. When this happens as we are preaching, we become so aware that it is not we who are speaking, but the Holy Spirit who has taken over.

We must speak by the enabling of the Holy Spirit. The anointing makes every message come alive. Paul said "the letter killeth, but the Spirit giveth life" (2 Cor. 3:6). We do not want to preach a "dead" sermon; we want it to be anointed, fresh, and alive. When this happens, we can feel the anointing come upon our mind, and the Holy Spirit takes us away from our notes and speaks through us. At the end of our message, we realize that we actually preached a far better sermon than the one we had prepared.

When we are preaching under the anointing of the Holy Spirit, we will say certain things and afterwards we will wonder why we said them. Yet at the end of the service, people will tell us that what we said was just for them and that it really ministered to them. We must be free because where the Spirit of the Lord is there is liberty, including a wonderful liberty to preach the gospel of Christ (see 2 Cor. 3:17). As we preach under the anointing of the Holy Ghost, men and women will be transformed by the very words that flow from our lips. Therefore, I recommend that you not only seek the Lord for the material for your message, but also for the anointing of the Spirit to declare it with power and authority.

2. THE SPIRIT OF WISDOM

The second of the seven Spirits of the Lord is the Spirit of wisdom. In our study of the Spirit of wisdom, we must first define *wisdom*. This is actually a very difficult task, because wisdom is a comprehensive word. The Hebrew word for *wisdom* is "chokmah." It means "to act wisely." Wisdom is the ability to make right choices, and, therefore, to live life skillfully. We are told that "the fear of the Lord is the beginning of wisdom," and "to depart from evil is understanding" (see Prov. 9:10, Job 28:28).

Wisdom is a gift from God. Ecclesiastes 2:26 declares, "For God giveth to a man that is good in his sight wisdom, and knowledge and joy." If we please the Lord, He will give us wisdom, knowledge, and joy. Wisdom is not given to everyone. In fact, Proverbs 17:16 says, "Why does a fool come with money in his hand to buy wisdom?" Obviously, wisdom cannot be bought with money. God gives wisdom to those who please Him.

I want to look now at seven aspects of wisdom which are contained in the book of Proverbs. There are seven things that the book of Proverbs tells us we must do in order to live a meaningful life. Proverbs 1:8-9 instructs us to obey our parents. Obeying our parents involves not only obeying our natural parents, but also those who have the spiritual oversight of us. Then in

Proverbs 1:10-19 we are warned to avoid bad company. In order to find wisdom, we must seek for it and love it with all of our hearts. Therefore, in Proverbs 1:20-2:22 we are exhorted to seek wisdom. A vital key to obtaining wisdom is kindness. Proverbs 3:27-35 deals with the subject of being kind. God desires for us to be kind to others (see Mt. 7:12). Another requirement to live life skillfully is to keep and guard our hearts (Prov. 4:23-27). There is a warning in Proverbs 5:1-14 to not commit adultery, and an admonition in Proverbs 5:15-23 to be faithful and loyal to our spouses.

1. Obey your parents (Prov. 1:8-9)
2. Avoid bad company (Prov. 1:10-19)
3. Seek wisdom (Prov. 1:20 - 2:2)
4. Be kind (Prov. 3:27-35)
5. Guard your hearts (Prov. 4:23-27)
6. Do not commit adultery (Prov. 5:1-14)
7. Be loyal to your spouses (Prov. 5:15-23)

Proverbs 14:1 is a very solemn and serious warning to wives: "Every wise woman buildeth her house: but the foolish plucketh it down with her hands." In my forty years of ministry, I have often had to counsel couples with broken relationships. It has been very heart-breaking. To my amazement, I have never found a case where there was one *completely* innocent party. Quarrels in marriage usually require two parties.

When I was an assistant pastor in France, the pastor's wife told me that the scripture which meant the most to her was Proverbs 14:1. I said to her, "Well, God must have given it to you for a reason." At that particular moment, the reason was not very clear. Sometime later I left France and went to Switzerland for several years, and then I went on to the United States. While my wife and I were teaching at a certain Bible school in the East, the Lord spoke to me during break time at the college, saying: "I am going to send you back to Europe for a short time, and what you see in Europe you will declare around the world. Your heart is going to be broken while you are there."

The Lord taught us many things during this trip to Europe. Among other things, soon after returning, I understood why the pastor's wife had received that scripture from the Lord many years before. Unfortunately, this word had never become rooted deeply within her heart. As a result, her husband, who was one of the leading pastors in France at that time, committed adultery. His sin was uncovered, and yet the sad thing is that he did not stand up alone at the time of his confession. His wife had to stand up by his side and admit that she was also guilty. She confessed that because she had not loved and cared for her husband properly, he turned to another woman in search of love. This lady did not build up her house in wisdom, and because she did not, it was torn down!

My wife's mother built up her house in wisdom. People from all over the world who stayed in her house would say to her, "There is such peace in this home." She was a very kind and wise woman. Through wisdom, her house was built up.

The Seven Pillars of Wisdom

Wisdom is multifaceted. In Proverbs 9:1 we see seven particular *pillars of wisdom*: "Wisdom hath builded her house, she hath hewn out her seven pillars." These seven pillars of wisdom are enumerated for us in James 3:17: "But the wisdom that is from above is first pure, then peaceable, gentle, and easy to be entreated, full of mercy and good fruits [or works], without partiality, and without hypocrisy."

The Seven Pillars of Wisdom

1. **Pure** - to have a heart with motives that are clean and pure
2. **Peaceable** - to live in peace with others to the best of our ability
3. **Gentle** - being sweet to all
4. **Easy to be entreated** - being gracious when people ask us for our help when it is inconvenient
5. **Full of mercy and good fruits** - mercy is always accompanied by good works and acts of kindness
6. **Without partiality** - not showing favoritism
7. **Without hypocrisy -** to be real and true in every area of our lives

The Spirit of wisdom was manifested in the life of King Solomon. It was an abiding anointing and mantle that was always with Solomon. Because of this anointing upon his life, he has been known throughout the ages for his wisdom. There is a reason why Solomon was so wise. Since God is not a respecter of persons, there is a definite reason why some people have wisdom and others do not. The reason is that Solomon had a heart that desired and loved wisdom. His parents, David and Bathsheba, had taught him the priceless value of wisdom. In fact, the first nine chapters of Proverbs are the teachings of Solomon's parents in his formative years. We read the words of

David to Solomon in Proverbs 4:5-7: "Get wisdom, get understanding: forget it not; neither decline from the words of my mouth. Forsake her not, and she shall preserve thee: love her, and she shall keep thee. Wisdom is the principal thing; therefore get wisdom: and with all thy getting get understanding." It was because of this godly instruction by his father that Solomon asked for wisdom when the Lord met him in Gibeon and told him He would give him whatever he asked for (see 2 Chron. 1:7-12, 1 Kgs. 3:5-12).

The consequence of this prayer for wisdom by Solomon is seen in First Kings 4:29-31: "And God gave Solomon wisdom and understanding exceeding much, and largeness of heart, even as the sand that is on the sea shore. And Solomon's wisdom excelled the wisdom of all the children of the east country, and all the wisdom of Egypt. For he was wiser than all men; than Ethan the Ezrahite, and Heman, and Chalcol, and Darda, the sons of Mahol: and his fame was in all nations round about." Because of his love for wisdom, wisdom opened up its many riches and treasures to Solomon.

The Spirit of wisdom in Solomon's life was expressed through his judgment of the two women who came before him laying claim to the same child (1 Kgs. 3:16-27). Solomon's judgment to cut the baby in half, knowing that it would reveal who was the real mother of the child, was extraordinary. As a result of this "all Israel heard of the judgment which the king had judged; and they feared the king: for they saw that the wisdom of God was in him, to do judgment" (1 Kgs. 3:28). The king's judgment made all the people of the land marvel with awe.

The wisdom God placed in Solomon's life can also be seen through the many songs and proverbs which he authored (1

Kgs. 4:32). King Solomon wrote 3,000 proverbs. About 800 of these are now contained in the book of Proverbs. He also wrote 1,005 songs, five of which are retained in the Song of Songs. Princes and nobles from around the world came to hear the matchless wisdom of Solomon. Solomon revealed the character and wisdom of God seen through His creation. He spoke about the trees and the animals, and the truths of the Godhead which they illustrate (1 Kgs. 4:33).

There is an expression of truth in everything God created. The caterpillar, for example, has thirteen segments. This speaks of man who was born in sin and rebellion. Caterpillars have twelve eyes, which speak of government. God's ultimate purpose is for man to have dominion over the whole earth and to rule and reign with Him. Through the chrysalis of the caterpillar, we can see how God transforms us into the beautiful image of His Son. The caterpillar spins himself a cocoon, and it is in this place of confinement and darkness that his nature is transformed. Then at the appointed time, the little butterfly releases some formic acid which burns a hole in the cocoon and out from that chrysalis there comes an object of great beauty—the butterfly that soars into heavenly places. In this same manner the Lord works in our lives. It is during our "prison" (or cocoon) experiences that God changes our nature, gives us a new heart, and clothes us with the beauty of Jesus.

We do not necessarily have to be placed in a literal prison or jail, but the Lord confines us and puts us in a corral so that we feel like we are in prison. Many of the great men of God in the Scriptures like Joseph, Jeremiah, and Paul spent time in literal prisons. Do you see the wonderful truths that can be illustrated through the life cycle of the caterpillar? All nature shows forth the glory of God!

The Spirit of wisdom is different from the baptism of the Holy Ghost. This is seen by the fact that the Apostle Paul exhorted the Ephesian believers who were already baptized in the Holy Spirit to pray for the Spirit of wisdom in Ephesians 1:17: "That the God of our Lord Jesus Christ, the Father of glory, may give unto you the Spirit of wisdom and revelation in the knowledge of him." We need to cry out for the Spirit of wisdom. In Ephesians 3:10 we see that one of the primary purposes of the Church is to manifest the wisdom of God. As Christians we should pray, "Lord, anoint me with the Spirit of wisdom so that I can be a wise person and live life skillfully."

Wisdom is the utmost prerequisite for leadership. When Moses was going to pass on to Joshua the leadership of the children of Israel, he laid his hands upon him and imparted the Spirit of wisdom to him (see Deut. 34:9). Therefore, when we are in positions of leadership, we should ask the Lord for the Spirit of wisdom so that we can guide and lead our congregations into fresh pastures and bring them into the place that God has ordained for them.

Wisdom can be received through the laying on of hands, as in the case of Joshua. For years I have cried out to the Lord, "Give me wisdom, and anoint me with the Spirit of wisdom." Lately, this prayer which was birthed in my heart by the Spirit has increased in fervency and frequency. Years ago, my wife and I went to visit Kathryn Kuhlman in her hotel room when she was in Los Angeles preparing to speak at the Shrine Auditorium. We took with us the Spirit-filled, Anglican Bishop of Singapore who was a good friend of ours because Kathryn had told me that she would like to meet him. We had a very pleasant time with her, and just as we were about to leave she said to our friend, "Let me pray for you." When she laid her hands on him, he went down and was slain in the Spirit. Then she turned to me, put her hands on my forehead and said one word, "wisdom." I went down as well. When I came back up she prayed again that I would receive wisdom. Then she asked me to introduce this Bishop of Singapore at her healing meeting that night in front of seven thousand people.

Those of you who knew Kathryn Kuhlman know that she was a terrible tease. We sat on the platform, and as I was preparing to introduce my good friend from Singapore, she said to me before the whole auditorium, "Before you introduce the bishop, would you like to tell everyone what you thought I would look like before you met me?" I became so embarrassed. My English background didn't help me any either. I had told Kathryn in her hotel room that I had gone to one of her meetings in Pittsburgh years before and had seen the Lord above the auditorium where she ministered, and I saw the word "Healer" underneath His feet. This experience helped me to know that she was authentic because once I got inside, I was shocked by her long, flowing garments and all her other eccentric qualities. Being English, I expected her to be a very quiet, demure little lady who was very prim and proper. However, I knew that the Lord was working through her and that the Lord was pleased with her life. When I shared what I thought she would be like, the whole crowd erupted into laughter. After I stopped blushing, I introduced the bishop; then the service continued and the power of God was manifested in a tremendous way.

The point I am trying to make is that God gives us the desires of our hearts. For years I had prayed for wisdom, and so when Kathryn Kuhlman (who normally prayed for healing) laid hands on me, she prayed that the Lord would give me the Spirit of wisdom. The Lord does give us the desires of our hearts. If we seek the Lord for the Spirit of wisdom and we desire it with all of our hearts, He will give us that precious anointing. Let us meditate on wisdom. It is the most important thing in life. Those who are void of wisdom ruin their lives and have many heartaches. May God grant that we are a wise and discerning people who have the Spirit of wisdom!

3. THE SPIRIT OF UNDERSTANDING

We now come to the third of the seven Spirits of the Lord—the Spirit of understanding. Understanding means to grasp the significance of a subject or an event, realizing why God is doing what He is doing in any given circumstance. Understanding also comprehends why certain things happen to people.

The Spirit of understanding refers also to the ability to interpret dreams and visions, as in the case of Daniel. When speaking of the four Hebrew children that were in captivity in Babylon, the Word of God says, "As for these four children, God gave them knowledge and skill in all learning and wisdom: and Daniel had understanding in all visions and dreams" (Dan. 1:17).

When a person has a vision from God, in reality, only God can interpret that vision. The author is the one who knows what it means. God-given prophecies and manifestations, and even the Scriptures, can only be interpreted by the Lord for He is the author of them (2 Pet. 1:20-21). Dreams, visions, and prophetic words require the Spirit of understanding to correctly interpret them. I have known many people who have ruined their lives completely because they did not correctly interpret dreams and visions they received from the Lord. Regarding the interpretation of visions and dreams, we have the classic example of Nebuchadnezzar's dream. He saw an image with a golden head, a silver breastplate, brass loins, iron legs, and feet and toes of clay and iron. It was a very simple dream, but it required the Spirit of understanding that God had given to Daniel to interpret it. Who else but God could have interpreted that vision? The correct interpretation of that dream was that the head of gold represented the Babylonian Empire, the silver breast was the Persian Empire, the brass loins symbolized the Grecian Empire, and the iron legs were the Roman Empire. Obviously, God alone who knows the future could have given the right interpretation to this dream. Therefore, if you have a vision or dream, be very careful that you have the correct interpretation. Go to your pastor or someone who has the Spirit of understanding and ask him to give you the correct interpretation.

Another aspect of understanding is the ability to judge and discern in matters pertaining to administration and government. King Solomon asked the Lord in First Kings 3:9 to give him an understanding heart so that he could rightly judge the people of God. May God cause us to be like the tribe of Issachar of old, who "were men that had understanding of the times and knew what Israel ought to do" (1 Chron.12:32). We need to pray for understanding; for it is such an important aspect of the manifestation of the Holy Spirit. Like the children of Issachar, we want to be those who know what the Church should do in these last days, and be able to clearly point the way.

4. THE SPIRIT OF COUNSEL

The Spirit of counsel is the fourth of the seven Spirits of the Lord. There are people in the Church who are given the ministry gift of a counselor. One of the titles of the Lord Jesus is Counselor (Isa. 9:6). A counselor is one who resolves problems, guides, and determines what should be done in any given situation. The Spirit of counsel is divine, not human. When a person has problems, he should not be counseled with human wisdom, or even with scripturally-based principles (though Scripture must never be contravened). We must hear from the Lord what His will and counsel is for each specific person and situation. We must obtain a quickened word from the Lord for each individual person.

Many years ago I was a faculty member of a certain Bible school. Several of the students at this college were former drug addicts who had been gloriously delivered from their lives of sin. They became famous virtually overnight and were invited to many churches to give their testimonies, and some even became film stars. However, the major drawback was that their testimonies glorified their former life of sin. The Lord spoke to me: "Tell them to stop glorifying Satan by their testimonies and to start glorifying Me. Otherwise, they will fall back into their life of sin." They promised me that they would do as the Lord had said, but, unfortunately, shortly thereafter they succumbed again to the pressure of speaking about their former lifestyles.

During the summer break from Bible school that year, all of these young men fell back into sin, just as the Lord said they would if they did not heed the warning. When school was in session again the next fall, some of the students came and told me one day that the leader of this group of former drug addicts was going "cold turkey" to get off drugs. I went rushing to his dorm room, fully determined to give him a good piece of my mind, for I had firmly warned him. However, as soon as I entered the door to his room, the spirit of prophecy fell upon me. To my amazement, instead of rebuking him, which I had every intention of doing, I told him that God was yet going to use him mightily and give him a large church.

This prophecy has since come to pass. Today, he pastors a church of several thousand people and frequently preaches on television. This young man needed my encouragement, not my rebuke. If I had followed my own reasoning, I would have rebuked him, and he probably would have quit school in disgrace and never entered the ministry. Can you see how important it is for us to speak under the anointing? We must always give *God's* counsel—not what *we think* people need to hear!

As well as the future, the Spirit of counsel can also reveal the past. At times, God may reveal to us why certain things have happened to people. When counseling people concerning a certain bondage in their life, the Lord may reveal to us through the Spirit of counsel a particular bondage that has been passed on to them by their parents or grandparents. This information reveals the key to their problem and helps bring deliverance.

For example, a certain man we knew could never seem to succeed financially, no matter what he did. He could not understand why. In a counseling session, the Lord revealed that the reason for this was that his parents had taken a vow of poverty and that this curse was still affecting him. We prayed with him and he was set free from that curse of poverty. Then he was blessed in his business endeavors.

The Spirit of counsel is so gentle and kind. After all, it is a part of the Holy Spirit. Therefore, we should be very careful when we counsel. Job's friends counseled him in the wrong way. They were very harsh, critical, and judgmental, which is completely contrary to the nature of the Spirit of counsel. They said to him: "Now, we know that if a man is upright, God prospers him, and if a man sins, God's judgment comes upon him. Job, God's judgment has fallen upon you. You have lost your children and all your wealth, and you are reduced to nothing. Therefore, you must be a hypocrite!" That was their human logic, but how did God see the situation?

Looking at it from the Lord's point of view, Job was one of the three most righteous men who ever lived, and now God was allowing him to pass through a trial that was going to lift him up even higher and give him an eternal name of honor. The story of Job could not have ended with his friends misunderstanding his trial and wrongly applying scriptural principles. Fortunately, God placed another man in their midst who was anointed with the Spirit of counsel, and he would declare the real reason for Job's trial. This man's name was Elihu. He did not speak with human reasoning. Elihu spoke the counsel of the Lord; and because he did, God confirmed his words. At the end of his trial, Job was given a double portion, which was totally different from what Job's three friends had predicted would happen.

Therefore, we should be careful before we counsel someone. Things are not always as they appear, as in the case of Job. That is why we must hear from the Lord, and not simply rely upon principles. Also, before you counsel someone, make sure it is your office and ministry; for only a God-ordained office will have an anointing. If we have that office, let us ask the Lord for the Spirit of counsel that we might say exactly what He wants us to say. When God anoints you with the Spirit of counsel, you become the mouthpiece of God in that particular situation.

We need to be men and women who have the answers for people's needs and questions! People should not have to turn to the world or to psychology for the questions they have about life. The Church should have the answers, and these answers are obtained through the Spirit of counsel.

5. THE SPIRIT OF MIGHT

The Spirit of might is the fifth Spirit of the Lord. This Spirit is always associated with Samson, whose name has since become synonymous with strength. Therefore, to get a picture in our minds of how the Spirit of might operates, let us now consider some of Samson's special feats.

In Judges 14:5-9 he slew a lion, and the swarm of bees out of the carcass of that lion provided him with honey. From this incident we have the proverb, "Out of the strong came forth sweetness." We should desire to be sweet and to show forth the sweetness, gentleness and kindness of Christ. However, it is only *the strong* who are able to be sweet.

I remember driving along a certain road in the state of New York many years ago with my wife. We stopped to eat at a little roadside restaurant, and I will never forget what I saw at this place. There were two dogs inside. The one dog, which was very large, was stretched out lazily upon the floor. As we entered the restaurant he just opened his eyes, looked at us, and then shut his eyes again. However, there was another tiny, little dog that barked and barked and barked as we ventured further into the dining area. He would not stop barking until finally his master forced him to stop.

This story gives us a good illustration of the above mentioned proverb. The little dog was barking because he was afraid and insecure. Yet, the big dog was sweet and good-natured. Not only did he not bark at us, but while we were eating, we watched with amazement as he allowed a little child to crawl all over him and even pull his mouth open. Out of the strong comes forth sweetness. Therefore, we want to major in the Lord's strength.

On another occasion, recorded in Judges 15:3-5, Samson caught three hundred foxes and tied their tails together in pairs. Then he fastened a torch to every pair of tails. After he lit all the torches, he turned them loose into the fields of corn owned by the Philistines. As a result, all their fields were burned up and destroyed.

There must have been a tremendous anointing upon Samson to enable him to do this. Think of it! He had to run extremely fast to catch all those foxes, and then he had to hold them very tightly as he lit a torch between their tails. Can you imagine what a monumental task it must have been to tie all their tails together? What a scene this must have been! Certainly, the Spirit of might was operating in the life of Samson, and it gave him supernatural strength.

With the jawbone of an ass Samson slew one thousand men (Judg. 15:14-17). Then he took the gates of the city of Gaza and ran with them up to Hebron, which is a distance of about twenty or thirty miles (Judg. 16:1-3). At his death he killed three thousand men by pulling down two supporting pillars, causing the house to crumble upon them (Judg. 16:26-30). Actually, he inflicted more damage to the enemy at his death than during his whole lifetime.

The Spirit of might was also upon the prophet Elijah. After Elijah announced that rain was about to fall, Ahab wanted to get back to Jezreel as quickly as possible (1 Kgs.18:46). Because Ahab was a king, he had to have a forerunner to run ahead of him. Therefore, in humility and great strength Elijah ran before the chariots of Ahab. These chariots were equipped with the finest and fastest horses in all of Israel, yet from Mount Carmel to Jezreel the prophet outran them all. This was not a feat of human strength or ability. It was the Spirit of might upon Elijah. We can also see the Spirit of might upon the Lord Jesus Christ when He cleansed the temple at the beginning and end of His earthly ministry (see Jn. 2:13-17, Mt. 21:12-13). The anointing of might came upon Jesus as He entered the temple and overturned all the tables of the money lenders and chased them out of the temple all by Himself.

Joel 2:7 speaks prophetically of the last day Church in this way: "They shall run like mighty men; they shall climb the wall like men of war; and they shall march every one on his ways, and they shall not break their ranks." The Church of Jesus Christ will march triumphantly in the last days and see the devil flee before them, for they will be anointed with the Spirit of might!

6. THE SPIRIT OF KNOWLEDGE

Now I would like to look at the sixth Spirit of the Lord, the Spirit of knowledge. This is the ability given by the Holy Spirit to know events in the past, present, and future. This anointing was manifested in the life of the Lord Jesus Christ when by the Spirit He saw Nathanael underneath the fig tree (Jn. 1:47-50). As Nathanael was coming toward Him, Jesus said to him, "Behold an Israelite indeed, in whom is no guile!" To this Nathanael replied, "Whence knowest thou me?" Jesus answered him by saying, "Before that Philip called thee, when thou wast under the fig tree, I saw thee."

The Lord saw Nathanael under that fig tree in a vision. So often the Spirit of knowledge operates through visions, which enable us to see events that are in the past or that are going to take place in the future. Under the anointing of the Holy Spirit, we see events as the Lord sees them.

For example, the Apostle Paul, who had never been to the city of Colosse, wrote to the believers in the Colossian church, "For though I be absent in the flesh, yet am I with you in the spirit, joying and *beholding* your order, and the steadfastness of your faith in Christ" (Col. 2:5). Paul was watching the Colossian church, and he saw everything they were doing just as though he were there in person. Yet, in actuality, Paul was writing this from a Roman prison cell many hundreds of miles away as the Spirit of knowledge enabled him to see what was going on in the Colossian church.

One evening many years ago I was in South Africa. By the Spirit, I walked through a church thousands of miles away in New Zealand. Amazingly, I saw everything that was taking place, and I actually heard what people were saying in the board meeting of the church. I might add here that it certainly was a very revealing board meeting!

When you see heavenly things, it is as if you are in heaven because they are so clear to you. Many years before my wife went on to be with the Lord, I saw her in heaven coming to greet me at the time appointed for me to go to heaven.

The Spirit of knowledge operated in the lives of the Old Testament prophets. The Holy Spirit is the author of the Old Testament as well as the New Testament (see 2 Tim. 3:16, 2 Pet. 1:20-21). How did He communicate His message to the Bible authors? In some instances, He caused them to literally see the events about which they wrote . We have a perfect illustration of this in Isaiah 13:1: "The burden of Babylon, which Isaiah the son of Amoz did see." Before his very eyes, Isaiah saw events that were going to happen to Babylon, including the fall of Babylon many years before it even became a world power.

The Spirit of knowledge can make things so real that you can actually hear what is happening. The Spirit of knowledge operated in this manner in the life of Jeremiah, for he said in chapter 4:19-21: "My bowels, my bowels! I am pained at my very heart; my heart maketh a noise in me; I cannot hold my peace, because thou hast heard, O my soul, the sound of the trumpet, the alarm of war. Destruction upon destruction is cried; for the whole land is spoiled: suddenly are my tents spoiled, and my curtains in a moment. How long shall I see the standard, and hear the sound of the trumpet?" By the Spirit of knowledge, the prophet Jeremiah actually heard and experienced the things that would take place many years ahead into the future. Jeremiah saw the land of Israel spoiled and he heard the war cries. It was all taking place before his very eyes, and he could hear what was happening with his ears.

In 1973 my wife and I visited Israel and stayed in a hotel on the Mount of Olives. During the night, the Lord showed me the fall of Jerusalem in the last days. I saw the Arab armies surrounding Jerusalem on the hills, and then breaking into Jerusalem. In this vision Jerusalem was almost completely overrun when the Lord returned. I saw this by the Spirit of knowledge.

Just consider for a moment how John wrote the book of Revelation. He wrote it by the Spirit of knowledge as he literally saw the events which he wrote about take place, including the Lord's coming. I remember when the Lord showed me one aspect of His second coming. The heavens rolled away, and the face of Jesus appeared in the skies. The interesting thing is that it was not the face of the compassionate Christ. It was a face filled with divine anger. And I saw people looking at that face and crying out in anguish for the mountains and rocks to fall upon them to hide them from His face (cf. Rev. 6:14-17).

The Spirit of knowledge can also reveal events from the past to us, including things that took place in the Scriptures. At times the Lord may give us visions of the life and ministry of Christ upon earth. We can see things that are present, even as the Lord saw Nathanael under the fig tree. We can also see things in the future. We need to cry out to the Lord for the Spirit of knowledge that we might know what is upon His heart and mind!

7. THE SPIRIT OF THE FEAR OF THE LORD

Finally, we come to the seventh Spirit of the Lord which is the Spirit of the fear of the Lord. This is the anointing that is poured out upon a nation, community, or an individual; it is marked by great conviction of sin and a fear of displeasing the Lord. This is the Spirit that comes upon people during revival and makes them afraid to sin. The fear of the Lord causes men to know if they are on or off the path of God.

An example of the Spirit of the fear of the Lord being poured out upon whole cities was that of Jacob and his household traveling from Succoth to Bethel (see Gen. 35). Simeon and Levi had slain all the men of Shechem for defiling their sister Dinah. Moved by fear of revenge by the inhabitants of that area, Jacob took up camp and headed toward Bethel. The Lord protected Jacob and his family as they passed through all the cities of that area, for God had poured out the Spirit of the fear of the Lord upon all the inhabitants of the land and they were afraid to harm or touch anyone of the house of Jacob.

This same spirit also enabled Israel under the command of Joshua to conquer the land of Canaan. Rahab, an inhabitant of the land, said to the two men who were sent to spy out the land, "I know that the Lord hath given you the land, and that your terror is fallen upon us, and that all the inhabitants of the land faint because of you" (Josh. 2:9). The fear of the Lord caused the inhabitants of the land of Canaan to tremble and fall before the armies of Israel.

There was an extraordinary outpouring of the Spirit of the fear of the Lord in the New Testament Church. During this time of revival, we are given a glimpse of what it was like in the early Church: "And great fear came upon all the church, and upon as many as heard these things. And by the hands of the apostles were many signs and wonders wrought among the people; and they were all with one accord in Solomon's porch. And of the rest [dared] no man join himself to them: but the people magnified them" (Acts 5:11-13). Because of the fear of the Lord, which was occasioned by God's judgment upon Ananias and Sapphira, there was great conviction of the Holy Spirit upon the people. Only the very sincere in heart came to church.

I have known situations similar to this. There was a very godly church in northern England that no one would attend until everything was made right in their lives with the Lord. The fear of the Lord was upon that church. There was tremendous conviction of sin. If anyone present had done anything wrong, it was revealed through the preaching or through prophecy. Can you see what a transformation takes place in people's lives when the Spirit of the fear of the Lord is poured out upon them?

The fear of the Lord was manifested in a very sovereign way in the country of Wales in the early nineteen hundreds when there was a national revival. Nearly fifty years after that revival, I was privileged to spend some time with a pastor who had been in that move of God. He was responsible for revival coming to his hometown. As we were walking down the streets of his hometown, he told me many things that happened during that revival. He pointed to one tavern after another that had been shut down because of the move of God that swept across the whole nation of Wales. Such tremendous conviction of sin and fear of the Lord came upon people that the tavern owners ran out of customers and were forced to close. The town cinema also went out of business because of a lack of interest in movies. The theater owner even donated the use of the building to the church. This is just a small picture of what happened in towns all over the nation. Taverns throughout the country closed down. The fear of God was so great upon the cities of Wales that those in the taverns could not even lift their drinks up to their lips because of the conviction of the Holy Spirit. In fact, I was told that it was not uncommon to see men sobbing and literally crawling on their hands and knees to get to church for prayer.

The fear of God can fall upon a whole nation and cover it. Many years ago when I was in Sweden, I listened to the testimony of one of the leading Pentecostal leaders in the nation at that time. He said that during revival in Sweden it was as though the whole nation was blanketed by the Spirit of the fear of the Lord. Men and women would be convicted of their sins in the middle of the night. They would get out of bed and walk until they found a church that was still open, so they could receive prayer and a release from the burden of their sin.

I believe that God is going to repeat this in nation after nation in the last days. We need to begin to cry out for the Spirit of the fear of the Lord to be upon our lives, upon our localities, and upon the nations of this world. This is the only way that the last day Church can be perfected. May we look forward with anticipation and prepare our hearts for the last day move of God!

SUMMARY OF THE SEVEN SPIRITS OF THE LORD

The Spirit of the Lord is the unction from God that enables us to preach and teach.

The Spirit of Wisdom enables us to make right choices in every area of our lives.

The Spirit of Understanding enables us to comprehend the reason why certain courses of action are necessary.

The Spirit of Counsel gives us direction in any given circumstance in life's trials.

The Spirit of Might releases God's power in the realm of the miraculous.

The Spirit of Knowledge reveals events past, present, and future as God views them.

The Spirit of the Fear of the Lord produces conviction of sin and promotes a reverential and holy life in the believer. This anointing causes sinner and saint alike to know if he is on or off God's path for his life.

Part Four

THE BAPTISM OF THE HOLY SPIRIT

In Part Four we are going to consider the baptism of the Holy Spirit. This blessed experience is the key and the secret to knowing the Holy Spirit and partaking of all of His wonderful blessings. Without this vital experience, we will never know all the riches and depths of the Holy Spirit. It is the baptism of the Holy Spirit that really awakens our spiritual senses and enables us to become spiritual people. It is through this experience that the Holy Spirit comes to dwell within us, empowering us to walk in the Spirit.

We must remember, however, that the baptism is not synonymous with sanctification or holiness—for a person can be carnal and also have the baptism of the Holy Spirit. Yet it is one of the greatest tools to aid us in our quest for true holiness. Therefore, let us now look at this exciting subject in detail, using the following topics:

A. Promised in the Old Testament
B. New Testament Fulfillment and Realization
C. Speaking in Other Tongues
D. How to Receive the Baptism of the Holy Spirit
E. Conditions to Receiving the Baptism of the Holy Spirit
F. For Whom is the Baptism of the Holy Spirit
G. The Progressive Experience of the Baptism of the Holy Spirit

A. PROMISED IN THE OLD TESTAMENT

The first point I would like to make is that the baptism of the Holy Spirit was promised in the Old Testament. For any doctrine to be true, it must be able to be proven from the Old Testament as well as the New Testament. Ample proof that the baptism of the Holy Spirit is a gift from the Lord is seen in Isaiah 28:11-12, where the prophet says: "For with stammering lips and another tongue will he speak to this people. To whom he said, This is the rest wherewith ye may cause the weary to rest; and this is the refreshing: yet they would not hear." Through the prophet Isaiah, the Lord clearly promises the baptism of the Holy Ghost with the initial evidence of speaking in other tongues. The Apostle Paul quotes this verse in First Corinthians 14:21 to confirm the authenticity of speaking in tongues. Yet, the prophet Isaiah also warned that many would not hear the message, but would reject it.

The baptism in the Holy Spirit is a "refreshing." It can cause the weary to find rest in their souls. It enables believers to express in another language the conflicts that are in their hearts and minds, and find release from them. Yet, many believers are taught to refuse the very remedy God has provided for their soul.

In Acts 1:4, just before His ascension to heaven, the Lord Jesus Christ gave His disciples specific instructions to wait in Jerusalem for "the promise of the Father." What was this promise of the Father? Well, it goes back to Isaiah 44:3, where God the Father made this promise to His Son Jesus: "For I will pour water upon him that is thirsty, and floods upon the dry ground: I will pour my spirit upon thy seed, and my blessing upon thine offspring." The Father promised the Son that He would pour out His Spirit upon His seed. His seed are all those who believe and call themselves by His name. The Apostle Peter also referred to this "promise" of the Holy Spirit by God the Father in his sermon on the day of Pentecost in Acts 2:33. "Therefore being by the right hand of God exalted, and having received of the Father the promise of the Holy Ghost, he hath shed forth this, which ye now see and hear."

Peter went on to say in Acts 2:39, "For the promise is unto you, and to your children, and to all that are afar off, even as many as the Lord our God shall call." This is also a very wonderful blessing for parents, for they have the privilege of passing on this experience to their children. The promise is unto our children as well as unto us. Praise the Lord for this special promise.

There is a third passage in the Old Testament in Joel 2:28 which also speaks of the experience of the baptism of the Holy Spirit: "And it shall come to pass afterward, that I will pour out my spirit upon all flesh; and your sons and your daughters shall prophesy, your old men shall dream dreams, your young men shall see visions." Peter quoted this verse in Acts 2:16-17 on the day of Pentecost, saying that the baptism of the Holy Spirit and the signs that accompany it are the fulfillment of the prophecy of Joel.

"But this is that which was spoken by the prophet Joel; And it shall come to pass in the last days, saith God, I will pour out of my Spirit upon all flesh: and your sons and your daughters shall prophesy, and your young men shall see visions, and your old men shall dream dreams." Thus, we have adequate confirmation that the baptism of the Holy Ghost was promised in the Old Testament, and that this promise was first realized on the day of Pentecost in Acts chapter two.

B. NEW TESTAMENT FULFILLMENT AND REALIZATION

In the New Testament, there was a promise given through John the Baptist concerning the ministry of the Lord Jesus as the Baptizer in the Holy Ghost. John said in Matthew 3:11, "I indeed baptize you with water unto repentance: but he that cometh after me is mightier than I, whose shoes I am not worthy to bear: he shall baptize you with the Holy Ghost, and with fire." John clearly stated that Christ would baptize us with the Holy Ghost.

The Lord Himself declared after His resurrection in Mark 16:17 that there are certain experiences that should follow a person's conversion: "And these signs shall follow them that believe; In my name shall they cast out devils; they shall *speak with new tongues*." After we are born-again, we should be filled with the Holy Spirit, and then continue to speak in other tongues on a regular basis. This is something the Lord has provided for every believer. Therefore, to reject it is to cut ourselves short of everything that God has ordained and purposed for our lives!

When was the baptism of the Holy Spirit first realized? The realization of the promise came during the Feast of Pentecost while the disciples were gathered in the upper room. Acts 2:1-4 records this outpouring of the Holy Spirit: "And when the day of Pentecost was fully come, they were all with one accord in one place. And suddenly there came a sound from heaven as of a rushing mighty wind, and it filled all the house where they were sitting. And there appeared unto them cloven tongues like as of fire, and it sat upon each of them. And they were all filled with the Holy Ghost, and began to speak with other tongues, as the Spirit gave them utterance."

Because the disciples were filled with the Holy Spirit on the day of Pentecost, speaking in tongues has been termed the "Pentecostal experience." Since the beginning of the twentieth century there has been a renewal of speaking in other tongues called the "Pentecostal movement."

C. SPEAKING IN OTHER TONGUES

Speaking in other tongues is a tremendous sign. It is the outrushing of the Spirit of God through the believer. All the manifestations of the Spirit (such as prophecy, healing, and miracles) were demonstrated in the Old Testament in one form or another, except speaking in other tongues. The Lord reserved this phenomena for the outpouring of the Spirit of God on the day of Pentecost to serve as an unmistakable sign that confirms that a person has received the baptism of the Holy Spirit. What happened on the day of Pentecost had never happened before; God was doing a new thing.

There are basically three aspects of the manifestation of tongues: (1) speaking in other tongues as the initial evidence of the baptism of the Holy Spirit; (2) speaking in tongues in our prayer life and worship; and (3) the gift of tongues for the edification of the Church.

When we speak in tongues, we are: (1) speaking unto God and speaking the mysteries of God (1 Cor. 14:2); (2) declaring the wonderful works of God (Acts 2:11); (3) magnifying the Lord (Acts 10:46); and (4) edifying our spirits and strengthening our inner man (1 Cor. 14:4, Rom. 8:26-27).

Let us now consider several aspects of this wonderful blessing of God.

1. The Initial Evidence of the Baptism of the Holy Spirit

How do we know for sure that we have been baptized in the Holy Spirit? We must look at the textbook, which is the Word of God, to see whether our experience coincides with the biblical experience. First of all, we must ask ourselves: What happened to people in the Bible when they were filled with the Spirit, and what was the outward sign that they had been filled? The answer is that they began to speak with other tongues. That is how we know when we have been filled with the Spirit.

Let me illustrate my point. When we are baptized in water, something happens—we get wet. It is the same with the baptism of the Holy Ghost. The evidence, or proof, that someone has been filled with the Spirit is that he begins to speak with other tongues. Until he does, he has not yet been baptized in the Holy Ghost. Let us be very clear about that. The outpouring of the Holy Spirit on the day of Pentecost was identified with speaking with other tongues. This was the initial evidence that they had been baptized in the Holy Ghost—they were filled with the Spirit and began to speak with other tongues.

Speaking of the outpouring of the Spirit of God upon the day of Pentecost and the baptism of the Holy Spirit, Peter said in Acts 2:33, "Having received of the Father the promise of the Holy Ghost, [the Lord] hath shed forth this, which ye now *see* and *hear*." The baptism of the Holy Spirit is clearly accompanied by audible and visible signs. The Jews could *hear* and *see* the disciples speaking in other tongues. Speaking in tongues is an unmistakable sign to let the believer know he has received that for which he has been seeking. The scriptural accounts of people being baptized in the Holy Ghost consistently declare that they began to speak with other tongues. Let us now examine these accounts with an open and teachable heart. Acts 2:4 says, "And they were all filled with the Holy Ghost, and began to speak with other tongues, as the Spirit gave them utterance."

We can also read about the Spirit of God that was poured out upon the house of Cornelius and the Gentiles in Acts 10:44-46. "While Peter yet spake these words, the Holy Ghost fell on all them which heard the word. And they of the circumcision which believed were astonished, as many as came with Peter, because that on the Gentiles also was poured out the gift of the Holy Ghost. *For they heard them speak with tongues*, and magnify God." The reason that Peter and his companions knew that Cornelius and his household had been baptized in the Holy Ghost was that they heard them speak with other tongues.

In Acts chapter eight, Philip the Evangelist went to the city of Samaria and preached Christ. Many signs and wonders, including healings, were performed by him. Among the many converts was a man named Simon who had bewitched the people of Samaria with sorceries. Convicted by Philip's preaching, this man gave his life to the Lord and was baptized in water. He continued with Philip and marveled at the miracles that were seen through his ministry.

Seeing revival continue to break out in the city of Samaria, the apostles in Jerusalem sent Peter and John to help Philip with this great harvest. When Peter and John came and prayed for the new converts, they received the baptism of the Holy Spirit. Before this, these blood-washed believers had only been baptized in water. The argument that some have made against speaking in tongues as the initial sign of the baptism of the Holy Spirit is that this account does not mention that the new converts spoke in other tongues when they received the Holy Spirit. However, if the reader carefully observes what happened *after* these disciples received the baptism, this account actually confirms that speaking in other tongues is indeed the initial evidence of the baptism of the Holy Spirit. In Acts 8:18-19 we read, "And when Simon saw that through laying on of the apostles' hands the Holy Ghost was given, he offered them money, Saying, Give me also this power, that on whomsoever I lay hands, he may receive the Holy Ghost."

Simon, who was well accustomed to signs and wonders himself, saw something so miraculous happen when the disciples received the Holy Spirit that he was willing to pay money for that power. We must take note here that Simon did not offer money for the convicting power that Philip had in his preaching or the healings he performed. He offered money for the obvious power Peter and John had when they prayed for people to receive the baptism in the Holy Spirit. Simon, who had moved in the realm of the supernatural for many years, must have seen mighty signs manifested with the occurrence of the baptism of the Holy Spirit. Therefore, this passage also proves that something must happen when people receive the Holy Spirit. Thus, we could say with assurance that Simon heard people speak in other tongues when they received the baptism of the Holy Spirit. There is an outward manifestation of the Holy Ghost that is apparent to others when someone is filled with the Spirit.

Acts 19:1-6 is the record of Paul's missionary trip to Ephesus. Paul asked the Ephesian believers in Acts 19:2, "Have ye received the Holy Ghost since ye believed?" This passage also offers conclusive evidence that the baptism of the Holy Ghost is clearly a separate experience from salvation. The two are not the same. These believers were saved and water baptized, but they had not yet been filled with the Holy Spirit (Acts 19:2-4). Then in Acts 19:6, after Paul laid his hands upon them, “the Holy Ghost came on them; and they spake with tongues, and prophesied.” In this case, those who were filled with the Spirit prophesied and spoke in tongues. As we have said before, speaking in tongues is not necessarily the only sign of the infilling of the Spirit, but it is the initial evidence. In the scriptural accounts, it was a sign that always accompanied people being filled with the Spirit, whereas prophecy did not.

The Apostle Paul was born-again when the Lord Jesus appeared to him on the road to Damascus (see Acts 9:4-6). Paul asked, “Who art Thou, Lord?” The Lord replied, “I am Jesus whom thou persecutest.” Paul’s response was, “Lord, what wilt Thou have me to do?” The Lord answered, “Arise and go into the city and it will be told thee what thou must do.” This was Paul’s salvation experience. Three days later Ananias said to Paul in Acts 9:17, “Receive thy sight, and be filled with the Holy Ghost.” It was here that he received the baptism of the Holy Ghost. Then he was later baptized with water. Therefore, salvation and the baptism of the Holy Ghost are different. They are *two separate experiences.*

Speaking in other tongues is the initial evidence of the baptism of the Holy Spirit. You can be *anointed* by the Holy Spirit, but that does not necessarily mean that you have the *baptism* of the Holy Spirit. The baptism of the Spirit and the seven Spirits of the Lord are different. As we have said in previous chapters, the first Spirit of the Lord is the anointing to preach. A person can be anointed to preach the gospel without being baptized in the Holy Spirit. Several well known evangelists speak under an anointing. You can feel the anointing when they preach, but they state publicly that they are not baptized in the Holy Ghost. Therefore, you can be anointed with the seven Spirits of the Lord and not be filled with the Holy Spirit. John the Baptist was anointed by the Holy Spirit and the Holy Spirit came upon him when he was in his mother's womb. However, he did not have the baptism of the Holy Spirit, nor did he speak in other tongues, because the Holy Spirit was not given until the day of Pentecost.

The Holy Spirit is instrumental in our salvation. Christ clearly states in John 3:5, "Except a man be born of water and of the Spirit, he cannot enter into the kingdom of God." It is through the agency of the Holy Spirit that we are born-again, but that is not the same experience as being baptized in the Holy Ghost. After His resurrection, the Lord breathed on the disciples and said to them in John 20:22, "Receive ye the Holy Ghost." This was their new birth experience. However, this was not the infilling of the Holy Spirit. Forty days later, just before His ascension to heaven, He told His disciples, "*Ye shall be baptized with the Holy Ghost not many days hence*" (Acts 1:5). Christ was referring to the day of Pentecost when the disciples would be baptized with the Holy Ghost. Their new birth experience was when He breathed on them.

In the Old Testament era before the cross, devout believers did not have the born-again experience that we know today. They walked uprightly and obeyed the commandments and it was counted to them for righteousness. But after the cross, we are saved by faith in the shed blood of the Lord Jesus. We become a new creature in Christ. This is what the disciples experienced in John 20:22. But it was not until the day of Pentecost that they were baptized in the Holy Spirit. Therefore, salvation and the baptism of the Holy Ghost are clearly two separate experiences. A person must be saved before he can be baptized in the Holy Spirit.

The day of Pentecost ushered in a new era. Before that time the Holy Spirit came *upon* men and anointed them to do certain things, and the Holy Spirit was *with* them. But at the baptism of the Holy Spirit, the Holy Spirit enters *into* our hearts and dwells *inside of* us. Jesus said of the coming Holy Spirit, "For he dwelleth *with you*, and *shall be in you*" (Jn. 14:17). Before the day of Pentecost, the Spirit of God came upon people and walked with them. But since that outpouring of the Spirit, He comes to dwell in us when we are baptized in the Holy Ghost.

We cannot look to an experience to form a doctrine. Some people say that they know believers who do not speak in other tongues who are more upright and honest than Pentecostal believers who do speak in tongues. Thus, they conclude that those who are more upright, even though they do not speak in other tongues, must be baptized in the Holy Spirit. You cannot argue on the basis of your personal experience or the experience of others. The only basis for our arguments is the Word of God. Make sure you formulate your doctrine from the Word of God, not from people's experiences. Otherwise, you will err in your doctrine. Experiences should only confirm what the Scriptures teach.

2. A Known or Heavenly Language

The gift of tongues is either a known language, or a heavenly language, as seen by the words of Paul in First Corinthians 13:1: "Though I speak with the *tongues of men and angels*." In Acts 2:5-11 people from many different countries heard the disciples speaking in their own languages. The record of this is in Acts 2:11: "We do hear them speak in our [languages] the wonderful works of God." Therefore, when we speak in tongues we are declaring the wonderful works of God in a foreign earthly language or in a heavenly language.

I distinctly remember a certain prayer meeting I attended at the church where I was an assistant pastor in France many years ago. I really needed answers from the Lord for certain things, so I prayed freely in English because I knew that no one there would be able to understand me. Then the senior pastor, who didn't even know one word of English, spoke in tongues. Well, much to my surprise, he spoke in perfect English and answered all of my questions and petitions with great detail.

I remember another time when my wife and I went to Yugoslavia. The pastor of the church where we ministered had just been released from jail a few days before we arrived because someone from within the church had betrayed him and had turned him in to the Communist authorities. Unfortunately, the assistant pastor was the one accused of being the traitor. During one of the services, I heard this assistant pastor praying in German. This did not seem strange to me because there were many people in Yugoslavia at that time who spoke German.

I was very perplexed, however, when I spoke to him in German after the service and he did not respond. Those who were with me told me that he did not speak even one word of German. I exclaimed quickly, "What do you mean he doesn't speak German? I heard him with my own ears speak in German." They replied, "That is the language he speaks when he speaks in tongues." I was then able to understand from his prayers that he was not the traitor. He had been saying in German, "Jesus, He is my Lord; Jesus, He is my Lord." No man can say that Jesus is Lord but by the Holy Ghost. Speaking through an interpreter, I said to him, "You are innocent, aren't you?" When I said this he began to weep. My point is that when he spoke in other tongues, he was speaking in the known language of German, even though he didn't know German.

Another time, at a convention in North America, a man from Uruguay was speaking in French while he was being prayed for. I quietly whispered to the pastor who was laying hands on him, "This man is speaking in French." He quickly responded: "He is not speaking in French. He can't possibly be; he doesn't know French. He's speaking in Spanish." I replied, "Well, listen to him, and see if you can understand what he is saying." He listened closely and then said to me: "You're right. He's not speaking Spanish." I then confidently replied, "I know. He's speaking in French—I know French too." It was beautiful to hear the Holy Spirit pray through this man as he was reciting the psalms in tongues and magnifying the Lord.

In a particular service many years ago, my sister-in-law spoke out loud in tongues. Afterwards, a missionary came up and told her that when she spoke in tongues she was speaking in the language of Hindi.

I am reminded of another story that concerns a Canadian pastor. He once told me that he knew a sure way to judge prophecy. He recounted to me what would frequently take place in his church. There was a certain person in his church who would from time to time give a message in tongues, and the language he spoke when he spoke in tongues was Hindustani.

Well, there was also a retired missionary lady at this church who had ministered for many years in northern India where they speak Hindustani. Because she knew the language, she could understand what this man was saying when he gave a message in tongues. However, she would never give the interpretation; she would wait for someone else to interpret in English. Obviously, she knew whether or not the correct interpretation was given; and she would tell the pastor whether it was right or not.

One time in a convention in Switzerland, I felt the anointing very strongly and I spoke out in tongues during the worship service. I thought for sure that someone was going to interpret my tongues, but to my horror, no one did. I was very embarrassed because I had been teaching our Bible school students that when they give a message in tongues, it should be interpreted. Yet, the Lord tests us. After that service, as I was trying to leave quickly to avoid seeing too many people, an American missionary lady came up to me and said: "I am of Swedish descent. When you spoke in other tongues during the service, you spoke in perfect Swedish. I understood every word you said, and the Lord was speaking to me personally." I can assure you that I felt very relieved after she told me that!

We need to speak frequently and fluently in tongues. Our tongues are an actual language, as indicated in Acts chapter two. Therefore, like learning any language, we must develop our vocabulary in our spiritual tongues. Some people, however, never mature in their language. They keep repeating the same little phrases and words over and over again. That is fine for someone who has just received the Holy Spirit, but if our language has not enlarged after ten years, we are in a sad spiritual state.

When a child first begins to speak, his parents are overwhelmed with joy. However, if he were still repeating the same three or four words when he was twenty years old, his parents would be terribly disappointed. We should practice speaking in tongues every day so that we can speak fluently. We want tongues to just flow out from us. And as we continue to speak in tongues, God will give us a new prayer language in other tongues. First Corinthians 12:10 tells us that there are different kinds of tongues. In the natural, if a person is diligent and studies hard, he can learn many languages. It is the same in the spiritual life. If we are diligent to seek the Lord and use the language in other tongues that God has already given us, He will give us new languages.

3. The Key to Power, Revelation, and the Anointing

Speaking in other tongues is the key to power, revelation, and the anointing. Christ declared to His disciples in Acts 1:8, "But *ye shall receive power, after that the Holy Ghost is come upon you*: and ye shall be witnesses unto me both in Jerusalem, and in all Judea, and in Samaria, and unto the uttermost part of the earth." The baptism of the Holy Spirit is power to witness and preach for Jesus. This baptism enables us to overcome the spirit of fear. It transforms someone who is timid into a bold and flaming witness for the Lord. Acts 4:31 illustrates this: "They were all filled with the Holy Ghost, and they spake the word of God with boldness." Jesus said in Luke 24:49, "And, behold, I send the promise of my Father upon you: but tarry ye in the city of Jerusalem, until ye be endued with power from on high." The prime feature of the baptism in the Holy Ghost is *power*. Speaking in other tongues develops the power of the Holy Spirit in our lives. As we speak in tongues, we are building ourselves up and strengthening our inner man (1 Cor. 14:4).

Speaking in other tongues is also the key to having the anointing of God. Those who spend time every day in the presence of the Lord and speak in other tongues will *drip* with the anointing and presence of God in their lives. They are noticeably different from others who lack this relationship and daily communion with the Lord. The beautiful fragrance of the Lord is upon their lives, and it is obvious to others. Every time you come in contact with people like this, you feel as if you were in the very presence of God.

When I was an assistant pastor in France, we were ministering among the Pentecostal churches in the country. Basically, the messages revolved around salvation, water baptism, the baptism of the Holy Ghost, and perhaps the elementary principles of the doctrine of Christ (see Heb. 6:1-3). But there was a certain pastor who had an extraordinary grasp of the Word of God as well as tremendous revelation. He ventured out where other pastors feared to tread, speaking under a tremendous anointing from obscure and isolated portions of the Word of God that no one else preached from and scarcely read.

Being young at that time, some of my colleagues and I said to him, "Pastor, would you tell us what books you use for study so that we can acquire the knowledge you have." This dear pastor replied: "I only have a few reference books. Actually, what I do is I spend about two hours every morning from eight o'clock to ten o'clock praying in the Spirit in tongues. As I pray, I start to get revelation and the messages flow."

In other words, when this pastor spoke in other tongues and worshipped the Lord in tongues, he was speaking mysteries to the Lord, and the Lord was opening up his mind to the wonders of God's Word (see 1 Cor. 14:2). I have never forgotten this pastor's shining example. I would recommend that each of you pray and worship in other tongues every day, especially before you study the Word of God, so that the Scriptures are opened up to you, even as they were to this great man of God.

Before preaching or studying for a message, we should speak in tongues. This enables our spirit to be revived and our mind to be quickened; and then the message that God has for us flows. This has always been a practice of mine. Whenever I am studying a portion of the Word of God that is complicated and the right interpretation is not clearly discernible, I will break from my study to pray and worship the Lord in tongues until I am sure that I have received the correct interpretation of the passage I am studying. Therefore, one of the purposes of speaking in other tongues is to obtain revelation.

Many years ago when my wife and I were in the western United States ministering in several denominational churches, I was preaching on different aspects of the power of God and the anointing. The meetings began to get crowded and people became really excited about what God was saying. On the last night of these meetings, the Lord spoke to me, "Now tell them where this power comes from—the baptism of the Holy Spirit." I said to the Lord, "But Lord, You know that if I tell them where the power comes from they will reject the message." The Lord's response was: "They are not on trial, you are. I know what they will do; I want to know if you will obey Me or not."

That night I preached on the baptism of the Holy Spirit; and sure enough, there was an uproar. Most of the people rejected the message. As a result, the city became so divided that denominational Christians would not even walk on the same side of the street as Pentecostal believers. There is much more to this story, but the point I am trying to make is that the Lord clearly spoke to me and said that a Christian's key to power is the baptism of the Holy Spirit and speaking in tongues.

D. HOW TO RECEIVE THE BAPTISM OF THE HOLY SPIRIT

Let us now consider how we receive the Holy Spirit. In his sermon on the day of Pentecost, the Apostle Peter tells us the three things we must do to receive the baptism of the Holy Spirit.

He said in Acts 2:38, "Repent, and be baptized every one of you in the name of Jesus Christ for the remission of sins, and ye shall receive the gift of the Holy Ghost." In order for people to receive the baptism of the Holy Spirit, they must first repent and have a genuine new birth experience whereby they know they are redeemed by the blood of the Lamb of God who died for them upon the cross. Repentance literally means "to have a change of mind, and to turn around and walk in the opposite direction." Therefore, people must forsake their old lifestyle and begin to walk in the ways of God.

The next requirement is that they must be water baptized, or in some cases, be willing to be water baptized. For example, the house of Cornelius repented at the preaching of Peter, gave their lives to the Lord, and were filled with the Holy Spirit while Peter was still preaching. Afterwards, they were water baptized. The Apostle Paul himself was filled with the Spirit before he was water baptized. I, too, was baptized in the Holy Spirit before I was water baptized, but I was willing to be baptized in water and had already put my name down on a list to be water baptized. Peter tells us that if we repent and become born-again, and we are water baptized, then we are candidates to receive the gift of the Holy Spirit.

It is the Lord Jesus Himself who is the Baptizer. It is He who baptizes us with the Holy Ghost. John the Baptist made this point very clear in Matthew 3:11. A man cannot baptize himself or anyone else with the Holy Ghost. Men and women can certainly be the *instruments* used to lay hands upon people and pray for them to receive the baptism of the Holy Spirit. However, they will not receive the Holy Spirit until the Lord sovereignly baptizes them. Neither does one receive the baptism of the Holy Spirit by repeating certain words or phrases spoken by another person, or by following a formula. It is only the Lord who can baptize with the Holy Spirit. The Lord must be present for someone to receive the Holy Spirit. Therefore, we want to be in an atmosphere of prayer and worship so that the presence of the Lord will come and people will be baptized with the Holy Ghost.

One of the most precious things about the baptism of the Holy Spirit is that everyone's experience is unique and different. There is no set pattern for receiving the baptism. Many people in the Scriptures received the Holy Spirit when someone prayed for them and laid hands on them (see Acts 8:17, 9:17, 19:6). However, on the day of the original outpouring of the Spirit of God the disciples were filled with the Spirit as they were sitting down waiting for the Lord to move in their midst (Acts 2:2-4). The household of Cornelius received the Holy Spirit as Peter was preaching (Acts 10:44). We can also receive the Holy Spirit all by ourselves. We do not necessarily have to be in a church building or in a service. I received the Holy Spirit while I was all alone in the hills of England.

Nonetheless, it is a good idea to have someone who is baptized with the Holy Spirit pray for you to help you and guide you through it. This is very helpful, because most people don't know what to do and they have doubts and questions. Therefore, if someone is there to explain to you how to receive, it is much easier for you.

Speaking in tongues is a gift of the Holy Spirit, but there is also the human element involved. We have to do the speaking with our vocal chords. This is our part. However, the words are given by the Spirit. Acts 2:4 says, "They began to speak with other tongues, as the Spirit gave them utterance."

The Holy Spirit wants to come *into* us and flow *out* through us. It is a good idea to start by praising the Lord and worshipping Him in our native language. Then by faith we yield our vocal chords unto the Lord and begin speaking in a new language. We do not have to think about what we say, or formulate the words in our minds because it is a language that we cannot understand. The Holy Spirit bypasses our minds and intellect and speaks through us. We should not try to make up the words or copy someone else's tongues. It is as we speak by faith, that the Holy Spirit will give us the words.

E. CONDITIONS TO RECEIVING THE BAPTISM OF THE HOLY SPIRIT

The Scriptures make it abundantly clear that there are certain conditions for receiving the baptism of the Holy Spirit. There is a reason why some are filled with the Spirit and others are not. Since the Lord is not a respecter of persons, it therefore depends upon people's hearts.

1. Obedience

Peter said in Acts 5:32, "And we are his witnesses of these things; and so is also the Holy Ghost, whom God hath given to them that *obey* him." Quite often the Lord will not give the Spirit to people until they put certain things right in their lives and do what He is telling them to do. For example, after I was led to the Lord by a Pentecostal believer in England, I joined a certain church and began attending services there regularly. One day the pastor of the church announced that they were going to be having a water baptismal service for all those who were interested. He made an appeal for everyone who was not baptized in water to put their names down on a list. I was not really interested in getting water baptized because I felt that I was seeking for something better. I wanted the baptism of the Holy Spirit. However, the Lord told me that I had to be water baptized before He would fill me with the Holy Spirit. So I put my name down on that list; then I went to southern England on vacation where the Lord baptized me in the Holy Ghost. When the Lord saw that I had obeyed Him by signing up to be water baptized, He filled me with the Spirit.

Sometimes the Lord requires us to do certain acts of obedience before He will baptize us in the Holy Ghost. Many times they are very little things. A pastor in England whom I knew many years ago had been earnestly praying to receive the Holy Spirit. Yet no matter how hard he tried, or how long he prayed, he could not receive. Then one day the Lord spoke to him to release a bird that he had caught and placed in a cage. Just as soon as he let that bird out of the cage, he was instantly filled with the Spirit.

2. Believing

In order to receive the baptism of the Holy Spirit we must believe. John 7:39 says, "But this spake he of the Spirit, which they that *believe* on him should receive: for the Holy Ghost was not yet given; because that Jesus was not yet glorified." We must believe the Lord and believe that the baptism of the Holy Spirit is a gift from God in order to be filled with the Spirit. If there is unbelief in our lives, we will not receive.

3. Desire

We must also have the desire in our hearts to be baptized with the Holy Spirit. The Lord fills everyone according to his desires. He gives us the desires of our heart (see Psa. 37:4). The Lord Jesus said in John 7:37, "If any man thirst, let him come unto me, and drink." Therefore, having rivers of living water flowing out from our innermost being and receiving the baptism of the Holy Spirit is rooted in our *desire* (see John 7:37-39). Only those who are thirsty and desire to receive the Spirit are going to be filled. We must be thirsty. Paul tells us in First Corinthians 12:31 to "covet earnestly the best gifts." The gifts of the Holy Spirit are not given to people who do not have any interest in the things of God. The Apostle Paul also said in First Corinthians 14:1, "Follow after charity, and desire spiritual gifts."

The reason some people never receive the Holy Spirit is because they simply have no desire for it. They are content with the spiritual plateau on which they have settled. This is a terrible state to be in! Let us hunger and thirst for the fullness of the Holy Spirit in our lives, for if we do, we will surely receive.

4. Persistence

Another condition to receiving the baptism of the Holy Spirit is that we must persistently ask the Lord for it and persevere in prayer until we receive it. In Luke 11:1 the disciples asked the Lord to teach them to pray. In response to this, He spoke a parable on the subject of importunity. "Which of you shall have a friend, and shall go unto him at midnight, and say unto him, Friend, lend me three loaves; For a friend of mine in his journey is come to me, and I have nothing to set before him? And he from within shall answer and say, Trouble me not: the door is now shut, and my children are with me in bed; I cannot rise and give thee. I say unto you, Though he will not rise and give him, because he is his friend, yet *because of his importunity* he will rise and give him as many as he needeth" (Lk. 11:5-8).

In Luke 11:9-10 the Lord said (reading from the original Greek): "Ask [and keep on asking], and it shall be given you; seek [and keep on seeking], and ye shall find; knock [and keep on knocking], and it shall be opened unto you. For every one that asketh receiveth; and he that seeketh findeth; and to him that knocketh it shall be opened." The verbs in this passage are in the present progressive tense. In other words, we must ask and continue asking in order to receive. Jesus then went on to say in Luke 11:13, "If ye then, being evil, know how to give good gifts unto your children: how much more shall your heavenly Father give the Holy Spirit to them that ask [and keep on asking] him?" If we ask and we keep on asking, and if we insist and will not be denied, then the Lord will hear our desperate cry and fill us with His Spirit.

We must take hold of the Lord as Jacob did when he wrestled with Him, and say to Him: "I will not let You go unless You bless me. I will not stop praying until You fill me with the Holy Spirit." But if our attitude concerning the baptism of the Holy Spirit is that we can take it or leave it, we are never going to receive. The baptism of the Holy Spirit is an experience that we must *insist* upon having in order to obtain it. It does not come to the passive.

Some people say, "If the Lord wants to fill me with the Holy Spirit, He knows where I live and He can come and fill me when He wants to." Those who have this mentality are never filled with the Holy Ghost. They live their whole life not openly opposing the baptism of the Holy Spirit, but never experiencing it because of a lack of perseverance to obtain it. Those who only ask once are not going to receive. This separates the sincere from the insincere. God does this so that only those who *really* want to receive will be filled with the Spirit.

F. FOR WHOM IS THE BAPTISM OF THE HOLY SPIRIT

The baptism of the Holy Spirit is for every believer in every generation. It is for the Church of Christ today. We must not compromise on this issue. People cannot scripturally say that speaking in other tongues is not for today. Peter said in Acts 2:38-39: "Repent, and be baptized every one of you in the name of Jesus Christ for the remission of sins, and ye shall receive the gift of the Holy Ghost. For the promise [referring to the baptism of the Holy Spirit] is unto you, and to your children, and to all that are afar off, *even as many as the Lord our God shall call*."

Peter clearly stated that speaking in other tongues was for his generation and for their children, and that it was also for all those "afar off." Then he states that the baptism of the Holy Spirit is for "as many as the Lord shall call." This means that the baptism of the Holy Spirit is for every believer in every generation. Christ declared in Mark 16:17, "And these signs shall follow them that believe; In my name shall they cast out devils; they shall speak with new tongues." Therefore, you should be assured that this experience is for you too!

G. THE PROGRESSIVE EXPERIENCE OF THE BAPTISM OF THE HOLY SPIRIT

The English word *baptism* is an Anglicized word. It is derived from the Greek word "baptizo." The translators of the King James Version of the Bible belonged to many different denominations, and they could not agree on the doctrine of water baptism. Some said that it meant complete immersion, others believed in sprinkling, and still others practiced splashing with water or pouring water on the head. Therefore, they simply transliterated the Greek word "baptizo." However, in the transliteration, the true meaning and force behind this word was lost. This Greek word actually means *to fully immerse*. It was the word used for a ship that had sunk and was completely covered and filled with water. It was also used for a garment that had been dyed. The dyeing liquids would completely saturate that garment and would therefore affect the color of every thread of the material.

By understanding this deeper meaning, we can see that the Lord's desire is not only to baptize us *once* in the Holy Spirit and give us the gift of tongues. Rather, He wants us to be *fully* immersed with the Holy Spirit, so that every area of our life is covered with the presence and anointing of the Spirit. This is the ongoing vision and progressive experience of the baptism of the Holy Ghost.

The Apostle Paul said in Ephesians 5:18, "And be not drunk with wine, wherein is excess; but be ye filled with the Spirit." This verse in the original Greek reads like this: "Be ye *being* filled with the Spirit." Therefore, there is a progressive infilling of the Holy Spirit. For this to be shown as a scriptural truth, we must see an account in the Word of God where believers were filled with the Spirit more than once.

The same disciples who were baptized in the Holy Spirit on the day of Pentecost in Acts 2 were filled again in Acts 4:31. "And when they had prayed, the place was shaken where they were assembled together; and they were all filled with the Holy Ghost, and they spake the word of God with boldness." There is an initial infilling of the Holy Spirit whereby we begin to speak in new tongues in a language that we have never spoken before.

However, there is also a progressive infilling of the Holy Spirit. This is what we want to seek the Lord for. We must desire to be filled with all the fullness of the Spirit.

In England, the process of pouring more oil into your engine when it is low is called "topping up" your oil level. This is how we should seek to be when it concerns being refilled with the Spirit. We do not want to run low on the anointing of the Holy Spirit, but we want to have a continual and ever-increasing infilling of His Spirit so that our lives overflow with His presence and anointing.

Part Five

THE GIFTS OF THE SPIRIT

Part Five of this book concentrates on the nine gifts of the Holy Spirit which are enumerated in First Corinthians chapter twelve. The nine spiritual gifts are blessings that are freely given to us by the Lord. They cannot be earned. The gifts are given by God with one main objective in mind—to bring edification to the Church (1 Cor. 12:7, 14:12).

The five ministry gifts of Christ spoken of in Ephesians 4:11, which are callings to the fivefold ministry, are different from the nine gifts of the Spirit. Ministry gifts cannot be obtained through prayer; they are only given to those whom God has sovereignly called to the ministry. No man can take this honor unto himself (Heb. 5:4). The nine spiritual gifts, on the other hand, are for every Spirit-filled believer. We are exhorted to seek the Lord for them. The nine gifts of the Spirit are a means whereby every Christian can be fruitful and a blessing to the Church, even if he is not called to the fivefold ministry.

Paul said in First Corinthians 12:1, "Now concerning spiritual gifts, brethren, I would not have you ignorant." The Lord wants us to understand the workings of the Holy Spirit in the realm and experience of the baptism of the Holy Ghost. God's express intention is that every believer should experience the fullness of the Holy Spirit and have a flow of the gifts in his life.

In verses eight through ten of First Corinthians chapter twelve, Paul lists the nine gifts of the Holy Spirit: "For to one is given by the Spirit the word of wisdom; to another the word of knowledge by the same Spirit; To another faith by the same Spirit; to another the gifts of healing by the same Spirit; To another the working of miracles; to another prophecy; to another discerning of spirits; to another divers kinds of tongues; to another the interpretation of tongues." Actually, these nine gifts can be grouped into three categories: the gifts of guidance, the gifts of power, and the gifts of utterance. The gifts of guidance include the word of wisdom, the word of knowledge, and the discerning of spirits. The gifts of power incorporate the gift of faith, the gifts of healing, and the working of miracles. The gifts of utterance consist of prophecy, tongues, and interpretation of tongues.

THE NINE GIFTS OF THE HOLY SPIRIT

Guidance

1. Word of wisdom
2. Word of knowledge
3. Discerning of spirits

Power

4. Faith
5. Gifts of healing
6. Working of miracles

Utterance

7. Prophecy
8. Tongues
9. Interpretation of tongues

Paul mentioned a very important point concerning the spiritual gifts when he said in First Corinthians 12:29-30: "Are all apostles? are all prophets? are all teachers? are all workers of miracles? Have all the gifts of healing? do all speak with tongues? do all interpret?" God gives different gifts to each person. It would be extremely rare for someone to have all nine gifts in operation at the same time, but it is possible if we consider someone of the caliber of the Apostle Paul.

We do not instantly receive all nine gifts of the Spirit when we are baptized in the Holy Spirit. This is very clear, for the Apostle Paul told the Spirit-filled believers at Corinth to covet and pray for the gifts. Paul would not have told them to seek for the gifts if they were already *resident* within them. Therefore, we become candidates to receive the spiritual gifts after we are baptized in the Holy Spirit. However, we only receive them as we earnestly seek the Lord for them.

In verse eleven Paul continues, "But all these [are the work of one and the same Spirit], dividing to every man severally as he will." It is the Holy Spirit who determines *which* gifts we receive and *when* we receive them. To those who have received the baptism of the Holy Spirit, the spiritual gifts are imparted as He wills.

Paul said in verse seven, "But the manifestation of the Spirit is given to every man to profit withal." These gifts are for *our* profit as well. We are blessed when we exercise these gifts, and they also are a blessing to the Body of Christ. We profit *with all.*

We must remember that although the nine gifts of the Holy Spirit are one hundred percent divine and perfect, they are used by vessels that are human and natural. Therefore, the operation of the gifts is not infallible because the channels are not infallible. This can be clearly seen from nature. There might be a body of water that is absolutely pure and clean. However, even though the source is pure, if that water is to be channeled to people, it must pass through pipes (or channels) that may be rusty or dirty. As a result, the water will come out tainted by the channel. It is the same way with the spiritual gifts. The source (the Holy Spirit) is divine, but because the vessels used are human, mistakes can be made.

Many times mistakes are made because of a lack of teaching about the gifts, or because of a lack of practice of the gifts. Some people at times may embellish the message the Lord has given them. Generally, this will not do too much damage. However, there are others who operate in the gifts from their own spirit with wrong motives to give others the impression that they are very spiritual. It becomes a thing of pride to them. This is very serious. Nevertheless, we must not judge the gifts by the one who receives and uses them, but by the One who gives them—the Holy Spirit. If you remember this truth, it will save you a lot of frustration and confusion.

The gifts of the Holy Spirit are His personal gifts to His children. They produce godly character in those who use them with right motives. Although we may be very imperfect in many areas of our lives, we can still receive the gifts of the Holy Spirit, and as we use them our character is being changed from glory to glory.

The Word of God says, "He that watereth shall be watered also himself" (Prov.11:25). As we begin to move in the gifts of the Spirit and pour out to others, we will receive more of His Spirit. We receive a blessing as we bless others!

For example, when we pray for the sick and they are healed, it makes us feel better even though we may be perfectly healthy. When we prophesy, we get a greater understanding of God's ways. We feel good in our hearts after we have given a prophecy. Even if the prophecy was for the church and did not have any real application to our own lives, we still feel very refreshed in our spirits. By the same token, those who operate in the word of wisdom actually become recipients of God's wisdom, and they become wise people.

Everyone who would be used effectively in the realm of the gifts of the Spirit must understand that wisdom is the underlying factor in all manifestations of the Holy Spirit. Wisdom must govern the power and the operation of the spiritual gifts! Psalm 104:24 says that "all the Lord's works are done in wisdom." Therefore, power must be subjugated to wisdom, and operate only as directed by wisdom.

For example, it is true that the creation of the heavens and the earth was a manifestation of God's awesome power. However, this power was cradled in wisdom (see Jer. 51:15). It was wisdom that set everything in order. Can you see how power must only be used in conjunction with wisdom?

Consider for a moment the tremendous power of dynamite. One stick of dynamite alone is very powerful. Yet, unless it is used *wisely* it can cause great damage and harm. In like manner, if the power of God and the gifts of the Holy Spirit are not used with wisdom, they can tear down rather than edify and build up.

The healing power of God is governed by wisdom. There is a specific time for people to be healed. Everything God intended to accomplish in one's life through the trial must be completed first. In the case of Lazarus, God's purpose was for him to die, so that through his death and resurrection he might bring even greater glory to the Lord. Had Jesus not been in tune to the Spirit and to His Father, He could have altered God's plan for Lazarus.

The gifts of the Holy Spirit must be accompanied with wisdom and a sensitivity to the Holy Spirit and His will. We must only use the gifts when it is the Lord's time—not whenever we want to use them. There is a time to speak in tongues, a time to interpret, a time to prophesy, and a time to heal, and there are also times when we should not use these gifts. Another thing to remember is that the gifts are intended to accomplish the Lord's purposes—not ours. They are intended to bring Him the glory alone. Wisdom enables us to channel power in the right direction and use it only for God's purposes.

One of the most important aspects of teaching on the gifts is the need for humility. Yet, the emphasis on humility is often neglected. Without humility of heart and mind, the Christian will never experience the fullness of the Holy Spirit and never be used effectively to any great extent in the realm of the spiritual gifts. We must be humble enough to accept the gifts the Lord chooses to give us and wait in expectation for the other gifts. Also, it requires great humility to use these gifts only when the Lord tells us to, and to use them only for God's glory.

We must always have the humility of heart to ask the Lord what His will is in every situation, because the way God operates varies from situation to situation. Be careful not to limit God to a form. The prophet Isaiah had the humility of heart to use a bunch of figs to heal King Hezekiah. Since Isaiah had already been used to cause the sun to go back ten degrees, he could have reasoned that he did not need figs to heal the king. However, he was humble and he knew where his power came from. We must accept whatever means God chooses to heal us or to speak to us. This was the problem in the heart of Naaman. He wanted the prophet Elisha to heal him miraculously. Therefore, he was offended when Elisha simply told him to go wash in the Jordan seven times in order to be cleansed of his leprosy (see 2 Kgs. 5:8-14).

If we are to know God's will, we must have a close relationship with the Lord and be sensitive to the Spirit. The key to the life of the Lord Jesus can be seen in Isaiah 50:4: "The Lord God hath given me the tongue of the learned, that I should know how to speak a word in season to him that is weary: he wakeneth morning by morning, he wakeneth mine ear to hear as the learned." The spiritual gifts progress and mature in our lives as we draw closer to the Lord, for it is in the secret place of the most High that we have our ears opened to hear the burden and message of the Spirit for the Church.

We need to spend time waiting silently in the presence of the Lord. We need to become good listeners. So often we cannot hear the Lord speak to us because we are doing all the talking. Waiting upon God is the thought of waiting in absolute silence before a monarch.

I remember when I was child, I went with my father to see King George VI of England. My father had a private audience with the king, and before we were taken to see him we were told not to speak when he came into the room until he spoke to us first. This is a vital aspect of the devotional life of every Christian. We should spend time in the presence of the King of Kings waiting quietly with an attentive ear to hear Him speak to us.

In actuality, it is the anointing that develops the spiritual gifts. Therefore, they operate through the life of one who is anointed by virtue of his spending time with the Anointed One—the Lord Jesus Christ. If we are quiet and at rest in our spirits, and we are seeking the Lord daily, we will have an open heaven and the gifts will freely operate in our lives. We will be in tune to the Spirit and we will be able to manifest the gifts, which will bring edification to the Body of Christ, and give a word in season to those who are weary.

Another major factor with the gifts of the Spirit is *desire* on the part of the believer. Paul exhorts us to "covet earnestly the best gifts" and to "desire spiritual gifts" (see 1 Cor. 12:31, 14:1). In order to receive the spiritual gifts, there must be an immense desire for them in our hearts, and we must be actively praying for them. God does not give the gifts to the passive believer who is satisfied and is not seeking for something new from the Lord.

All of the gifts operate by faith. Because of this we are often afraid to step out into something new in order to exercise the gifts. We are afraid that we will make a mistake, and we are worried about what people will think of us and say about us if we do. The fear of man is a snare. Our only desire should be to have God's approval upon our lives and to function in the gifts that He has chosen for us.

Faith cannot exist where there is fear! The problem of fear and timidity that plagued Timothy, the dearly beloved spiritual son of Paul, also hinders us from having a flow in the gifts of the Spirit. It is essential to ask the Lord to free us from the bondage of fear so that faith will *ignite* the gifts and cause them to operate in our lives.

An unchanging principle of God's Word is this: "Unto every one that hath shall be given, and he shall have abundance: but from him that hath not shall be taken away even that which he hath" (Mt. 25:29). These are the words of Jesus in His parable of the talents. In the parable there were servants who used what their master had given them, and therefore they were rewarded with more. However, there was also another servant who did not use what the Lord had given him because he was fearful. He hid his talent in the ground. As a result, the Lord took it away from him.

As we practice using the spiritual gifts that the Lord has given us, He will give us more. On the other hand, if we do not use the gifts but allow them to become dormant, God will take them away from us. It is just that serious! Timothy was told to "stir up the gift of God" which he had been given through the laying on of hands (2 Tim. 1:6).

One of the main purposes of this book is to challenge all of us to begin flowing anew in the spiritual gifts. It is not intended to be just an *academic* study of the gifts of the Holy Spirit. My desire is that each one of us will begin to seek the Lord afresh for the spiritual gifts. We want to be honest with ourselves and ask ourselves this eternally important question: Why am I not exercising the spiritual gifts, and why do I not have a flow in the use of these gifts?

We are held responsible by the Lord for not exercising the gifts of the Spirit, just as the man in Matthew chapter 25 was responsible for not using his talent. What are we going to do with what God has given us? May the Lord grant that we all have a release in the gifts so that we may bring forth much fruit for His glory and honor!

The gifts operate in an atmosphere of worship. So often there is a lack of the spiritual gifts in Pentecostal churches because they are not worshipping in the Spirit and in tongues. They sing nice songs that have good words and nice tunes, but they never enter into worship. There is no time devoted to worshipping the Lord in the Spirit. This limits the moving of the Spirit in their congregations. True worship prepares the way for the gifts of the Holy Spirit to operate. This is true for our personal lives as well. As we worship the Lord and wait upon Him in our homes and throughout the day, the gifts will operate more often through us. We should speak in tongues every day. Otherwise, we will experience a spiritual drought.

In addition to this, anointed music releases the moving of the spiritual gifts. In First Samuel 10:5b-6 the prophet Samuel told Saul, "And it shall come to pass, when thou art come thither to the city, that thou shalt meet a company of prophets coming down from the high place with a psaltery, and a tabret, and a pipe, and a harp, before them; and they shall prophesy: And the spirit of the Lord will come upon thee, and thou shalt prophesy with them…"

This company of prophets had musical instruments with them, and as they played unto the Lord, the Spirit of God moved and the spirit of prophecy flowed. In Second Kings 3:15-16, when the minstrel played, the hand of the Lord came upon Elisha and he began to prophesy. First Chronicles 25:1-7 speaks of several men of God who "prophesied with harps, psalteries, and cymbals." Anointed music and worship releases the spiritual gifts and brings a liberty in the Spirit.

In conclusion, let us review several of our main points concerning the operation of the spiritual gifts.

Eight Things the Spiritual Gifts Depend Upon

1. Wisdom
2. Humility
3. Sensitivity to the Spirit
4. Communion with the Lord
5. Desire
6. Faith
7. Practice
8. An atmosphere and life of worship

The Apostle Paul concludes his teaching on the spiritual gifts in First Corinthians 14:40 by saying, “Let all things be done decently and in order.” This guideline governs the use of all the gifts. Regrettably, one of the major drawbacks of the Pentecostal movement has been that so many Charismatic believers fail to do things decently and in order. This has greatly discouraged many evangelical believers from entering into the Pentecostal experience.

For example, under normal circumstances it would be out of order for a person to get up and start prophesying as loud as he can while the pastor is preaching. This would totally interrupt the flow of the Spirit. In a service, we must function in the gifts when there is a specific time allotted for them to be used. We should always wait for the appropriate time to share what God has spoken to us. Paul makes it very clear that everything should be done decently and in order.

1. THE WORD OF WISDOM

The first gift of the Holy Spirit is the word of wisdom. Just as wisdom is the principal thing (Prov. 4:7), so the word of wisdom is one of the greatest manifestations of the Holy Spirit.

Since we have already studied wisdom in great detail in Part Three under the Spirit of wisdom, we will not dwell upon it very much in this section. I would just like to say that wisdom could be defined as "the right application of knowledge." Knowledge alone is not sufficient. You might know a certain fact, but not know what the solution is or what to do about it. The word of knowledge reveals a fact, but it is another thing to know what to do with that knowledge. Therefore, wisdom is the ability to know what to do in any given situation. The word of wisdom and the word of knowledge often function together.

Paul exhorts us in his first epistle to the Corinthians not to be content with having just one gift of the Spirit. Often several spiritual gifts must flow together in order to solve a problem. For example, one who has the gift of the discerning of spirits might discern the presence of an evil spirit in a certain person. The word of knowledge might reveal the reason why that spirit governs or possesses that individual. However, even with these two gifts in operation, we still need something more. We need the word of wisdom to know how to deal with the situation and to give us the key to a breakthrough and deliverance. This is the priceless value of the word of wisdom! It gives us the keys for situations, decisions, and people's lives.

It must be clearly understood that the word of wisdom is different from the Spirit of wisdom. The word of wisdom is given for a specific circumstance or situation. In contrast, the Spirit of wisdom is a continuous, abiding anointing. The Spirit of wisdom does not only operate when there is a necessity, as the word of wisdom does. The word of wisdom is normally for the benefit of a church or an individual, whereas the Spirit of wisdom is the governing factor of one's own personal life.

The way in which the word of wisdom comes can vary drastically from person to person, and situation to situation. We can receive a word of wisdom through a prophecy, impression of the Holy Spirit, vision, or dream. Also, it can come through the agency of a visitation by an angel, as it did with Paul in one case (see Acts 27:23-24). Therefore, let us be sensitive and open to hear from the Lord in any way He chooses, for the word of wisdom can be manifested in a number of ways.

The life of Paul is interwoven with one manifestation after another of the gifts of the Spirit. An excellent illustration of this occurred when Paul was en route to Rome to stand trial before Nero. While on board the ship a terrible storm came up. Paul received a word of wisdom. He said to the centurion and the soldiers in Acts 27:31, "Except [the shipmen or sailors] abide in the ship, ye cannot be saved." They were in a real predicament and they were considering their options. The crew was attempting to abandon ship, but Paul gave them a word of wisdom from the Lord and told them what they had to do in order to be preserved. He warned that unless the ship crew stayed on board, the rest of the passengers would not make it. Thus, this word of wisdom benefited everyone on the ship.

Paul certainly knew what it meant to live a Spirit-filled life. The careful reader will notice that Paul received either a word of knowledge or a word of wisdom at many junctures in his voyage to Rome. For example, Paul warned of coming disaster in

Acts 27:10, "Sirs, I perceive that this voyage will be with hurt and much damage, not only of the lading and ship, but also of our lives." Paul could have only known this by a word of knowledge.

The primary purpose and function of the word of wisdom is to give guidance and direction to a corporate assembly of believers or to an individual. It is given so that the Church might know what to do in every situation it faces. Many years ago my wife and I were the directors of a Bible school in Switzerland. At one point we had to make a major decision that would determine the future direction of the Bible school, and we just did not know what to do. In desperation, we called for a day of prayer and fasting. The students and faculty joined us as we prayed for the solution, but they were not told all the complexities and details of the situation.

Then the Lord revealed through one of the students the direction we should take, down to the most minute detail. We knew it was the Lord speaking because only the Lord could have revealed to her all the many facets of our dilemma. This student received a vision from the Lord, and it showed us exactly what we should do. This was the word of wisdom in operation, giving us a sense of direction. Before the prayer meeting, we had known all the facts, but we did not know what to do. However, the word of wisdom enabled us to apply the facts in the right way and go in the direction the Lord desired for us. The word of wisdom causes us to know what we should do in a given situation.

We must live by the word of wisdom, and by hearing from the Lord at all the major crossroads in our lives. Those who live by principles *alone*, however good they may be, will inevitably miss the Lord at some point in their life. The reason for this is that God often requires us to do things that go contrary to human wisdom and logic. David did not rely upon principles or statistics. He sought the Lord every time before he went out to battle against the Philistines, and the Lord's battle plan for him was different each time.

Christ did not heal everyone the same way, and we need to understand that there is not just one correct way to heal people. This applies to virtually every area of the Christian life. So many Christians become legalistic and bound to routines and principles. By doing this, they leave no room for the Holy Spirit to operate in their lives in a new and fresh way. We must be open to hear what the Lord's will is for us and what direction He wants us to take. Thus, we can see the importance of the word of wisdom for our personal lives as well as for the Church.

2. THE WORD OF KNOWLEDGE

The word of knowledge can reveal to us the past, present, or future—an event that took place in the past, an event that is taking place now, or something that will happen in the future. This gift is desperately needed in the Body of Christ today; for when it is in operation, this gift dispels all confusion and indecisiveness. It makes everything crystal clear. The word of knowledge pinpoints the problem or need.

I would like to illustrate this gift by telling a little story that took place when I was a young man. The Spirit of God was moving in a very special way in a certain Pentecostal church which I attended near London. I particularly remember one Sunday morning the Lord gave me a prophecy during worship. Later that day while I was riding back to church on my bicycle for the evening service, I had a vision of one of the ladies from the church preparing for supper. As she was putting the knives and forks on the dinner table, she said to the Lord, "If that prophecy which was given by that young man this morning was for me, please prompt him to tell me." Therefore, I knew that the message I would have to deliver to her that evening was, "Yes, sister, that prophecy this morning was for you." However, as events unfolded, I did not even have to say one word to her. During the worship service that night while we were all worshipping the Lord, I felt led to open my eyes. When I opened them, I noticed that this particular lady was looking right at me. I then turned my head in her direction, looked at her, and nodded my head in an affirmative manner. That nod was all it took for her to know that the prophecy was for her. She smiled at me and turned around. This was a word of knowledge that I received, and it came in the form of a vision.

The word of knowledge can operate in many kinds of situations. I have also seen it operate in the realm of judgment. There was a certain elder in a church who was opposing the pastor, and God was very displeased with him. I had a vision, and in this vision I saw that this elder was going to die. He and his wife were going to move into another house, but while they were in the process of moving he was going to become ill and be taken to the hospital. I saw that his wife would move into the house, but he would die in the hospital. The Lord even showed me the approximate time that all this would take place. To this elder's misfortune, all of this came to pass exactly as I saw in the vision, and he died. This, of course, was a word of knowledge concerning something in the future.

In certain circumstances, the word of knowledge is used to give direction. I remember a situation years ago in France in which this was the case. A certain lady visiting a church for the first time received a vision during the service. She then shared it with the church. It was a quite remarkable word of knowledge. She saw a piano that was in someone's living room, and the impression she received from the Lord was that this piano should be given to the church.

This service was the only one she ever attended, and she did not know any of the circumstances about the church. However, through the word of knowledge she gave confirmation to a certain member to donate his piano to the church. Actually, the man had already spoken to the pastor about giving the piano, but he was not sure whether he should. This word of knowledge confirmed to him God's will and gave him direction, which resulted in a blessing for that church.

A word of knowledge reveals a small part of God's infinite knowledge. It is not all-inclusive. Also, there is a difference between the word of knowledge and the Spirit of knowledge. The Spirit of knowledge is an abiding anointing that releases a continuous, unceasing flow of God's knowledge. As in the case of Solomon who had the Spirit of knowledge and wisdom, the queen of Sheba could ask him question after question and he was able to answer every one of them (1 Kgs. 10:3). The word of knowledge does not function in this way. The word of knowledge operates sporadically. It will reveal a certain fact to you and then it will stop operating until God wants to reveal something else to you. It requires a definite manifestation of the Spirit of God each time. Sometimes you will get a revelation and sometimes you will not.

We can see a personal application of the word of knowledge in Acts chapter 21. As the Apostle Paul was journeying to Jerusalem, he stopped along the way at Caesarea for several days. While he was there, a certain prophet named Agabus came from Judea. He took Paul's girdle, bound his own hands and feet with it, and said, "Thus saith the Holy Ghost, So shall the Jews at Jerusalem bind the man that owneth this girdle, and shall deliver him into the hands of the Gentiles" (Acts 21:11). This was a word of caution for Paul—if he went to Jerusalem he would be imprisoned by the Jews. This was a word of knowledge given as a prophecy.

The word of knowledge can have a personal or national application. In Acts 11:27-30, Agabus the prophet signified by the Spirit that there was going to be a great dearth throughout the whole world. Therefore, the word of knowledge can reveal the destinies of individuals and nations. More importantly, the word of knowledge can also reveal things that are going to happen in the Church.

Something that is extremely important to remember concerning the word of knowledge is that you must understand from the Lord whether or not you should share it with others. Just because you receive a word from the Lord does not necessarily mean He wants you to declare it. There are times when the word of knowledge should be declared, and there are other times when it must not be shared with others. Let me try to explain my point.

Many years ago, when my wife and I were in Switzerland, I had a vision of a certain person in that country. However, I did not share with him what I had seen. Eight years later, I was sitting on the platform of a church in Los Angeles. As I was meditating upon the Lord and praying, I had the same exact vision of that person I had seen eight years before in Switzerland. When I got up to the pulpit to preach, I asked if that person was in the auditorium. Sure enough, he was present. Once again, I did not share this vision with him or others. There was a reason why I didn't. In this vision the Lord revealed to me what this person was going to do. There are times when it is harmful to tell people certain things about their future, and I knew by the Spirit that this was one of those times.

The word of knowledge is potentially very dangerous. That is why we must be so careful when using this gift. If the Lord reveals someone's past to us for a certain purpose, we must never reveal it except under very special circumstances. Perhaps the Lord will show us a certain sin that once bound that person. If he has repented of it, then we must not bring it up again. Also, God might show us hurts and bad memories from their childhood that cause them to do the things they do. However, unless we really hear from the Lord to share it, we should keep it to ourselves. Understanding things from people's past can be extremely helpful in counseling them and praying for them, but we must be sensitive to the Spirit in these cases.

Sometimes the word of knowledge will reveal to us that a certain person is going to try to make us do a certain thing. Knowing their motives and intentions will preserve us from untold sorrow and danger. At a certain church many years ago, there was a man who was always very nice to me. Because of his kindness, I began to trust him completely. Well, one night the Lord gave me a vision about him. In this vision, the Lord spoke to me that he was being friendly to me because he wanted to plot my destruction in a particular matter. I said to the Lord: "I don't like to think evil of others. I want to believe that everyone is upright. If this man is really seeking my downfall, please prove it to me." The Lord then showed me a telephone.

After a short period of time, this man called me, and I had that vision all over again as we talked. In the vision I saw a huge animal trap on the path he wanted me to take. Graciously, the Spirit showed me that I could walk around that trap and continue on my journey unharmed. Yet, I also understood by the Spirit of God that if I walked through the trap, it would permanently damage my walk with the Lord. God spoke to my heart: "Tell him 'no.' You cannot walk in that path." In this case, I also did not declare what I had seen because I knew he planted a trap for me.

By showing me the motives and plans of this man, the word of knowledge spared me from making a wrong decision. Obviously, I could not declare this vision because everyone around him thought he was a saint, even as I had previously thought before the Lord showed me otherwise. Can you see how extremely careful we must be not to share certain things with others? Jesus knew who Judas was all along, but He did not tell anyone. Even His apostles, who were closer to Him than anyone else, could not detect any mistreatment of Judas that would cause them to suspect him as the traitor. Jesus treated him the same as He did the other eleven. He even gave him the position of treasurer. Therefore, always pray before you share with others what the Lord has revealed to you.

At times, God shows us something about a person that we do not want to believe is true, even as I did not want to think evil of the man I have already mentioned. Therefore, God creates circumstances that show us something in the natural to confirm what He told us about them. The Lord may even quicken verses from the Bible to us to make it abundantly clear that they are not right before God. The reason God does all this is because He wants us to be sure in our hearts when He speaks something to us. Conversely, if the Lord speaks to us something very good about someone, He will also confirm it in like manner.

Another truth concerning the word of knowledge is the fact that a revelation can be one hundred percent correct but still not come to pass. There can be conditions to the word of knowledge. At times, the word of knowledge can reveal that a certain thing is going to happen, and it happens. At other times, there is a condition that is woven into the word of knowledge that must be met for it to be fulfilled.

For example, a word of knowledge could reveal that if a person continues walking on the path he is on, there will be certain consequences. However, if that person repents of what he is doing, the word of knowledge obviously will not come to pass. This does not mean that the word of knowledge was incorrect or untrue. It simply means that the person has changed his course, and therefore has avoided a catastrophe. This also applies to a word of knowledge concerning a blessing. If a person turns away from the path of God, he will not receive the blessing.

Because of the seriousness of the word of knowledge, the attitude of the person using the gift is very important. Jeremiah said, "Oh that my head were waters, and mine eyes a fountain of tears, that I might weep day and night for the slain of the daughter of my people!" (Jer. 9:1). When we receive a true word of knowledge from the Lord, we feel as God feels in the situation. Often there is sadness of heart and weeping that comes upon us when God reveals sin in the lives of individuals or nations.

We must not have any condemnation or criticism in our hearts when the Lord gives us a word of knowledge. The Lord does not reveal things to us so that we can say, "I knew all along that this person was going to fail and that he was no good." The word of knowledge operates in the lives of compassionate believers who do not have the "I told you so" attitude.

Paul said in Philippians 3:18-19, "For many walk, of whom I have told you often, and now tell you even weeping, that they are the enemies of the cross of Christ: whose end is destruction, whose god is their belly, and whose glory is in their shame, who mind earthly things." Paul was honest about the problems that were in these peoples' lives, but he was weeping for them. When the Lord gives us a word of knowledge and we are to declare it, we must be free of all criticism in our hearts. We must speak the truth in love.

I believe with all my heart that it is God's desire for us to have the spiritual gifts, particularly the word of knowledge. The word of knowledge is so important. However, the reason God cannot cause the word of knowledge to operate freely in many people's lives is because of a critical or harsh attitude.

Amos 3:7 reveals the heart of God. "Surely, the Lord God will do nothing, but he revealeth his secrets unto his servants the prophets." God wants to share His secrets with us and cause us to know what He is going to do before it happens. Yet, the problem lies in the fact that there are very few men and women who can be trusted with His secrets and His knowledge. God does not give the word of knowledge to those who gossip about people, for He is not a gossiping God. The Lord does not reveal things to those who cannot keep His secrets. If God tells us something that we are supposed to keep secret, and we share it with others, it may not come to pass. The secret to any strong church is the flow of the word of knowledge in the lives of the leaders, especially the pastor. The Lord uses this gift to reveal to the pastor what is happening in his congregation. God has been gracious to show my wife and me many things people were doing in the various churches we have pastored over the years, and this knowledge has saved us from many wrong decisions. However, God will not show things to pastors who gossip about people, because their tongues would destroy the church and scatter the sheep. In summary, there are two basic things we must do to have a free flow of the word of knowledge in our lives. We must cleanse our hearts of all criticism and condemnation, and we must be able to keep God's secrets.

3. THE GIFT OF FAITH

The gift of faith is different from the fruit of faith. The *fruit* of faith is necessary for salvation and the development of character. The *gift* of faith is the impartation of God's faith to accomplish His purposes in a *specific* situation or circumstance. We must realize that the gift of faith is not all-inclusive. We cannot use this divine gift whenever we choose. For example, by the operation of the gift of faith in response to the word of the Lord, we could command the heavens not to rain, and it would not rain. Yet, in the next breath we might attempt to command our car to start, and it would not. The gift of faith is given for one specific demonstration of the power of God. It takes a separate impartation of God's faith for each manifestation of this gift, and this gift only functions according to the will of God.

The gift of faith also operates in conjunction with other phenomena and gifts of the Holy Spirit, especially the gifts of healing and the working of miracles. However, the gift of faith is far greater power than miracles. It is far wider in scope and greater in power than miracles, for faith is the foundation for miracles. It is manifested in many different ways. This gift functions basically in the realm of the supernatural and the miraculous. It empowers us to do things that we could not do in our own human strength. It is imparted to us to do the impossible in times of great crisis, and when there are obstacles that are insurmountable. The gift of faith could be called "faith in action." With faith *all* things are possible! There is no limit to what faith can do.

The gift of faith operates in any aspect of the various names of the Lord. For example, one of the names of the Lord is Jehovah-Jireh, which means "the Lord your Provider." Therefore, the gift of faith functions in the realm of provision. To illustrate this, I will recount a little incident that happened to my wife and me many years ago. We did not have any food or fuel for heat and it was during the middle of winter. The Lord said to my wife, "I am going to provide food for you." She believed the Lord and declared it in faith. That faith in her heart produced the food. Three days later, a lady drove up to our house and delivered lavish and expensive food that we would never have bought for ourselves, and she also gave us enough money to buy fuel to heat the house.

The gift of faith is also manifested through another name of the Lord, Jehovah-Rapha, which means "the Lord your Healer." As we mentioned before, the gift of faith can operate in conjunction with other gifts of the Lord such as the gifts of healing. In Acts chapter three, as Peter and John went into the temple, they were confronted with a man who desperately needed to be healed. He had been lame since birth. Anointed with the power of the Holy Spirit, Peter took him by the hand, telling him to rise up and walk. He was instantly healed and went throughout the temple walking, leaping, and praising God. In Acts 3:16 Peter gives the reason this lame man was healed: "And his name through faith in [Christ's] name hath made this man strong, whom ye see and know; yea, the faith which is by him hath given him this perfect soundness in the presence of you all." Therefore, it was through the exercise of the gift of faith that this man was healed.

This type of faith is intricately linked with the moving of both natural and spiritual mountains. These mountains represent something that is opposing us and blocking us from fulfilling God's will. Christ declared in Matthew 17:20, "*If ye have faith* as a grain of mustard seed, ye shall say unto this mountain, Remove hence to yonder place; and it shall remove; and nothing shall be impossible unto you." When circumstances or people are opposing us from doing God's will, the gift of faith can cause them to be removed and be silenced.

Zerubbabel lived during the Restoration Era. There were many who were opposing the reconstruction of the temple, which God had commissioned Zerubbabel and Joshua to rebuild. Therefore, the Lord spoke to Zerubbabel in Zechariah 4:6-7: "Not by might, nor by power, but by my spirit, saith the Lord of hosts. Who art thou, O great mountain? before Zerubbabel thou shalt become a plain: and he shall bring forth the headstone thereof with shoutings, crying, Grace, grace unto it." The demonic powers and government officials that were blocking him from completing the temple were going to be removed, and this enormous *mountain of opposition* was going to become as a plain before him by the power of God through faith.

I firmly believe that there is no government on the face of this earth that can resist the power of faith. One of the acts of faith mentioned in Hebrews chapter eleven is that the heroes of faith "subdued kingdoms" by faith (Heb. 11:33). Faith is so great that it can force governments and countries to submit to the will of God. Faith can even cause the rise and fall of governments.

Real faith transcends natural laws! It is not subject to the elements of nature. Faith enabled the Lord Jesus to walk on the water and defy the laws of gravity. Faith is creative. Where there is no eye, faith creates a new eye. My wife and I have seen extraordinary miracles over the years in different parts of the world. We have seen people with missing legs be instantly healed by the creative power of faith, even restoring those missing body parts. Faith can also command lions' mouths to be shut, as Daniel did (Heb. 11:33). Can you see that there are no boundaries or limits to faith!

In a church service, this gift could operate with several of the other gifts in the following way. A word of knowledge might reveal that God wants to heal all those with cancer, then the gift of faith would release the gift of healing to heal all those with cancer. Faith cannot be easily categorized because it is so diverse.

The kingdom of God is with power (1 Cor. 4:20). Oh, how desperately we need to see the power of God restored to the Church today. Jesus promised that we would perform greater miracles than He did in His earthly ministry. But where are these promised miracles? After all, we don't just want to talk about the power of God and the moving of the Holy Spirit, we want to *experience* that power. The gift of faith is the key to seeing these promises fulfilled and seeing God's power manifested in the earth once again. It is the faith of God—His faith—that will cause the lame to walk and the blind to see. The faith of God can accomplish more in one second than all the human efforts and good intentions of a lifetime!

4. THE GIFTS OF HEALING

This particular gift is the anointing of God to heal every manner of disease, ailment, and sickness that exists. Actually, this gift is in the plural—*gifts* of healing. It is segmented and divided up according to the different needs and diseases of the human body. For instance, many ministers have been given the gift of healing to heal cancer. Yet, this particular gift will not heal heart problems. Another distinct manifestation of the gifts of healing is required to heal ailments of the heart. Certain ministers have the anointing to heal a particular disease, but they cannot heal other illnesses.

We must understand that the Lord is very specific when He says He wants to heal. In the Gospels, there were times when the Lord Jesus Christ healed all who were present, and there were other times when He only healed certain ones. If we want to hear God speak, the key is a close relationship with Him. By this intimacy with God, we will know which diseases He wants to heal in a given situation.

My wife and I have seen this firsthand in many countries around the world. When we were in New Zealand, we had a service virtually every night of the week because the Spirit of God was moving in such a great way in that country. In these meetings, the Lord would impress upon our hearts that He wanted to heal a certain illness, or a certain part of the human body on a particular night.

For example, one night the Lord would say, "I want to heal everyone here tonight who is lame." We would then simply declare this from the pulpit: "All those who are lame, please raise your hand. God is going to heal you tonight." Sure enough, they would all be healed. Another night, the Lord would tell us He wanted to heal other diseases. The important thing to grasp here is that we must move in accordance with the will of God. We can only declare that God is going to heal diseases that He has told us He will heal. The gifts of healing are very specific.

I believe that healings can take place in a meeting without the ministers even laying hands on the people. We also experienced this in New Zealand. We would say to the people in the meetings, which usually exceeded several thousand, "Call the secretary of the church and let us know if you have been healed." Well, would you believe we received complaints from the secretary every week? She said to us, "I have not been able to do anything this week because all I have been doing is answering the telephone and listening to one person after another give their testimony of healing."

We must be sensitive to the Holy Spirit and have that daily relationship with the Father that Jesus had. Christ knew when it was His Father's will to heal everyone, and when He wanted to just single out certain people. We have to know what the will of the Lord is in the service, and know which sicknesses He wants to heal in a particular meeting.

How do we know which diseases God wants to heal? God uses many signs to indicate whom He wants to heal. Sometimes you will see the name of the sickness in a mental picture. For example, you might see the word "deaf." After you have received your sign, you would declare that God wants to heal the deaf and those with hearing problems. Another possible sign is that you might feel in your own body the affliction that God desires to heal. At other times, you might sense that the Lord desires to heal everyone present.

Faith on the part of the one praying and the one being prayed for is essential. The Scriptures record that there were times when the Lord healed people because He saw that they had faith (Mt. 9:2). At other times, He was unable to do any mighty works because of their unbelief (Mk. 6:5-6).

We can see so many instances of the gifts of healing in operation in the Acts of the Apostles. In Acts 5:15-16 we read: "They brought forth the sick into the streets, and laid them on beds and couches, that at the least the shadow of Peter passing by might overshadow some of them. There came also a multitude out of the cities round about unto Jerusalem, bringing sick folks, and them which were vexed with unclean spirits: and they were healed every one." The anointing of the gifts of healing upon Peter was so great that he didn't even have to touch people and they were healed. Many were healed as Peter walked by them.

As seen in Acts 8:7, when Philip led a revival in the city of Samaria, remarkable healings took place: "For unclean spirits, crying with loud voice, came out of many that were possessed with them: and many taken with palsies, and that were lame, were healed."

An important factor to remember concerning the gifts of healing is that there is a price to pay to obtain the healing power of God, and to retain that power. Often, we will have battles in our own lives. The reason for these battles is that God wants to give us power over certain spirits and diseases. Yet, until we get power over them in our own lives, we cannot have the power over them in the lives of others (see Ex. 4:6-7). You will notice that those who have had great healing ministries have often been sick themselves. They have paid a price for that power over sicknesses.

Smith Wigglesworth, for example, had the power of God like few others ever had. There was virtually no sickness that was not healed through his ministry and he raised the dead on a number of occasions. Yet, for six years while he saw one miraculous healing after another in his ministry, he was suffering in his own physical body. He had terrible kidney stones for several years. Make no mistake about it—this suffering qualified him for the power he possessed. If we experience our message, we will have authority over the spirits of disease. I believe with all my heart in divine healing, but my wife and I have had to pass through some very painful trials over the years.

When we suffer in our own lives, compassion is developed in our hearts for others. The Scriptures repeatedly tell us what motivated and moved the Lord Jesus to heal those in need—it was compassion. Matthew 9:36 says, "But when [Jesus] saw the multitudes, he was moved with compassion on them, because they fainted, and were scattered abroad, as sheep having no shepherd." (See also Mt. 14:14, 15:32, 20:34, Mk. 1:41.) The gift of healing flourishes in the lives of those who are compassionate.

Healing is an integral part of the Gospel message. Healing is in the atonement, and it is for every believer. Isaiah 53:5 and First Peter 2:24 tell us that by His stripes we are healed. Every child of God has the right to ask his Heavenly Father for healing. When we are sick, we should immerse our minds with scriptures on divine healing.

There are three agencies that the Holy Spirit employs to heal—the Word of God, the prayer of faith, and the gifts of healing. However, we must not confuse these three agencies with one another. Any born-again believer can believe God for healing in the realm of the Word of God and the prayer of faith. Yet the gifts of healing only operate in the life of a believer who is baptized in the Holy Spirit.

We must realize that there is a difference between these three mediums of healing. The Word of God is certainly one avenue of healing. Psalm 107:20 states, "He sent his word, and healed them." The reading and preaching of the Word can bring healing. I remember a certain meeting in Germany many years ago in which the minister asked, "How many were healed tonight during the preaching of the Word?" A number of hands were raised, even though healing had not even been mentioned during the service. The Word itself is creative, and it has the power to heal.

The prayer of faith and the laying on of hands upon a person can also bring healing. James 5:14-15 says, "Is any sick among you? let him call for the elders of the church; and let them pray over him, anointing him with oil in the name of the Lord: And the prayer of faith shall save the sick, and the Lord shall raise him up."

Any Christian can pray for the sick and believe for the Lord to heal them, even if he doesn't have the gifts of healing. This comes by virtue of Christ's sacrifice upon the cross. Also, every local church should pray for the sick.

The gifts of healing, however, are different from these other two means of healing. The gifts of healing involve the anointing and power of the Holy Spirit which can heal every manner of disease. But this powerful gift can only be used by a Spirit-filled believer. I have seen it operate many times over the last forty years in which I have been in the ministry.

We witnessed very significant healings on a continual basis when I was the assistant pastor of a church in Marseilles, France. This city was one of the chief medical centers in the nation of France at that time. Actually, it was the last hope for anyone with fatal or incurable diseases; hospitals from all over would send their patients here when they could no longer help them.

I remember one four year old girl who could not walk. It was medically unexplainable and there was nothing that could be done for her. Her situation was hopeless. She was sent to Marseilles, and there the top doctors told her parents that they could not do anything for her either. All the doctors there agreed that she would *never* be able to walk.

Well, our church had a reputation throughout the whole city for healing, so her parents were told to try our church as a last resort. They came to our Sunday service, and after the visiting evangelist preached, we prayed for the sick. As I helped the evangelist pray for this little girl, he instructed her parents to let her feet touch the ground. And although they did not believe, they still followed his instruction. With a Holy Ghost confidence, the evangelist boldly said to her, "In the name of Jesus, walk." Miraculously, she began to take a few steps with her parents holding her arms.

Then the evangelist told them to let go of her, and told her to walk around the church. She began to walk without help from anyone, and continued walking all around the church. Everyone was amazed that night by the power of God. Even when there is no hope medically for someone to be healed and doctors have done all they can for a person, the gift of healing can heal him. There is no disease that cannot be cured by the power of God. Only believe, dear ones!

There was also a lady in the church who had been diagnosed with cancer. She spoke to me one day and said: "Pastor, the doctors have told me that I have cancer, but I believe that God wants to heal me. Will you pray for me?" I assured her that I would be happy to. At the next service, when the invitation was given for prayer, she came to the place where I was standing at the front. Smiling, she declared to me in faith, "I believe I am going to be healed tonight." As I prayed for her, I felt an awesome anointing come upon her. A few weeks later she joyfully informed me that when she returned to the doctor for a checkup, he could not find any trace of cancer. It was completely gone!

Another time when we were in India for a service, we saw tremendous healings take place. The organizers of the meeting had advertised a healing service. Before I even got up to the pulpit to preach, the evangelist who had invited me to preach asked for any children who were deaf to come forward. Three deaf children who came forward were instantly healed, and this miracle of healing really got the crowd's attention. Then I preached on blind Bartimaeus.

After my sermon, we had an altar call. I emphasized to the people that the most important thing in life is to make it to heaven. Four hundred people gave their lives to the Lord that night. I then told the people: "Jesus said while He was upon earth, 'What would you that I do unto you?' Blind Bartimaeus knew exactly what he needed; he needed his eyesight restored. Jesus is here tonight to heal everyone who is sick." All the ministers divided up into prayer teams. My wife and I prayed for many people, and they were all healed by the power of God.

I will just recount the healing of one man in particular. He was in a miserable state. He was lame, with his right leg bent up.

When we prayed for him to be healed in the name of Jesus, his leg was completely restored and he danced all around. Experiences like these really increase your faith!

May we begin to seek the Lord afresh for this gift to flow in our lives and in our churches so that many people might be healed for the glory of God. We want "the power of the Lord to be present to heal" everywhere we go (Lk. 5:17). Let us look to the Lord as the Sun of righteousness arises with healing in His wings!

5. THE WORKING OF MIRACLES

The fifth gift is the working of miracles. First of all, we must consider what constitutes a miracle. The English word "miracle" is not the word used in the original Greek. The Greek word for *miracle* is "dunamos," which literally means "power." Miracles are really a demonstration of the power of God. Therefore, the definition of a miracle is *an act of power—something that can only be done through supernatural power*.

This helps us grasp the difference between miracles and healing. Miracles are not limited only to the realm of healing. They apply to every aspect of our lives in which we need a manifestation of God's supernatural power.

At times, we will experience miracles of provision. I would just like to recount a story to illustrate this. When we were pastoring a church of about three thousand people in New Zealand a number of years ago, the Lord spoke to us to buy a certain piece of land which was worth 1.2 million dollars. As you know, that is a lot of money. We asked the Lord, "How are we going to raise this much money?" The Lord replied: "The money will come in through faith. Sunday morning you will teach on faith and tell the whole congregation to believe Me for miracles of provision." That Sunday morning in obedience to His Word, I declared from the pulpit the direction the Lord wanted the church to take. I challenged everyone ages twelve and older to seek the Lord and believe Him for a miracle of provision so that we could buy this piece of land.

It is amazing what happened! Nearly everyone in the church began to experience miracles. Even children who were only twelve and thirteen years old experienced miracles of provision. People would give them money unexpectedly for no reason at all, or they would win art contests and give their prize money. Everyone in the congregation could hardly wait for the opportunity to give money for the building project. We received telephone calls from many parents saying, "Pastor, could you please lower the age of this fund raiser because my little eight year old child wants to be a part of it too?" We were overwhelmed by these testimonies, and so we assured them that anyone could participate.

One Sunday we had a cash service. A chest was placed at the front of the church, and everyone who wanted to give that morning put their money into it. One hundred and fifty thousand dollars came in that morning in cash. Also, many people felt the Lord tell them to pledge a certain amount without knowing where it was going to come from. With cash and pledges, the total that came in was over one and a half million dollars.

Miracles became common place for everyone in that church, and we accomplished the Lord's will through these miracles. Therefore, we should be encouraged in the Lord! God can perform a miracle for you in whatever situation you find yourself.

Miracles are linked with signs and wonders. Many times in the Scriptures we see these three words mentioned together (Acts 2:22, 6:8, 15:12, 2 Cor. 12:12, Heb. 2:4). Miracles can be used as a sign to illustrate a spiritual truth. The word *miracles* is used quite often in John's gospel, but it actually refers to a sign. The Lord always used miracles to teach truth. For example, He used the miracle of the feeding of the five thousand to illustrate that He is the Bread of Life.

Teaching people the pure Word of God and correct doctrine is necessary for proper spiritual growth. However, this alone will not usually convince people of the truth and cause them to walk in the ways of God. Miracles are absolutely needed to ground and establish our faith. Paul said in First Corinthians 4:20, "For the kingdom of God is not in word, but in power." He also said in this same letter to the Corinthians in 2:4, "And my speech and my preaching was not with enticing words of man's wisdom, but in demonstration of the Spirit and of power."

The Lord Jesus Christ taught the people, but He also manifested the power of God. Peter declared to the Jewish nation, "Ye men of Israel, hear these words; Jesus of Nazareth, a man approved of God among you by miracles and wonders and signs, which God did by him in the midst of you, as ye yourselves also know..." (Acts 2:22). Jesus exercised the power of God to perform miracles.

The early Church saw extraordinary miracles on a continual basis. It was an age of the miraculous. Tremendous things happened in the ministries of the apostles. Acts 2:43 records, "And fear came upon every soul: and many wonders and signs were done by the apostles." In Acts 6:8 we read, "And Stephen, full of faith and power, did great wonders and miracles among the people." Great miracles were also seen in the ministry of Philip. Even Simon the sorcerer, who was well accustomed to the realm of the supernatural, marveled at the miracles Philip performed (Acts 8:13).

In Acts 8:39-40 Philip was miraculously transported from one town to another. This is something I believe God is going to do time and time again in the last days. By His Spirit, the Lord will transport His ministers into countries that are closed to the gospel. Many people have seen this take place in visions. Being transported from one place to another was apparently a common event in the life of Elijah (see 1 Kgs. 18:12, 2 Kgs. 2:16).

The raising of the dead is another manifestation of this gift. While Paul was at Troas and was speaking for a particularly long time one night, a young man named Eutychus fell asleep. He had been sitting in the window of this third story building and fell to the ground, and he died from the impact of the fall. Immediately, Paul quit preaching and prayed for him, and by the power of God he came back to life (Acts 20:7-12). As a result of this miracle, the brethren were greatly encouraged (Acts 20:12). Miracles are a source of great encouragement to believers, and they strengthen our belief and trust in the Lord.

Miracles can be negative as well as positive. In Acts 13:8-12 Elymas the sorcerer was stricken with blindness by the words of Paul. In this case, a miracle was used to judge a man who was evil in the sight of the Lord. There were many extraordinary things that happened in the early Church!

Miracles open people's hearts to the preaching of God's Word. In Acts chapter 8, the Church began to fulfill her calling to world evangelism and missionary work. Just before the Lord ascended to heaven, He commissioned His disciples to preach first in Jerusalem and Judea, then in Samaria, and finally in all the nations of the earth (Acts 1:8). Up to this point they had ministered exclusively in Jerusalem and Judea. In Acts chapter 8 they began to fulfill their world-wide calling. It was through the miracles of Philip that people were prepared to receive the Word of God. Many were healed and others were set free from demonic oppressions. Acts 8:6 says, "And the people with one accord gave heed unto those things which Philip spake, hearing and seeing the miracles which he did." Miracles are the key to opening up new areas to the gospel.

Notable Miracles

The early Church was established and enlarged not just through miracles, but through *notable* miracles. It was miracles of great renown that drew people to the Church and propagated the message of the gospel of Jesus Christ. Without these miracles, the vision of world missions would have never been realized, the Church would never have grown, and the truth of Jesus Christ would have dwindled into obscurity.

When Jesus ascended to His Father's right hand, there were at least five hundred disciples who heard His commission and charge to wait in Jerusalem for the promise of the Father (see 1 Cor. 15:6). However, ten days later on the day of Pentecost there were only one hundred and twenty who remained. In only ten days after the Lord's ascension, He began to lose followers. Therefore, something extraordinary had to happen to draw people to the Lord. Three thousand believers were added to the Church on the day of Pentecost. This was a good beginning, but to continue the expansion of the Church, a notable miracle was needed.

In Acts chapter 3, as Peter and John were entering the temple, a lame man asked them for alms at the gate Beautiful. This man had been born lame, and every day he was carried to the gate of the temple to beg for alms. This man was recognizable to nearly everyone in Jerusalem. Therefore, when Peter healed him by the power of God and he leaped and danced all around the temple, everyone knew immediately that a phenomenal miracle had taken place.

"And all the people saw him walking and praising God: And they knew that it was he which sat for alms at the Beautiful gate of the temple: and they were filled with wonder and amazement at that which had happened unto him. And as the lame man which was healed held Peter and John, all the people ran together unto them in the porch that is called Solomon's, greatly wondering" (Acts 3:9-11). This miracle was something that became known to everyone.

The Jewish leaders said among themselves in Acts 4:16: "What shall we do to these men? for that indeed a *notable* miracle hath been done by them is manifest to all them that dwell in Jerusalem; and *we cannot deny it*." This healing of the lame man was a notable miracle that no one could deny. The Jews were trying to find some way to accuse Peter and John, but they could not because "beholding the man which was healed standing with them, they could say nothing against it" (Acts 4:14).

The interesting thing about the notable miracles in the Scriptures is that everyone knew the condition of the people who received the miracle. As a result, people had to give the glory to God. This notable miracle of healing in Acts chapter 3 caused many to believe in the Lord. We read in Acts 4:4 that "many of them which heard the word believed; and the number of the men was about five thousand." When this miracle made people attentive to listen to Peter's sermon, five thousand believed. This was more than on the day of Pentecost. In just an instant, five thousand people turned to the Lord! Oh, we must not limit the Lord. He will do great things in these last days.

Then in Acts chapter 5, Ananias and Sapphira were smitten by the Spirit of God for lying to the Holy Ghost. News of this miracle of judgment spread very quickly and it became known to many people, causing them to fear the Lord. "And by the hands of the apostles were many signs and wonders wrought among the people… And of the rest durst no man join himself to them: but the people magnified them. And believers were the more added to the Lord, multitudes both of men and women" (Acts 5:12-14). These notable miracles—healing of the lame man being healed and the slaying of Ananias and Sapphira—brought great fear, and attracted many people to the Church.

In Acts chapter 9, Peter performed two more notable miracles. As he was traveling along the coast of the Mediterranean Sea, he came to the city of Lydda. There he found a certain paralytic man named Aeneas who had been bedridden for eight years. Peter addressed him by name and said to him, "Jesus Christ heals you."

He was instantly healed and began walking. Because this man had been sick for eight years, many people would have known of his condition. Thus, when he was healed, there was no denying that he had been sick. The result of this notable miracle can be seen in Acts 9:35: "And all that dwelt at Lydda and Saron saw him, and turned to the Lord." This miracle caused two whole cities to turn to the Lord, bringing a tremendous harvest of souls because of one significant act of power.

While Peter was still at Lydda, certain disciples from nearby Joppa asked him to come to their city. They wanted Peter to pray for a godly woman named Dorcas who had suddenly become ill and died. These friends of Dorcas were full of faith. They believed that the power of God could raise her up. The early Church, and Peter in particular, had a great reputation for manifesting God's power. When Peter came to Joppa, all the widows showed him the clothes Dorcas had made for them. This woman was very beloved and was known for her ministry of helping others. Therefore, when she died, all the people who had been blessed by her labors of love were there weeping and lamenting her death.

In Acts 9:40 Peter went into the room where her lifeless body lay and, calling her by her Hebrew name, said to her, "Tabitha, arise." A resurgence of life instantly came into her body, and she opened her eyes. Peter then presented her alive to everyone. Dorcas was also a woman known by virtually everyone in the city of Joppa, and all of them would have known of her death. Therefore, when she was raised from the dead, the whole city gave glory to God. This notable miracle had a lasting effect upon the city of Joppa. "And it was known throughout all Joppa; and many believed in the Lord" (Acts 9:42). Many people turned to the Lord because of her restoration to life.

Seeing miracles take place was a common event in the life of the Apostle Paul. He went to Ephesus and stayed there for two years teaching daily in the school of a man named Tyrannus (see Acts 19). While he was there, "all they which dwelt in [the province of] Asia heard the word of the Lord Jesus, both Jews and Greeks." Ephesus became a key place for Paul. It was the capital city of the Roman province of Asia and because it was also the center of commerce and education, people from all over the province had to travel frequently to Ephesus. Paul had a mighty impact on this whole region. People who heard him preach or who were healed by him in Ephesus went back to their cities and spread the good news of the gospel. Many people who never even met Paul were transformed and turned to the Lord because of his shining light in Ephesus.

In addition to this, people from all over the province who could not come to Ephesus themselves would send handkerchiefs and pieces of cloth to Paul. When these handkerchiefs were placed on his body and taken back to the people, they were instantly healed and set free of their demonic oppressions. This can be seen in Acts 19:11-12: "God wrought *special miracles* by the hands of Paul: So that from his body were brought unto the sick handkerchiefs or aprons, and the diseases departed from them, and the evil spirits went out of them." It was through these extraordinary, notable miracles that God reaped a mighty harvest in this large province.

I do believe that there can be an impartation of the power of God through pieces of cloth. In the life of Paul, there was such a transmission of power. Great care should be taken, however, not to *market* this form of healing.

The Ministry of Jesus

I would like to now consider the life and ministry of Jesus. Acts 10:38 tells us that "God anointed Jesus of Nazareth with the Holy Ghost and with power: who went about doing good, and healing all that were oppressed of the devil; for God was with him." After the Lord was anointed at the Jordan River, He went about performing miracles. As we study His earthly ministry, we find that His power increased, and the miracles became even more extraordinary toward the end of His ministry. Because the Lord is the Head of the Church, and His life is a pattern for the Church, we can say with assurance that the power of God will be greater in the last day Church than in the early Church.

The ministry of Jesus is divided up into several notable parts in the Scriptures. The Lord's power increased significantly, as did His depth of teaching, especially in the last six months of His ministry, from October of the year A.D. 29 to April A.D. 30, when He was crucified. This last section of His life commenced with His appearance in the temple during the Feast of Tabernacles in John chapter 7. Throughout the Scriptures, the Feast of Tabernacles represents the last day outpouring of the Spirit.

The day after this seven day feast, which was a sabbath, Jesus forgave the woman taken in adultery in John chapter 8. He also performed a notable miracle on the man born blind in chapter 9. From this point on, the miracles increased and the Lord's power and anointing increased. The man he healed in chapter 9 became known to all. The Scripture declares, "Since the world began was it not heard that any man opened the eyes of one that was born blind" (Jn. 9:32).

Then, in John chapter 11, the Lord raised Lazarus from the dead four days after he had died, which was even a greater miracle. This was a notable miracle that no one could deny, and many believed on Him because of it (see Jn. 11:45, 12:11,17-19). After these two notable miracles, the Lord proclaimed in John 14:12, "He that believeth on me, the works that I do shall he do also; and greater works than these shall he do; because I go unto my Father." The Lord promised that we would do greater works than He did. Christ assured us that we would see incredible miracles in these last days.

Since the beginning of time, the Lord has repeated Himself again and again. The interesting thing is that every time God repeats Himself, He repeats it in a greater measure. In the beginning, the Lord created heaven and earth in Genesis chapter 1. Then in Revelation, the Word of God ends with the Lord creating a new heaven and a new earth, which will be more glorious than the first creation. The Lord ascended to heaven from the Mount of Olives, and when He comes again He will return in glory to the Mount of Olives. These are just two examples of the numerous times that God repeats Himself. Jesus cleansed the temple at the beginning of His ministry, and He cleansed it again at the end of His three and a half year ministry. This was a prophetic sign of God moving at the beginning and the end of the Church Age. It also revealed the principle—what the Lord does at the beginning of an era, He will repeat at the close of that era.

The point I am trying to make here is that what God did at the birth of the Church on the day of Pentecost and in the New Testament era, He will repeat again in the last days. However, He will move in the last days in greater power and force. Haggai 2:9 promises that "the glory of the latter house shall be greater than of the former house." Truly, the Lord has reserved "the best wine until the last" (Jn. 2:10). The supernatural power that the early Church experienced will be seen again by the last day Church, but in an even greater measure. As miracles brought multiplication to the early Church, so miracles will bring expansion to the last day Church.

I have seen many miracles in my lifetime, but I believe that the Lord is going to exceed everything He has done in the past. We are entering a new day in the Spirit and a new era—an age of the miraculous and the supernatural. A new wave of God's Spirit is about to be poured out upon His Church worldwide. We sense it wherever we go around the world. Former things will be forgotten because we will be so consumed by the goodness of God in these end times. Just as the last part of Jesus' earthly ministry was the greatest (the greatest power and depth of teaching), so the last days of the Church Age will be more glorious than the early Church. Teachers of righteousness shall arise, and "they that do know their God shall be strong, and do exploits" (Dan.11:32).

David's life is also prophetic of the last day Church. In fact, the last day Church is a restoration of David's Tabernacle (Amos 9:11, Acts 15:15-16). Before he captured Mount Zion and possessed the full inheritance that God had promised to Israel, David was told by the Jebusites, "Except thou take away the blind and the lame, thou shalt not come in hither" (2 Sam. 5:6). This signifies that unless we move in the realm of the miraculous, we cannot possess all that God has for the last day Church.

Can you see what a tremendous need there is for the gift of the working of miracles today? It is essential that we continue seeking the Lord earnestly day and night until we get a breakthrough in the realm of miracles. This is not a time to relax and get comfortable. This is a day of new beginnings. It is time to seek the Lord until He pours out His Spirit and the gift of the working of miracles upon the Church.

In closing, I would just like to say again that miracles apply to every aspect of our lives. Perhaps a simple personal illustration will help to encourage you. Many years ago my wife and I were traveling in Africa. We had flown from the Cameroons to Kinshasa, Zaire. From there we were to fly to Nairobi, Kenya. At that time, we needed a visa, but it was impossible to receive one in Zaire before the time we were due to leave. We boarded the plane and arrived in Kenya. We then presented ourselves to the immigration authorities with our explanation. They said that we could not enter the country without an onward ticket, which we did not have. They were threatening to send us back to Zaire, which would have caused serious difficulties for us. We sat down on a bench by immigration somewhat crestfallen. But from within, I heard the voice of the Holy Spirit say, "Expect a miracle." It came with such firmness and assurance that I was very confident there was going to be a divine intervention on our behalf. Nothing happened for several minutes, but the voice inside continued to encourage me—"expect a miracle." Then an Indian gentleman living in Kenya, who was a complete stranger to me, approached us and said: "I have just been told your predicament by the immigration authorities, whom I know. I am going to sign a document and be your guarantee, and the officials have agreed to permit you to enter Kenya." This was a divine miracle of provision. We were able to enter Kenya without money and without an onward ticket through the benevolence of a business man whom we had never met before. God had stirred his spirit to help us.

God is the God of miracles. My wife and I have seen His wonderful miracles so many times in our lifetime. What He has done for us, He can do for you. Expect your miracle, whether it be of healing, provision, or any other area of need. He is the faithful, wonder-working God whom we serve.

6. PROPHECY

Paul's exhortation to the saints of God was: "Desire spiritual gifts, but rather that ye may prophesy" (1 Cor. 14:1). Paul, therefore, placed a high premium on the gift of prophecy and exalted it to a high position. We should seek the Lord for a flow in all the gifts of the Spirit, but in particular, we should earnestly pray for the gift of prophecy. If a person is called to the ministry, he absolutely must have a release in this gift. The operation of this wonderful blessing is essential for the growth of the Church.

First Corinthians 14:4 tells us that those who prophesy are edifying the Church. A minister cannot meet the needs of everyone in his congregation in one sermon because everyone has different needs. People are all going through a different season in their lives. Therefore, God has provided a way for the specific needs of every believer to be met, and it is through prophecy.

The gift of prophecy is speaking for God and declaring His message. It is a divinely inspired utterance. Many times, prophecies will be quotations of Scriptures. A prophecy is a word from God usually given in the language of the congregation. The gift of prophecy is mentioned many times in Scripture. In fact, the whole Word of God is really a collection of prophecies and divinely inspired messages from God.

First Corinthians 14:3 clearly defines the three primary purposes of the gift of prophecy. "He that prophesieth speaketh unto men to edification, and exhortation, and comfort." *Edification* means "to build up and strengthen." *Exhortation* means "to encourage." *Comfort* means "to solace and bind up the wound." The gift of prophecy functions basically in these three realms.

Three Basic Purposes of the Gift of Prophecy

1. Edification - *to make strong*
2. Exhortation - *to encourage*
3. Comfort - *to bind up the wounds*

This realm of prophecy is *very elementary* compared to the prophetic mantle of a prophet. If we do not grasp this truth, we will be very confused about prophecy. There is a distinct difference between the gift of prophecy and the prophetic office. The office of a prophet is one of the five ministry gifts of Christ (Eph. 4:11). This is a calling to which not just anyone can aspire. It is only for those whom God has called to be prophets (see Heb. 5:4). One cannot just pray for the ministry gift of a prophet, he must be sovereignly called by God. Whereas anyone can prophesy in the realm of the gift of prophecy, and every Christian is exhorted to do so. We must make this distinction between these two *classes* of prophecy.

The anointing to prophesy concerning future events belongs to the office of a prophet, not to someone with the gift of prophecy. The gift of prophecy does not relate to predicting the future. To predict future events like Jeremiah's prophecy of seventy years of captivity belongs to the anointing of a prophet, not the gift of prophecy. The New Testament prophet Agabus declared that a worldwide famine was coming (Acts 11:28). This anointing to declare the future is reserved solely for those with the mantle of a prophet. We must know our place in the Body of Christ, know the gifts God has given to us, and flow in them. We must not try to function in an area that the Lord has not given to us.

Everyone who prophesies can loosely be called a prophet, but only in a very limited sense. He is only a prophet in the sense that he is speaking a message on God's behalf. However, a prophet in the truest sense of the word refers to one who has the ministry gift of a prophet. For example, when Saul was with a company of prophets, the Spirit of God was moving and he also began to prophesy. People were so amazed by this that they began to ask: "Is Saul also among the prophets?" Saul prophesied, but he was not a prophet (see 1 Sam. 10:9-12). This scripture makes that point very clear.

The anointing of someone who holds the office of a prophet is far greater than someone with the gift of prophecy. The anointing upon a prophet is in the realm of the seven Spirits of the Lord. Anyone can prophesy, but the mantle of a prophet is reserved for a select few. Paul said to the Spirit-filled believers at Corinth, "For ye may all prophesy one by one" (1 Cor. 14:31). The gift of prophecy is reserved solely for those who have the baptism of the Holy Spirit. Yet, it is also true that a born-again believer who is not baptized in the Holy Spirit can deliver the word of the Lord and give an utterance that has a prophetic *impulse*. However, it would not be the gift of prophecy.

In Numbers chapter 11, when the Lord took the spirit and anointing that was upon Moses and gave it to the seventy elders, they all began to prophesy. Two of them continued to prophesy for a very long time in the camp of Israel. When Moses was told that they were prophesying, Joshua asked Moses to forbid them. The reply of Moses was: "Would to God that all the Lord's people were prophets [or would prophesy], and that the Lord would put his spirit upon them!" (Num. 11:29). God's desire is that all His people prophesy. He wants there to be a continual flow of prophecy in His Church.

The promise of God for the Church Age and the last days in particular is seen in Joel 2:28: "I will pour out my spirit upon all flesh; and your sons and your daughters shall prophesy, your old men shall dream dreams, your young men shall see visions." God's Spirit is going to be poured out upon the Church and men and women will begin to prophesy under the anointing of the Holy Spirit. Notice that it says that your "sons" and "daughters" shall prophesy. Obviously, women can prophesy and preach too. Deborah was a prophetess (Judg. 4:4), and Philip's four daughters prophesied under the anointing (Acts 21:9).

As with all spiritual gifts, there is a development in the gift of prophecy. Romans 12:6 says, "Having then gifts differing according to the grace that is given to us, whether prophecy, let us prophesy according to the *proportion* of faith." There are degrees and levels of prophecy. Those who are new to the gifts of the Spirit will prophesy on a very simple level, whereas those who have been prophesying for many years will prophesy on a much higher level. This increase in depth of prophecy comes through years of practice and walking in the Spirit. We should seek the Lord for the development of the gift of prophecy in our lives. Studying the Word of God and waiting upon Him every day develops this gift within us.

As the gift of prophecy develops, the conditions of people's hearts can be revealed. The Apostle Paul spoke of this in First Corinthians 14:24-25: "But if all prophesy, and there come in one that believeth not, or one unlearned, he is convinced of all, he is judged of all: And thus are the secrets of his heart made manifest; and so falling down on his face he will worship God, and report that God is in you of a truth." I have actually seen and heard of this taking place on a number of occasions. In particular, I remember a certain church in Leicestershire, England. People would not attend that church without first making everything right in their lives because if they did not, they knew the condition of their hearts and the sins they had committed would be exposed through prophecy. I would like to give you one little illustration of this so that you understand what can happen as this gift develops.

The pastor of this church was a very godly man who moved in the gift of prophecy. In one service as he was preaching, he was saying to the Lord in his heart, "Lord, please give me an illustration for my sermon." Suddenly, before his eyes he saw a tenement house with five floors. He began to prophesy from the pulpit everything he saw. He declared: "You are living in a tenement house that has five floors. The tenants of each floor all have a different day of the week to wash their clothes and hang them out to dry on the clothes line. Just suppose that it is your day to wash clothes, and you have washed your clothes by hand and worked very hard. You go to hang up your wet clothes, and to your amazement people from another floor have hung up their clothes, but it is not their day to use the clothes line."

"What should you do as a Spirit-filled believer?" he continued. "Shouldn't you lift up your hands to the Lord in thanksgiving and say, 'Thank You, Lord, for this trial,' carry your soaking-wet clothes back up to your room and wait for another time?" The pastor then went on to finish his sermon. After the service a very irate lady came up to him. Shaking her finger at him angrily, she said, "Who told you what I did?" Surprised, this saintly pastor asked her, "What are you talking about, Sister?" She said to him: "Who told you that I became very angry when I found someone else's clothes hanging up to dry when it was my turn to do laundry? And who told you that I gave this person a piece of my mind? Was it sister so and so?" The pastor replied, "No one told me except the Holy Spirit, who was watching everything you did." That prophetic anointing revealed her heart and her sin.

When I was very new in the ministry and I had just arrived in France, I attended a certain prayer meeting with several ministers. I hardly knew any of these men, when suddenly the Spirit of God came upon me and I boldly prophesied these words, "How dare you come into My presence with filthy garments!" This prophecy really upset the prayer meeting, and I was totally ignorant of anything that was going on; but evidently there was a certain minister present whose life was not right with God. Can you imagine bringing forth a prophecy like this, especially being very young and in a foreign country among men who had been in the ministry for many years? It was a very uncomfortable moment, to say the least.

We are told that one of the primary aspects of the gift of prophecy is to bring edification and encouragement (or exhortation). When we are asking the Lord about something, or we are going through a difficult time, and someone gives a prophecy that meets our need, we feel so encouraged and refreshed. This reminds me of a time in my life when I attended a certain non-Pentecostal Bible school, and I was having a very hard time there. Fortunately, I found a little Spirit-filled church where I could go to meet with God. Meeting after meeting, God would speak to me through prophecy, helping me through this difficult period in my life.

When I attended another Bible college, the Lord brought me in contact with an elderly lady who had been a missionary for many years in India. She took me under her wing and she would pray for me quite often. As she prayed the spirit of prophecy came upon her, and she would prophesy over me. This was a time when the Lord spoke very profound things to me and strengthened me through her prophecies. On one particular day during this special time in my life, she said to me: "I have a friend in London who is blind. When you go to London, I think it would be nice if you stopped by to visit her." She made arrangements with her friend, and scheduled a certain day for me to visit her.

When I arrived at her home, which was in one of the poorest parts of London, I knocked on the door and introduced myself. She introduced herself, and said: "Please come in. I have been expecting you." She led me into her kitchen where, to my amazement, there was a hot iron on an ironing board and food being cooked on an open coal fire. I said to her: "I was told you were blind. How do you …?" She quickly reassured me that she was blind. "How then do you cook on an open fire and iron your husband's shirts?" Her miraculous testimony was this: "Well, the presence of the Lord is so strong and real here that He directs my hands when I iron clothes. And if I touch a hot coal while I am cooking, I just pray in the name of Jesus, and I don't get burned."

She then asked me to read the Word of God to her. After I had read the book of Colossians out loud to her, she said, "Let's pray." As she prayed, the Spirit of God came into that room and the gift of prophecy flowed through this lady in a marvelous way. She told me under the unction of the Holy Spirit where I had come from, the battles and struggles I had faced, and what God had in store for my life. These prophecies have stayed with me over the years and have been a source of great encouragement and comfort.

The Apostle Paul told his spiritual son Timothy to war a good warfare by virtue of the prophecies that had been pronounced over him (1 Tim. 1:18). Personal prophecies strengthen us for all the valleys and dark times we go through in life. Every time we receive a prophecy, we should commit it to memory and meditate upon it.

Now let us consider several practical aspects of the gift of prophecy. Many of these principles apply to the other vocal gifts as well. Whenever we receive a prophecy or word from the Lord, we must also ask Him for the correct interpretation.

For example, the Lord spoke to a certain pastor while he was praying for a gentleman who was on his death-bed, "He shall not die, but live." Immediately, the pastor thought this person was going to recover and not die. However, understanding that death is transitory, the Lord spoke this declaring that this person was going to make it to heaven and inherit eternal life. Do you see that a prophecy can be true, but the way we interpret it makes all the difference?

Another very important factor with prophecy is to know when to give it. Just consider for a moment how you would feel if you had the correct interpretation of a message in tongues and just as you were about to give it, someone else gave a totally different interpretation. (This could have been a prophecy they received which they thought was the interpretation of the tongues.) You would become confused and discouraged, thinking that you didn't hear from the Lord correctly. Do you see how important Paul's words are to do everything "decently and in order"? (See 1 Cor. 14:40).

When we prophesy or operate in any of the gifts of utterance, we should speak in our normal tone of voice. We do not have to shout. Volume is not equivalent to the anointing. We should speak in such a clear way that everyone will be able to understand what we are saying (1 Cor. 14:9).

Prophecy can come in many different ways. Many times our words will be spontaneous and totally unpremeditated. This happens to me often. I will feel the anointing to prophesy, but I don't have any idea what I am going to say. By faith, I open my mouth and begin to speak the message of the Holy Spirit. Other times we receive an impression from the Lord, a scripture, or a vision, and we know that we are to share it in the form of a prophecy.

As with all manifestations, prophecy can come from three sources: the Holy Spirit, the human spirit, or a Satanic spirit. Many were condemned in the days of Jeremiah and Ezekiel for prophesying things from their own spirits (see Ezek. 13:2, Jer. 23:16). Because prophecy is not always given by inspiration of the Holy Spirit, we must judge it. Paul makes this very clear in First Corinthians 14:29. "Let the prophets speak two or three, and let the other judge [or weigh carefully what is said]." We should judge prophecies and make sure that we feel the witness of the Holy Spirit in our hearts before we embrace them.

Another important thing to realize about prophecy is that there are usually conditions that we must meet in order for the prophecy to come to pass. If we receive a prophecy that tells us wonderful blessings from the Lord are coming, there are conditions for this to be fulfilled. That is why we should ask the Lord what is our end of the bargain when we are given prophecies. Therefore, by doing our part we can be certain that we are going to receive that which He has prophesied over us. Also, quite often prophecies are not fulfilled for many years. We must be patient and wait for God to bring prophecies to pass in His good time, but we must also do our part and fulfill the conditions to see them come to fruition.

In closing, let us realize that God is far more interested in using us to prophesy than we are. We need to begin to move out in faith and operate in this gift. It is a gift that God wants every Christian to have and to use. It is powerful! Prophecy is speaking for God. This is a tremendous blessing and privilege. Therefore, let us "desire the spiritual gifts, but rather that we may prophesy."

7. DISCERNING OF SPIRITS

Discerning of spirits is the seventh spiritual gift. The gift of discerning of spirits is different from discernment. Discernment is spoken of in Hebrews 5:14: "Strong meat belongeth to them that are of full age, even those who by reason of use have their senses exercised to discern both good and evil." Discernment is the ability to discern right from wrong, good from evil. It is a sign of maturity.

Spiritual discernment comes through exercising our spiritual senses, and through meditating on the Word continually. Isaiah 7:15 says of the Lord Jesus Christ, "Butter and honey shall he eat, that he may know to refuse the evil, and choose the good." Butter is the abundance of milk, which represents the Word of God, and honey represents revelation of the Holy Spirit.

Therefore, Christ learned discernment (knowing how to refuse the evil and choose the good) by feeding upon the Word of God. This is how we obtain discernment also. Spiritual discernment is something that is worked into our character and into our hearts over the years. Discernment, however, is not a suspicious mind. Some people always think that others are doing wrong. This is because their own hearts are not right. There is a difference between discernment and being overly suspicious.

Now I would like to distinguish the difference between discernment and the gift of discerning of spirits (1 Cor. 12:10). The gift of the discerning of spirits can be defined as a supernatural gift of the Holy Spirit used to determine the *source* or origin of spiritual manifestations. There are three sources for spiritual manifestations: the Holy Spirit, the human spirit, and Satanic spirits. This fact is taken from First Corinthians 2:11-12, where the Apostle Paul says: "For what man knoweth the things of a man, save the *spirit of man* which is in him? even so the things of God knoweth no man, but the *Spirit of God*. Now we have received, not the *spirit of the world*, but the spirit which is of God; that we might know the things that are freely given to us of God." Here the human spirit is spoken of as the spirit of man, the Holy Spirit as the Spirit of God, and Satanic spirits as the spirit of the world.

Three Sources of Spiritual Manifestations

1. The Holy Spirit
2. The human spirit
3. Satanic spirits

We cannot discern the origin of any manifestation unless the Spirit of God causes the gift of the discerning of spirits to function through us. The fact that we have this gift does not mean that we can use it any time we wish. It operates only when the Lord wants us to supernaturally know the source of a manifestation. However, there are things we can do to cause the gifts to flow in our lives more frequently.

The discerning of spirits also operates in the realm of our five senses. As we have already mentioned, Hebrews 5:14 speaks of exercising our *senses* to discern both good and evil. It is through our five senses that spirits are discerned.

1. Touch

Our first sense is the ability to touch. We can actually feel demons and angels at times. We can feel them with our body, our soul, or our spirit. Spirits and demons have characteristics. For example, spirits of lust feel lustful, and spirits of hate feel hateful. Sometimes we can feel their impression upon our mind and body. Other times, we might physically battle with demons.

Many years ago, a fallen angel whose appearance was very beautiful, like an angel of God, came into my room in London, England, and attacked me while I was in bed. He grabbed me by my throat, and I could feel his hands upon my neck as he was trying to kill me. I tried to defend myself, but my hands went right through him. It was only as my spirit cried out, "Jesus save me," that he left. My throat was sore for three days after this encounter. If the Lord shows us grace, we can also feel Him at times and touch Him. On one occasion, the Lord appeared to me and said, "Touch Me, I am altogether good."

2. Taste

We can actually taste evil spirits with the taste buds in our mouths. In the same way, we can taste the Lord at times. Psalm 34:8 says: "O *taste* and see that the Lord is good: blessed is the man that trusteth in him." John the Beloved was told to eat the Word of God, and when he did it tasted like honey in his mouth, but it was bitter in his inward parts (Rev. 10:9-10).

Certain spirits lodge in the mouth and on the tongue, such as the demons of unbelief and lust. We must be very careful what we use our mouths for, because if our mouths speak lies, sooner or later demons will inhabit our mouths and taint everything we say. When I was in the country of Côte D'Ivoire along the West Coast of Africa, I was asked to teach. In this seminar I had four different men interpreting my message in French. I was having difficulty with one of my interpreters, and all the other interpreters who spoke in various dialects were to interpret from what he was saying. I knew something was not coming out right because I could feel it in my spirit, but I could not pinpoint the problem. I felt he was not interpreting my words correctly, and I also felt that he was doing it on purpose. I was teaching from John 15, and I said to the Lord, "This is not flowing."

At that moment, as I turned to look at this interpreter who was standing right next to me, I saw a demon hanging on his lips. I finished my message, and afterwards I went to talk to the missionary who had invited me there. I said to him, "What was that interpreter doing while I was preaching?" He quickly admitted, "When you would say the word *wine*, he would translate it *coffee*." "Why didn't you correct him?" I inquired. "I can't," he sheepishly replied. "He is one of the senior pastors here." I then made my feelings known very clearly: "That is not right. He cannot interpret for me again." "If he doesn't, there is going to be trouble," he murmured. "No, there will not be," I immediately responded, "because we are going to do things right before the Lord. I am not going to have a lying spirit be my interpreter. We will pray, and he will come to us and confess." We then prayed that the Lord would prompt him to come confess to us what he had been doing. Before the next meeting, he came and confessed to us, not only what he was doing, but also the reason he had that demon in his mouth. After praying for him, he was gloriously delivered.

Our mouth can be the instrument of God's Spirit or Satan's spirit. David said in Second Samuel 23:2, "The spirit of the

Lord spake by me, and his word was in my tongue." At times when we preach or prophesy, we can actually feel the word of the Lord in our mouths. Isaiah 59:21 speaks of a special covenant God would make with us; a covenant we should earnestly desire. "As for me, this is my covenant with them, saith the Lord; My spirit that is upon thee, and my words which I have put in thy mouth, shall not depart out of thy mouth." We should seek God for anointed lips and words. Our heart's cry should be to proclaim the words of life and truth, and to be an oracle of God.

3. Sight

We can also see evil spirits when our spiritual eyes are opened. There are two forms of evil spirits: demons and fallen angels. Demons are earth bound. They do not have wings. They are the disembodied spirits of the former civilization before the creation of man. This is obviously so because demons always seek to dwell in a body; the reason for this is that they once inhabited a body. Demons are usually very ugly and deformed in shape. Fallen angels, however, are very different from demons. They are not earth bound. In their normal state, angels have wings and wear garments. However, both good and evil angels have the ability to transform themselves into men. This is proven from Hebrews 13:2, where Paul says, "Be not forgetful to entertain strangers: for thereby some have entertained angels unawares." No one would entertain an angel unawares if the angel appeared with his wings. I know of many cases when good angels transformed themselves into the form of human beings. Fallen angels have the same ability. They can transform themselves to look like people. They can also transform themselves to look like angels of light (2 Cor. 11:14-15). This is why John tells us to "try the spirits" (1 Jn. 4:1).

In Switzerland, while a certain pastor was preaching, my spiritual eyes were opened. I saw the angel of the Lord standing at his right hand, and on his left side was a very large demon with a crown on his head playing a fiddle. When this minister preached, the angel of the Lord was speaking through him. However, when he led in worship, the demon was leading the worship. We must be very careful of so called "Christian rock music," because it allows other spirits to influence and control our services.

Spirits can also manifest themselves as animals. Sometimes spirits like jealousy and envy take the form of animals. Animals represent certain things. Mice speak of uncleanness, and frogs represent false prophecy (cf. Rev. 16:13). In the same manner, the Holy Spirit manifests Himself as a gentle dove. We want to believe God to open our eyes to the spirit world, especially the good side.

4. Hearing

We can hear both fallen angels and true angels speak, either through a mental or an audible voice. There are many instances of this occurring in Scripture. The prophet Daniel had some remarkable encounters with angels that spoke to him. The archangel Gabriel spoke to him in Daniel chapter 8 and gave him understanding concerning certain future events. Gabriel also spoke to Zacharias in Luke chapter 1, telling him that he was going to have a son whom he would name John. This same angel was sent about six months later to Nazareth to speak to Mary about the birth of her Son Jesus. There were many other times when angels spoke to people in the Bible. I have personally heard angels, good and bad, speak to me on a number of occasions.

5. Smell

We can smell spirits too. Their odor is very unpleasant. Depending on the demon, the odor is different. By the same token, we can sometimes smell the sweet fragrance of the Lord. In Song of Songs 1:3 the Bride says to the Bridegroom, "Because of the savour of thy good ointments thy name is as ointment poured forth, therefore do the virgins love thee." Psalm 45:8 tells us some of the ointments which are associated with the presence of the Lord. "All thy garments smell of myrrh, and aloes, and cassia, out of the ivory palaces, whereby they have made thee glad."

The Body

There are spirits for each organ of the body. Cancer can be an actual spirit. One time just as I was about to pray for a certain man, I saw the spirit of cancer standing by his side. I asked him, "Are there any members of your family in past generations that had cancer?" He said, "Yes, cancer has passed on for many generations in my family." "I see the spirit of cancer by your side," I told him. "We are going to cast out that spirit of cancer, and we are going to pray for your healing. We are going to command that spirit of cancer to leave you and go to hell so that it does not pass on to your children." God not only healed him, but none of his daughters have had cancer.

We must realize that sometimes to heal a sickness, we must cast out the demon that is causing the illness. There is a spirit of gluttony that needs to be cast out of some people. I would like to relate a story I heard about Smith Wigglesworth, who could be quite demonstrative at times. A certain man with stomach pains came up to him in one of his meetings and asked for prayer.

Smith Wigglesworth laid his hands on him and commanded the pains to go away, and immediately this man was completely healed.

This miracle of healing took place on a Monday evening, but by Friday the pains had returned. He came to the service again and said to Wigglesworth, "You prayed for me Monday and the pains left, but now they have returned." Well, Smith Wigglesworth was a plumber, and he had very large, strong hands. With no warning, he pulled back his fist and hit that man in the stomach as hard as he could, shouting, "Come out you spirit of gluttony!" The man was not only delivered from stomach pains, but also from a gluttonous spirit.

This story illustrates the importance of the gift of discerning of spirits when we are praying for a person's healing. In reality, it might not be healing that a person needs, but deliverance from a spirit. A number of years ago, we prayed for a lady at a certain church, who was sick all through the meeting. By the gift of discerning of spirits, I saw a spirit curled around her bowels that was making her sick. It wasn't healing that she needed; she needed to be delivered of that spirit. The Holy Spirit spoke in tongues through me, and that spirit loosened its grip and went away. This lady felt so much better after she was set free from this demon. What took place was not a miracle of healing, but deliverance from an afflicting spirit.

In every part of the body there are spirits that lodge on certain organs to prevent their proper function or to overemphasize their function. For example, spirits for the stomach overemphasize the duty of the stomach. Certain people are overweight because of physical problems or other reasons, but other people have a spirit of gluttony. There are spirits for the emotions too.

We must be very careful that the spiritual gifts (and the gift of discerning of spirits in particular) do not become idols to us. The gift of discerning of spirits must be subjugated to the will of God. Do you know what happens when the discerning of spirits becomes an idol? All the preaching in a church revolves around demons, and the church becomes overbalanced on the negative side in the realm of the Satanic.

I know many pastors who open their service by binding Satan and casting him out, rather than giving all the glory to God. By doing this, they are actually giving praise and recognition to demons. One thing about Satan's kingdom is that they are all like him. Satan fell because he craved attention. This is also one of the primary characteristics of all who follow him, which includes demons and fallen angels. We should invite the Holy Spirit into our services. When ministers emphasize the kingdom of darkness more than the kingdom of light, the people become demon-conscious. They begin to see, or imagine, demons under every chair and in every corner. God desires His people to be Christ-conscious, focusing their attention and thoughts upon Him.

At one Bible school where I was given the subject of demonology to teach, there were spiritual manifestations from the kingdom of Satan all week long. Doors and windows would open and shut by themselves; floors creaked. The demons did not trouble me, however, because I said to them: "I am teaching demonology. Don't you dare come around me," and they didn't. However, the students were young, and they were susceptible to these things.

They would go to bed thinking of demons and sure enough they were not disappointed. Their hair would stand up on the back of their necks as the doors to their rooms opened by themselves. I warned them not to think about demons after the class because if they did, they would surely see them. We must not be ignorant about the kingdom of Satan. However, we must be Christ-centered, and know this irrefutable truth that "greater is He that is within us than he that is in the world." Remember, only one third of the angels fell, two thirds did not. Therefore, there are more angels that are for us than there are against us (see 2 Kgs. 6:16).

The Apostle Paul had the gift of discerning of spirits operating at a very high level in his life. Acts 16:16-18 gives us an excellent example of this while Paul was in Philippi. "And it came to pass, as we went to prayer, a certain damsel possessed with a spirit of divination met us, which brought her masters much gain by soothsaying: The same followed Paul and us, and cried, saying, These men are the servants of the most high God, which shew unto us the way of salvation. And this did she many days. But Paul, being grieved, turned and said to the spirit, I command thee in the name of Jesus Christ to come out of her. And he came out the same hour." It was by the gift of discerning of spirits that Paul knew this woman had an evil spirit of divination. Therefore, as seen in this case, the gifts can function outside of a church service.

By the discerning of spirits, Paul knew there was a spirit of divination in this woman. However, to know there is a spirit of divination is one thing, but to know what to do with that spirit is quite another. For a number of days, until he knew what to do, Paul allowed that spirit to manifest itself. We need to realize an important truth here—when we cast out spirits, it can cause a lot of trouble. After taking authority over the spirit in this woman, we see that Paul was thrown into prison.

We should weigh beforehand the result of every action we take very carefully. Suppose a minister discerns through the gift of discerning of spirits that a demonic spirit is manifesting itself within a certain lady in the church, which other people mistake for the Holy Spirit. Knowing there is a spirit is not enough. Remember, demons are gregarious. There would probably be the spirit of sympathy along with this demonic manifestation, and this spirit would have its tentacles in certain members of the congregation.

Therefore, if the minister rebukes this woman and tells her that she is operating under a false anointing, many people in the church would be offended because they thought her manifestations were from the Lord. Thus, the pastor must have great wisdom to deal with this situation.

We must always calculate what the end result will be of everything we do. Often, we need other gifts of the Spirit to operate with the gift of discerning of spirits, such as the word of wisdom to give us direction as to what we should do with a demonic spirit. There is a specific time to cast out demons and to bind fallen angels. We must hear from the Lord and move with great caution when dealing with spirits.

This gift of the discerning of spirits is greatly needed in the Church today. Many manifestations that are passing for manifestations of the Holy Spirit are not birthed by the Spirit of God, but by a demonic spirit. By the anointing of the discerning of spirits we can discern the source of these manifestations. Many times we need this gift to reveal to us what spirits are hindering our churches from growing. This gift will bring the answer and bring a release in our church and lives. May we pray for this priceless gift to function in our lives and in our churches.

8. THE GIFT OF TONGUES

The eighth spiritual gift, the gift of tongues, is always linked with the ninth gift, the gift of interpretation. These two gifts are intended and designed to be used together, not separately. The gift of tongues, as one of the nine gifts of the Holy Spirit, is very different from the personal language in other tongues we receive when we are baptized in the Holy Spirit. They are essentially the same in nature, but different in function and purpose. The tongues that accompany the baptism of the Holy Spirit are for our personal use and for our personal edification. The gift of tongues is used to bring edification to the church. This is basically the difference between our personal language in other tongues and the gift of tongues. One is for personal use and the other is for use in the Body of Christ.

Let us review again the three aspects of the manifestation of tongues: (1) speaking in other tongues as the initial evidence of the baptism of the Holy Spirit; (2) speaking in tongues in our prayer life; and (3) the *gift* of tongues, one of the nine gifts of the Spirit, for the edification of the Church.

The gift of tongues is a Holy Spirit-birthed message given in a language that is foreign to the speaker. It should be followed by an interpretation given in the language the congregation speaks. It is something that would usually be given in a church service or meeting. When we speak in tongues and worship in tongues privately or corporately in church, these are the tongues we received with the baptism of the Holy Spirit. When we were baptized in the Holy Ghost, no one interpreted our tongues. Our tongues become resident within us after we are baptized in the Holy Ghost, and we can speak in our personal tongues at any time we choose. The words are given by the Holy Spirit, but we initiate them and decide when to speak in this language. But this is not the gift of tongues; this is not one of the nine gifts. Everyone who speaks in tongues does not have *the gift of tongues*, or the faith that comes along with it to give a message in other tongues. The *gift* of tongues is something we receive after the tongues we receive with the baptism of the Holy Spirit, although it could be very shortly afterwards.

The gift of tongues is a message from the Holy Spirit for the church in general, or it can be for an individual. The Holy Spirit originates it, and chooses when we are to use it. We cannot give a message in tongues when we desire to do so; we can only use this gift when the Holy Spirit moves upon us to use it. However, we can use our personal language in tongues whenever we want, and we are encouraged to do so frequently.

Keep in mind, however, that we should *not* speak in our personal tongues when the congregation is silent during a time specifically allotted for prophecies and spiritual manifestations. This is the time when the *gift* of tongues should be used. We could speak in tongues quietly to ourselves during this time, but not out loud unless we have the gift of tongues. There are other times in the service (such as during the worship service or when praying for those in need) that we can speak in our *personal* tongues.

We must not confuse the gift of tongues with our personal prayer language. There has been much error in the Church concerning the gift of tongues because people have failed to recognize the difference between the two.

In First Corinthians 14:14 the Apostle Paul said, "For if I pray in an unknown tongue, my spirit prayeth, but my understanding is unfruitful." When we speak in our personal tongues that are resident within us, we are praying to God. Paul said in First Corinthians 14:18, "I thank my God, I speak with tongues more than ye all." Concerning his personal life and prayer language in tongues, Paul said that he prayed in tongues more than anyone. He realized that it was the secret to his power. From this verse, it seems as though every time Paul was alone he was speaking in other tongues. He is referring to the personal prayer language he received when he was baptized in the Holy Spirit. Paul is not referring to the gift of tongues here.

Then Paul continues in First Corinthians 14:19 to speak about the *gift* of tongues: "Yet in the church I had rather speak five words with my understanding, that by my voice I might teach others also, than ten thousand words in an unknown tongue." Here Paul is talking about the gift of tongues as a message. He tells us that to simply give a message in tongues to the whole church without giving an interpretation is not very useful. No one is edified because he cannot understand what is being uttered.

The gift of tongues is a message from God that should be followed by an interpretation so that the church or body of believers may be edified. In First Corinthians 14:13 Paul states, "Wherefore let him that speaketh in an unknown tongue pray that he may interpret." This is referring to the gift of tongues, which under normal circumstances should not be given without an interpretation. The interpretation may be given either by the same person or someone else. The person who gives a message in tongues should pray for the interpretation. If he does not receive the interpretation, someone else in the church should. I believe that we can also receive the interpretation of our personal tongues when we are praying to the Lord. I pray in tongues frequently, and I ask the Lord to give me the interpretation of what my spirit is saying—and He does.

Paul continues to develop the function of the gift of tongues in First Corinthians 14:5-6. "I would that ye all spake with tongues, but rather that ye prophesied: for greater is he that prophesieth than he that speaketh with tongues, except he interpret, that the church may receive edifying. Now, brethren, if I come unto you speaking with tongues, what shall I profit you, except I shall speak to you either by revelation, or by knowledge, or by prophesying, or by doctrine?"

When we speak in our personal tongues, we are edifying ourselves. But when we give a prophetic message in tongues to the church, we are edifying the church. Therefore, the gift of tongues, when given as a message to the church, should be followed by an interpretation so that the Body of Christ may be edified. The gift of tongues with the interpretation is basically the same as and equivalent to prophecy, and falls into the same three general categories as prophecy: edification, exhortation, and comfort (1 Cor. 14:3).

Tongues are a sign to unbelievers. "Wherefore tongues are for a sign, not to them that believe, but to them that believe not: but prophesying serveth not for them that believe not, but for them which believe" (1 Cor. 14:22). Let me recount a story to help make this point more vivid. In England many years ago, a devout Jew who was not satisfied with the Jewish religious practices of his day visited the Pentecostal church which I attended. He sat in the back row. During the service someone spoke in other tongues and then someone else interpreted his message in tongues into English. The impact upon this Jewish man was astounding.

The person who spoke in other tongues, which were totally foreign to him, spoke in perfect Hebrew. After the service this Jewish man came up to the pastor trembling and asked him, "What is in this place?" "What do you mean?" queried the pastor. This Jewish gentleman then surprised the pastor by this abrupt confession: "Why did that person speak in Hebrew during the service and tell me all my sins, even calling me by my Hebrew name? And why did this other person repeat it all in English?" In total shock, the pastor said to him, "No one spoke in Hebrew, especially not that man."

The Jewish man did not believe the pastor, so he spoke to that person in Hebrew until he was convinced that he did not know any Hebrew. The pastor assured this Jew that it was the Holy Spirit speaking through this man. The gift of tongues and interpretation operating together functioned like prophecy, and this man's heart was revealed (see 1 Cor. 14:24-25). May we all have a fresh hunger to seek the Lord for a new fluency of this precious gift.

9. INTERPRETATION OF TONGUES

As we have already mentioned, the ninth gift of the Holy Spirit is inseparably linked with the gift of tongues. This gift is its counterpart, and the two must be used together. The gift of interpretation is the supernatural understanding and interpretation of a message given in a foreign tongue.

Interpretation is different from translation. The interpretation is the sense and basic meaning of the message in tongues. The interpretation is not an exact word for word translation of the tongues. It gives the sense and general idea of the message. The message in tongues might be very short and the interpretation in our language very long because it could take several words to explain one word in an unknown language, or vice versa. Because the message comes through a human vessel, each interpreter will explain the message differently. The basic meaning is the same, but given with a different angle or slant to it. Therefore, it is possible for two people to receive the interpretation of a message in tongues and for them to express it in different ways. Nonetheless, it is the same message.

The interpretation of tongues, as with all the gifts of utterance, can come in a number of different ways. To name just a few, the interpretation can come to us spontaneously, or we can sense in our spirits what we should say, or we could have a vision and then give the impression of the vision. Visions can be in very vivid color like watching a movie; or in black and white; or in a simple mental picture or sketch.

We must be extremely careful with this third avenue for interpretations because visions usually portray *one* main idea. Many times, every part of a vision cannot be taken literally because there is one general theme the Lord is trying to express. Therefore, we must be very careful in our interpretations of visions, making sure that we clearly understand what God is trying to speak through them.

Remember, all the gifts of the Spirit operate through human channels. Therefore, the gifts, and the gift of interpretation in particular, are going to be colored by the personality, disposition, and make-up of the human vessel. Some years ago, when I went to visit a certain church, the minister who was a former student of mine, asked me to start the service because he was delayed. I opened the service and we began to worship. After worship, while everyone was silently waiting upon the Lord, I felt the wooden floor shake beneath me and I wondered what in the world was happening. To my surprise, when I turned around, I saw a very large person making a lot of noise and commotion, and then he gave a message in tongues.

Moments later, as I was pondering this rather fleshly display, the floor began to shake again. Then someone else gave the interpretation of this message in the same demonstrative way the other person gave the tongues. Almost immediately after, someone else prophesied in like manner. I thought perhaps I should say something to the church about this, but mercifully I didn't because the pastor arrived at that moment. But He apparently felt the anointing too, and soon the floor began to go up and down once again. His face became beet red and out came a prophecy. Now, I think I should say that all of the messages were correct, but there was a lot of excess involved too. It would have been much easier to hear what the Lord was saying if the vessels had been relaxed and did not go through all those other contortions.

As we have said before, we should operate in the vocal gifts just as we speak in normal, every day speech and in our normal tone of voice. The idea is to convey a message from the Lord to others, not draw attention to ourselves. We should make it easy for people to concentrate on the message, not on the messenger.

Once in Sweden there was a group of ministers on a platform. When a message in tongues was given, the man behind the pulpit gave the interpretation. As this man gave the interpretation, a woman minister on the platform was seeing visually, one slide after another, what the man was interpreting. The amazing thing was that, as the minister interpreted, she would see slides and then she would see blank ones. She got the message very clearly. There were a lot of human insertions in that interpretation. This man had become so carried away in his spirit that he embellished the interpretation. When he did this, the woman minister saw blank slides, meaning that what he was saying was not really part of the message from the Lord. Do you see how careful we must be with interpretation? It must be spoken under the anointing. Many people allow their spirits to be carried away in what they say. Sometimes we can feel so good under the anointing that we add our own thoughts and feelings. Unfortunately, some people who are upset with others in the church will at times say something to rebuke them, but it is not what the Spirit of the Lord is saying.

The Holy Spirit speaks through the vocabulary of the person speaking. The person who is very limited in his vocabulary will give a very simple interpretation or prophecy, whereas someone whose vocabulary is considerably larger will give a more erudite interpretation. However, both vessels are giving a correct interpretation from the Lord. A farmer will give the message in a different vocabulary than a scientist or college professor. Neither is wrong; the background of a person influences his delivery of the message. This is true in most cases. However, when Smith Wigglesworth spoke and preached, he dropped his *h's* and put them in places they did not belong, and made many other phonetic errors. Yet, when he prophesied under the anointing of the Holy Ghost, he prophesied in the King James language with very good pronunciation. God sometimes overrides our limitations.

The purpose of the interpretation is that people receive the message from God. Therefore, brevity and repetition are important. The Word of God repeats itself again and again from Genesis to

Revelation. The purpose of repetition is to impress a thought upon the mind and heart of the listener. We must try to make the interpretation as understandable as possible. Paul said in First Corinthians 14:9, "So likewise ye, except ye utter by the tongue words easy to be understood, how shall it be known what is spoken? for ye shall speak into the air."

The interpretation of tongues is a very important gift. It is essential for our understanding. Paul said in First Corinthians 14:14-20: "For if I pray in an unknown tongue, my spirit prayeth, but my understanding is unfruitful. What is it then? I will pray with the spirit, and I will pray with the understanding also: I will sing with the spirit, and I will sing with the understanding also. Else when thou shalt bless with the spirit, how shall he that occupieth the room of the unlearned say Amen at thy giving of thanks, seeing he understandeth not what thou sayest? For thou verily givest thanks well, but the other is not edified. I thank my God, I speak with tongues more than ye all: Yet in the church I had rather speak five words with my understanding, that by my voice I might teach others also, than ten thousand words in an unknown tongue. Brethren, be not children in understanding: howbeit in malice be ye children, but in understanding be men."

Unless the gift of tongues is interpreted, no one is blessed, because no one understands what was said. The gift of interpretation enlightens our understanding, enabling us to clearly comprehend what the Spirit of God is saying. If the Church is ever to come into all that God has for her and move in the direction He is leading, the gift of interpretation must begin to function.

In closing, may I say this—God is a very competent businessman. A businessman does not invest money into firms that do not produce. In the same way, God does not give more spiritual gifts to those who do not use what He has already given to them. The key to receiving more spiritual gifts is to use what we already have, then seek the Lord for new ones. If we use and develop the gifts we already have, we will become candidates to receive more. May God cause the spiritual gifts to begin to operate in a fresh way in our lives and in our local churches, so that we may be used to bring glory to the Lord of Hosts!

Part Six

THE FRUITS OF THE SPIRIT

In Part Six we are going to study the nine fruits of the Holy Spirit spoken of in Galatians 5:22-23. These nine *fruits* of the Spirit are different from the nine *gifts* of the Spirit. This chapter deals with God's character being developed in our lives by the fruits of the Spirit, so that we may be transformed into His image and bear His likeness.

INTRODUCTION

I would like to direct your attention to Galatians chapter 5, where the Apostle Paul contrasts the seventeen works of the flesh with the nine fruits of the Holy Spirit. Following the list of the seventeen works of the flesh (which, if practiced, will prohibit us from inheriting the kingdom of God) are the nine fruits of the Holy Spirit in Galatians 5:22-23. "But the fruit of the Spirit is love, joy, peace, longsuffering, gentleness, goodness, faith [or faithfulness], meekness, temperance: against such there is no law." These nine fruits, which are aspects of God's character that should be worked out in our life, are contrasted with the nine gifts of the Holy Spirit.

The Balance Between the Gifts and the Fruits

Let us consider for a moment the balance between the gifts of the Spirit and the fruits of the Spirit. In Matthew 7:21-23 the Lord Jesus said: "Not every one that saith unto me, Lord, Lord, shall enter into the kingdom of heaven; but he that doeth the will of my Father which is in heaven. Many will say to me in that day, Lord, Lord, have we not prophesied in thy name? and in thy name have cast out devils? and in thy name done many wonderful works? And then will I profess unto them, I never knew you [I never had an intimate relationship with you]: depart from me, ye that work iniquity." This warning is addressed to those who have the gifts of the Holy Spirit. It is only those who are baptized in the Holy Ghost who can prophesy, for prophecy is one of the nine gifts of the Spirit. Casting out devils and the working of miracles are also works of Spirit-filled believers.

These verses became very real to my wife and me a number of years ago at a certain Pentecostal convention. There was a particular minister there who was twisting the Scriptures to condone sin in the lives of believers. This, of course, is an abomination to the Lord. My wife and I became very sick in our hearts. At the end of his message, he made an appeal to those who wanted to accept Christ as their Savior. Many responded and were saved. Countless others were filled with the baptism of the Holy Spirit and healed that night because of this man's ministry. However, the whole time this was taking place, my wife and I were absolutely disgusted in our hearts.

When we returned to our room where we were staying for this convention, we opened the door and the Lord Jesus was standing there in person. I have never seen Him so sad. His head was hanging down on His chest. He did not speak one word to us, but His head went from side to side. As His head moved, the Holy Spirit thundered the words from Matthew 7:22-23 into my heart: "Many, many will say to me in that day, Lord, Lord, have we not prophesied in thy name? and in thy name have cast out devils? and in thy name done many wonderful works? And then will I profess unto them, I never knew you: depart from me, ye that work iniquity." The message was eternally clear—we are not accepted on the basis of our gifts, but our character and fruits.

The warning in Matthew 7:21-23 actually flows out of an exhortation given by the Lord in the preceding verses that we are all known by our fruits. "Ye shall know them by their fruits. Do men gather grapes of thorns, or figs of thistles? Even so every good tree bringeth forth good fruit; but a corrupt tree bringeth forth evil fruit. A good tree cannot bring forth evil fruit, neither can a corrupt tree bring forth good fruit. Every tree that bringeth not forth good fruit is hewn down, and cast into the fire. Wherefore by their fruits ye shall know them" (Mt. 7:16-20). After speaking about the fruits, the Lord then goes on to give the warning about not relying upon our gifts, such as prophecy and the working of miracles, for acceptance in His sight. It is the fruit of the Spirit in our lives that makes us pleasing to Him.

Let us now put into true scriptural perspective the balance between the gifts and the fruits. With great skill, the Apostle Paul clearly describes the difference between the two in First Corinthians chapter 13. He says in verses 1-3: "Though I speak with the tongues of men and of angels, and have not love, I am become as sounding brass, or a tinkling cymbal. And though I have the gift of prophecy, and understand all mysteries, and all knowledge; and though I have all faith, so that I could remove mountains, and have not love, I am nothing. And though I bestow all my goods to feed the poor, and though I give my body to be burned, and have not love, it profiteth me nothing."

Paul goes on to say in verse 13, "And now abideth faith, hope, love, these three; but the greatest of these is love." Then Paul resumes his theme on the gifts of the Spirit in First Corinthians chapter 14. In verse one of chapter 14 he said, "Follow after love, and desire spiritual gifts."

We should desire spiritual gifts. Certainly, we need to speak in tongues for our own edification and enlightenment so that we are built up in the most holy faith. Also, we need to seek the gift of tongues for the edification of the Church, as well as seeking all the other spiritual gifts. In the final analysis, however, we could have all nine gifts operating in our lives, but still be rejected by the Lord if we do not walk in holiness and have the fruits of the Spirit worked out within us.

The spiritual gifts do not really profit us unless we walk in love, which encompasses many of the other fruits of the Spirit and many other aspects of God's character. With this in mind, let us now consider the nine fruits of the Spirit in detail.

The Nine Plants That Parallel the Nine Fruits

I would like to look with you now at another set of *nines* in the Word of God which are analogous to the nine fruits of the Spirit. It is found in the Song of Songs 4:12-14, where King Solomon, speaking under the unction of the Holy Spirit, describes the Bride of Christ. "A garden enclosed is my sister, my spouse; a spring shut up, a fountain sealed. Thy plants are an orchard of pomegranates, with pleasant fruits; camphire, with spikenard, Spikenard and saffron; calamus and cinnamon, with all trees of frankincense; myrrh and aloes, with all the chief spices." Solomon lists nine beautiful plants that he observed were growing and flourishing in the garden of the heart of the Bride of Christ.

These nine plants are symbolic of the nine fruits of the Spirit, and they correspond to the nine fruits in descending order. The interpretation of each plant can be seen by comparing each plant with its corresponding fruit. Therefore, every time we read the Word of God and we see one of these plants mentioned, we can understand what it represents and what the Lord is saying in that particular passage.

THE NINE FRUITS COMPARED WITH THE NINE PLANTS

Galatians 5:22-23	Song of Songs 4:12-14
Love	Pomegranates
Joy	Camphire
Peace	Spikenard
Longsuffering	Saffron
Gentleness	Calamus
Goodness	Cinnamon
Faithfulness	Frankincense
Meekness	Myrrh
Temperance	Aloes

* Each herb answers to one of the fruits of the Spirit.

How the Fruits are Developed in our Lives

The fruits of the Spirit are developed, as the Lord said in John 15:1-4, through the following four steps:

1. Through pruning (or purging) by the Heavenly Father. This is accomplished through severe trials and bitter experiences (Jn. 15:2).

2. By being thoroughly cleansed by obedience to the Word. Christ said in John 15:3, "Now ye are clean through the word which I have spoken unto you." (See Eph. 5:26, 1 Pet. 1:22).

3. Through abiding in Christ, which is accomplished by keeping the commandments. The Lord instructed us in John 15:10, "If ye keep my commandments, ye shall abide in my love; even as I have kept my Father's commandments, and abide in his love."

4. Through Christ abiding in us, which is accomplished as His words abide in us (see Jn. 15:4, 15:10).

To the degree that these four aspects of the Christian life are developed in us, we shall bring forth fruit, more fruit, and much fruit. Thus, our Heavenly Father will be glorified (Jn. 15:8).

The Nine Fruits are Developed through Contrast

Another very important factor concerning the development of the fruits of the Spirit in our lives is that the fruits are developed through contrast and through opposing forces. The fruits of the Spirit are really only brought to perfection through their opposites.

- **Love -** is developed through loving those who hate and despitefully use us.
- **Joy -** is developed by those who pass through the valley of Baca (sorrow) and make it a well of joy from which others may draw strength, as the joy of the Lord is their strength.
- **Peace -** comes to maturity as the Christian is placed in situations of confusion and he permits peace like a river to flow from his soul.
- **Longsuffering -** can only come to maturity through very long and arduous trials, where human strength fails and the divine suffer-

ing manifested by the Christ of Calvary flows through and from our spirit.

• **Gentleness -** shines forth in the midst of the rude and uncouth, the ungrateful and the unthankful.

• **Goodness -** manifests its fruit amongst the wicked with their cruel and deceitful acts.

• **Faithfulness -** is seen at its best when confronted by failure and betrayal of those we trusted most.

• **Meekness -** comes to its fullness, and causes all to marvel, when confronted by anger to which one does not respond.

• **Temperance -** is self-will graciously exercised amongst those of unrestrained lusts, passions, and desires in which one manifests beautifully disciplined tastes.

The Nine Fruits are Developed through Contrast

Love	Hatred
Joy	Sorrow
Peace	Confusion
Longsuffering	Prolonged Trials
Gentleness	Unthankfulness
Goodness	Wickedness
Faithfulness	Betrayals
Meekness	Anger
Temperance	Self-will; unrestrained desires

* The fruits of the Spirit are brought to perfection through opposing forces.

1. LOVE

The definition of love is commitment. Love is not based on feelings, although feelings do flow as the fruit of love matures. Therefore, love starts in the will, or the spirit, and then flows to the soul, the area of our emotions. Finally, it is expressed by the outward actions, such as acts of touching and kindness. Those acts of kindness can be exemplified by the giving of ourselves to the one whom we love. Love is best expressed in the character, nature, and action of God Himself. God is love (1 Jn. 4:8,16). Love is the summation of God's character. It is the warmth that emanates from His heart to all His creation. His perfect love is manifested toward us in this very familiar verse we all know so well: "For God so loved the world that He gave His only begotten Son that whosoever believeth in Him should not perish but have everlasting life" (Jn. 3:16).

The Apostle Paul said in Romans 5:8, "God commendeth his love toward us, in that, while we were yet sinners, Christ died for us." Just before this he stated in Romans 5:6, "For when we were yet without strength, in due time Christ died for the ungodly." God was in Christ seeking to reconcile the world unto Himself. Christ was the expression of the Father's love in this way—He was the sacrificial Lamb of God who was slain before the foundation of the world for the sins of the world. God had to pay a tremendous price in order to redeem us. Only His Son was qualified to pay that price, because it had to be *God* who paid the debt. It was God who wanted to redeem us. Therefore, God had to pay, and the price it cost Him was His own Son. His own Son had to become sin for us.

Not only that, but we read in Isaiah 53:10 that it pleased the Father to bruise Him. In other words, the Lord Jesus had to be baptized with the baptism of suffering of which He forewarned His disciples. He had to suffer in His *body* those physical wounds, bruises, and stripes. He had to suffer within His *soul* when He was put to grief. The Lord was the Man of Sorrows acquainted with grief, and He had to suffer in His *spirit* the agony of being separated from His Father.

As we contemplate this, we realize that the price God paid for our redemption is *eternal*. Why? Because when Christ was resurrected, He was resurrected in the same body in which He went to the cross. The only difference was that His body was *glorified* after the resurrection. This is why He could say to Thomas after His resurrection, "Reach hither thy finger, and behold my hands; and reach hither thy hand, and thrust it into my side" (Jn. 20:27). Thomas was able to behold His nail-scarred hands.

When the Lord Jesus returns at His second coming, He will still have those wounds in His body. In fact, the book of Zechariah tells us that the Jews will ask Him when He comes again, "What are these wounds in thine hands?" (Zech. 13:6).

The Father has to look at these wounds for eternity, and know that it was ultimately He who sent His Son to Calvary to die for the sins of the world. What an eternal price He paid for us! He has to look eternally upon His Son, whom He permanently marred because of His love for us. Oh, how He loves you and me!

Therefore, when we are asked to love God, there are two ways we show our love for Him. First, we love God by giving our body as a living sacrifice to Him. Secondly, we show our love to God by giving our dearest possession or loved one to Him, even as the Father gave His only begotten Son and Abraham gave his dearly beloved son, Isaac.

The Pomegranate

I would like to look now at the fruit that epitomizes love—the pomegranate. From the pomegranate, we can see many truths about love. A pomegranate has a very thick rind. It must be pierced to release its grenadine juice. If true love is really to be developed in our lives, in like manner we must be pierced and hurt by the ones we love the most.

When Jesus appears on the Mount of Olives to deliver the defenders of Zion at His second coming, He will cry out: "See now that I, even I, am he…I live forever" (Deut. 32:39-40). The Jews will respond, "O Lord, we have waited for Thee" (cf. Isa. 26:8). They will be filled with joy because their Messiah has come to deliver them. As He comes nearer, they will look at His nail-scarred hands and ask Him, "What are those scars in Your hands?" He will reply, "Those with which I was wounded in the house of my friends" (Zech. 13:6).

True love can only be fully developed through the piercings of the sword. Mary was told that a sword would pierce her own heart in order that the thoughts of others might be revealed. In this way, love and compassion would be developed in her heart for others (see Lk. 2:35).

Love is only fully developed between a husband and wife when some real tragedy enters their lives, such as one of the partners becoming very sick. When this happens, the sword goes into the other's heart. But it is then that true love is manifested. The love between my wife and me grew greatest during the last four years of her life when she was paralyzed and suffered from heart problems. During this time she was in constant pain and agony. Sometimes there can also be tragedies in a moral sense, as in the case of Hosea's wife. When his wife Gomer was unfaithful to him, the *sword* pierced Hosea's heart. This produced a deep love for the backslider. From this tragic situation, the beautiful book of Hosea was birthed.

Remember, the pomegranate must be pierced in order for the juice to flow forth. Paul's statement in Galatians 6:17 does not mention love by name, yet it is very important in our understanding of love. "From henceforth let no man trouble me: for I bear in my body the marks [or the stigmata] of the Lord Jesus." Sometimes when we go through deep suffering, we can feel the spear going into our hearts, even as Christ experienced. At times, we can feel the nail prints of the Lord in our hands or in our feet. This was the experience of St. Francis of Assisi. On other occasions, we might feel as though thorns are being forced upon our mind. All this is necessary for the love of God to be truly developed in our lives. We must love those who have wounded us. This is *true* love.

The Love Relationship Between Christ and His Bride

Three aspects of the love relationship between Christ and His Church can be seen in the Song of Songs.

1.) In Song of Songs 2:16 the Bride says, "My beloved is mine, and I am his." The Bride feels that her Bridegroom belongs to her. She is possessive of Him. When a bride first gets married, she takes her husband around and says, "He is mine." This is a very one-sided, selfish stage of marriage.

2.) Later in life the Bride says, "I am my beloved's, and my beloved is mine" (Song. 6:3). With a greater depth of maturity, the Bride begins to realize that the bride was created for the bride-groom. She realizes that she belongs to him first and foremost, and that secondarily, he belongs to her. I remember when I first became the pastor of a certain church, there was a very domineering lady in the church who introduced herself to me, and then introduced her husband by saying: "This is *my* husband. He belongs to me." Unfortunately, this was true; for she dominated him and gave the orders in their home.

3.) The third step in a marriage relationship can be seen by the words of the Bride in Song of Songs 7:10: "I am my beloved's, and his desire is toward me." This is the whole goal of marriage—for the bride to win her husband's love and affection. Throughout all her life, Leah could never win the affections of her husband Jacob. In the natural, the bride has to make herself attractive to her husband. In the same way, we must make ourselves attractive to the Lord Jesus, our Heavenly Bridegroom. Esther made herself beautiful for the king, and because she did, she was chosen to sit on the throne with him.

Two of the ways that the Lord Jesus won His Father's heart while He was upon earth can be seen in Psalm 91:14. "Because he hath set his love upon me, therefore will I deliver him: I will set him on high, because he hath known my name." As the Lord won His Father's heart, so we will win the Lord's heart by setting our love upon Him and by knowing His names.

Speaking prophetically and symbolically of the Bride of Christ, Psalm 45:10-11 says: "Hearken, O daughter, and consider, and incline thine ear; forget also thine own people, and thy father's house. So shall the king greatly desire thy beauty: for he is thy Lord; and worship thou him." We must forget where we have come from and our former lifestyle before salvation, so that the Lord may desire our beauty. It is the same in marriage. If the wife is constantly desiring to go back to her parents, her husband will become discouraged, because he should be the object of her love. In the same way, our Heavenly Bridegroom must be the supreme object of our love, and we must forget our past and abandon ourselves in His arms.

The Four Greek Words for "Love"

When we consider love, we must keep in mind that there are in actuality four Greek words that are translated "love" in our English Bible. The first Greek word for love is *eros*, which means the love and affection between husbands and wives. *Storgé* is the second Greek word, and it refers to family love, the love between parents and children. This aspect of love is so important for the stability of the Church.

Unfortunately, not only has the love between husbands and wives deteriorated at a drastic rate over the past several decades, but also the love between parents and children. We can even read in the newspapers stories about children murdering their parents, and parents killing their children. This is why the Lord is going to send the prophet Elijah to the earth in the last days with the specific mission of restoring the relationship and love between parents and children (see Mal. 4:5-6).

Another Greek word translated "love" is *philo*. This word expresses the love that friends have for each other. This form of love is exemplified by the relationship between David and Jonathan (see 1 Sam. 18:1-4, 20:1-23).

The fourth aspect of love is revealed through the Greek word *agape*, which means "unconquerable benevolence." This is God's love. It is the type of love that God wants to develop most of all in our hearts. *Agape* love is not human; it is divine. Human love can be symbolized by honey, which is very sweet. The one characteristic of honey that exposes its real nature is that fire changes its composition. Honey loses its sweetness when it is heated. In the same way, human love is very superficial. Whenever there is a test or a difference of opinions, human love burns up; it does not last. Friends can become the worst of enemies over one small ordeal if their relationship is based solely upon human love. Human love cannot pass through the fire of God. Remember, everything, including our works, will be tested by fire (see 1 Cor. 3:13-15).

When I was a student in Bible school, there was a certain housekeeper on the staff of the college who was very sweet. However, some of the students teased her too much, and her human kindness gradually began to show its true colors. As a result, on one particular day I remember so well, she exploded in a rage of fury in front of the students. Human love, however sweet it may be, does not last when it passes through fire and is placed under pressure. We want the fruit of God's love. In actuality, all our relationships should be grounded upon divine love rather than these other forms of love. Let me prove this from the Word of God. In Ephesians 5:25 we see God's standard for husbands. "Husbands, love your wives, even as Christ also loved the church, and gave himself for it." The word Paul uses here when he tells husbands they should love their wives is not *eros*, which is the human, natural affection between a husband and wife, but *agape*, which is divine love.

The love also that parents have for their children must be divine. One reason for this is that parents must punish their children sometimes. Remember, divine love does what is best for others, which many times is not what pleases them, but is what is in their best interest. Divine love will enable us to punish our children when they are wrong so that we may spare them from hell. Human love, on the other hand, tends not to punish children. But this only leads to their destruction in the end.

We must also have God's love for our friends, not just human, soulish love. Otherwise, the relationship will not withstand the confrontations that come in life. God joins us to people for His purposes, that we might strengthen each other. Also, He often has a long-term goal in mind, perhaps intending in the future for us to work together in some capacity of ministry. The love that God wants to work out in our lives, seen in Galatians 5:22, is *agape* love. It is a fruit of the Spirit.

THE THREE DUTIES OF LOVE

True love can be divided scripturally into three parts: (1) love for God; (2) love for our neighbors; and (3) love for our enemies. Remember, love is not an option. It is a commandment.

1. LOVE FOR GOD

The first and greatest commandment of the Word of God is found in the words of the Lord Jesus Himself in Matthew 22:37-38. "Thou shalt love the Lord thy God with all thy heart, and with all thy soul, and with all thy mind. This is the first and great commandment." The first commandment of the ten commandments given by the Lord in Exodus chapter 20 was: "Thou shalt have no other gods before me." There must never be anyone or anything that comes before God in our lives. He must be the One whom we love more than any other. King David brought this out so poignantly when he said in Psalm 27:4, "One thing have I desired of the Lord, that will I seek after; that I may dwell in the house of the Lord all the days of my life, to behold the beauty of the Lord, and to inquire in his temple." This thought of fulfilling the first commandment is to have a singleness of heart so that we are wholly devoted to the Lord, even as a bride is dedicated to her bridegroom.

We must have the same cry that came forth from the lips of King David in Psalm 40:8: "I delight to do thy will, O my God: yea, thy law is within my heart." The Lord said to my wife one time, "There is something greater than doing My will." My wife replied to the Lord, "What can be greater than doing Your will, Lord?" He said, "It is to *delight* to do My will." When we are married, we should *delight* to please one another. It is a pure delight and joy to do God's will, whatever it may be, to those who love Him with all of their hearts.

Sacrifice of Ourselves

In actuality, keeping this first commandment of the Lord is the fulfillment of Romans 12:1, where Paul said, "I beseech you therefore, brethren, by the mercies of God, that ye present your bodies a living sacrifice, holy, acceptable unto God, which is your reasonable service." By the grace and mercy of God, we are called to offer our lives unto Him as a living sacrifice. We are called to be priests, even as Christ was called to be a priest after the order of Melchizedek. Christ offered up a love sacrifice to His Father by giving His own body.

Therefore, in a very real sense, this is what we have to offer up as an expression of our love to God. We have to sacrifice our own body and our own life. This truth has its roots in the voluntary sacrifices made by the Israelites of old. (See Leviticus chapters 1-8.) Our love for the Lord is expressed through the willing sacrifice of our lives unto Him. This is the first aspect of love for God.

Sacrifice of What is Most Precious to Us

The second aspect of love for the Lord is giving that which we treasure the most unto the Lord. This is the real test of love. It could mean we have to give to the Lord our wife, family, children, ministry, calling, or a number of other things. These tests vary from person to person. The Father gave the One He loved the most, His Son Jesus, who was the one thing He could not replace.

This second aspect of love for God is exemplified by Abraham's sacrifice of his son Isaac. Abraham was told by God in Genesis 22:2, "Take now thy son, thine only son Isaac, whom thou lovest and offer him for a burnt offering." This was a great demand that was placed upon Abraham. Isaac was his son of promise. Abraham already had Ishmael, but he was not the true son. The true son was Isaac because God had told Abraham: "In Isaac shall thy seed be called." Everything God had promised to Abraham and everything he had lived his whole life for was wrapped up in Isaac. However, the Lord asked him to offer his beloved son. Why? Because God wanted love to be perfected in the heart of His servant Abraham. The love of God is only fully developed in our lives as we offer these two sacrifices—the sacrifice of ourselves and that which is most precious to us.

The Lord said to me many years ago, "Give me your wife." It was said in such a way that I knew the cost was going to be phenomenal, and I couldn't do it at that time. Later, I was slain in the Spirit in a meeting and the Lord looked down upon me and said, "Now, about your wife, who loves her most, you or Me?" I had to acknowledge, "Well, You do, Lord." Then He asked me, "Who has the greatest power to look after her, you or Me?" I was on the floor, and I could not move. I was really slain in the Spirit; and I might add that no one had pushed me over, either. In this state of absolute weakness, I meekly replied to the Lord, "You, Lord." "Then don't you think you had better give her to Me?" He asked. I knew when the Lord said this that it was going to be a very, very costly sacrifice.

By the Lord's grace, I have come to know in a very small way how the Father felt when He sacrificed His Son. For a period of over seventeen years (and really all of her life) my wife suffered continuously. She spent a lot of time in hospitals either for surgery or recovery. It tore every fiber of my being. The whole time the Lord constantly spoke to me, "It pleases Me to bruise her."

My wife was born with a very weak heart. She was told by the doctors when she was a child that she would not live past the age of a teenager, but God extended her time upon earth for many years. We had an acceptance of this long trial because the Lord had told my wife when she was very young, "I have made you this way for a purpose." For us to truly love God and have His love perfected in us, we must know the fellowship of *His* sufferings.

Love is Predicated Upon Obedience

True love is predicated upon obedience. The Lord Jesus said in John 14:21, "He that hath my commandments, and keepeth them, he it is that loveth me: and he that loveth me shall be loved of my Father, and I will love him, and will manifest myself to him." The proof of our love for the Lord is that we obey Him and keep His commandments. This is seen in family life too. The child that loves his parents obeys them. If we truly love our Heavenly Father, we will prove it by obeying Him.

Then the Lord continued to speak about this truth in John 14:23-24: "If a man love me, he will keep my words: and my Father will love him, and we will come unto him, and make our abode with him. He that loveth me not keepeth not my sayings." Those who do not obey the Lord do not truly love Him. Yet, there is a tremendous promise given to those who love and obey Him. The Lord says that He will manifest (or openly reveal) Himself to them.

Rooted and Grounded in Love

Paul proclaimed in Ephesians 3:17-19: "That Christ may dwell in your hearts by faith; that ye, being rooted and grounded in love, May be able to comprehend with all saints what is the breadth, and length, and depth, and height; And to know the love of Christ, which passeth knowledge, that ye might be filled with all the fulness of God." In order to be filled with all the fullness of God and go on to perfection, we must be rooted and grounded in love so that everything we do springs from love. As Christians, we want God's best. And this is His very best—to be filled with His love.

The Love of God Constrains Us

Paul said in Second Corinthians 5:14, "For the love of Christ constraineth us." This is what the outrushing of love from our hearts does, it constrains us. The ultimate reason people fail is because there is not a complete, wholehearted commitment of love for the Lord in their lives. There is family, employment, career or something else that comes before the Lord in their lives, and they do not truly love Him with all of their heart, soul, and mind. When this is the case, there comes a strong magnetic pull in the spiritual realm that draws them off course because their love and affections are not centered on Him.

2. LOVE FOR OUR NEIGHBORS

The second duty of love is contained in the second commandment given by the Lord. After the Lord gave the first and greatest commandment which is to love God with all of our hearts, He gave a second commandment in Matthew 22:39. "Thou shalt love thy neighbour as thyself." This is a quotation from the book of Leviticus, the Old Testament handbook of the priests (see Lev.19:18). This commandment is predicated upon and flows out from our love for God. John, who is called the Apostle of Love, declared in his first epistle: "If a man say, I love God, and hateth his brother, he is a liar: for he that loveth not his brother whom he hath seen, how can he love God whom he hath not seen? And this commandment have we from him, That he who loveth God love his brother also" (1 Jn. 4:20-21).

We are going to divide this theme of loving our neighbor into four parts. First of all, in order to fulfill this commandment, we must have self-acceptance. Secondly, we must practice the Golden Rule. Thirdly, we must consider the question of who our neighbor is. Fourthly, we want to consider the love that restores.

Self-acceptance

A careful study of the words of Jesus reveals that we are to love others as we love ourselves. In order to fulfill this commandment and love others, we must first love ourselves. We should be at peace with ourselves, and have a joyful acceptance of ourselves as the Lord has created us.

I think this is brought out so beautifully in Psalm 139:14, where King David said, "I will praise thee; for I am fearfully and wonderfully made." We are made by God according to His good pleasure and we are what is best for us. Therefore, we should say to the Lord, "Thank You, Lord, for making me just like I am." If we hate ourselves and the way we look, we will hate everyone else too.

Many people have difficulty accepting themselves. I have heard a number of people say: "I don't like myself. I really hate my life. If only I were like someone else, things would be so much better."

There is a strong warning in Isaiah 45:9-10 to those who have this same mentality: "Woe unto him that striveth with his Maker! Let the potsherd strive with the potsherds of the earth. Shall the clay say to him that fashioneth it, What makest thou? or thy work, He hath no hands? Woe unto him that saith unto his father, What begettest thou? or to the woman, What hast thou brought forth?"

Many people say to the Lord, "Why did You make me like this?" Even the great prophet Moses said to the Lord in a moment of discouragement, "I cannot speak; I am not eloquent. ' God responded, "Who hath made man's mouth? or who maketh the dumb, or deaf, or the seeing, or the blind? have not I, the Lord?" (Ex. 4:11). You would think that eloquence of speech would be a prime requirement for a leader, but it isn't in God's eyes. Paul was not a great orator either. Some of Paul's opponents said his speech was contemptible (2 Cor. 10:10). Because the Greeks idolized the great orators of their time, they thought Paul's speech was boring.

We cannot say to our parents, "Why did you make me like this?" or, "It's all your fault that I am the way I am!" Instead, we must have a holy acceptance of ourselves. We should worship the Lord and say to Him, "Lord, You have made me just the way You want me to be." This applies to the color of our eyes, our hair, and everything else about us.

When Amy Carmichael was a very young girl, she looked at her brown eyes and brown hair, and became very sad because she knew other little girls who had blue eyes and light-colored hair. In her distress, she knelt down by her bed one day and prayed to the Lord, "Lord, please give me blue eyes." She got up from her knees and looked in her mirror with great expectation, but she sadly found that her eyes were still brown. Then she began to realize that perhaps God wanted her to have brown eyes. Later on, when she went to be a missionary in India, she fit right in with the Indians because she had brown eyes. This is the reason the Lord specifically created her with that color of eyes. He knew her calling, and He knew that brown eyes were necessary in order for her to be accepted by the Indians and fulfill her calling. God has a reason for everything He does. Thus, the first step to loving others is to love and accept ourselves the way God made us.

Practice the Golden Rule

Secondly, in order to fulfill this second commandment, we must practice the Golden Rule found in the words of Jesus in Matthew 7:12. "Therefore all things whatsoever ye would that men should do to you, do ye even so to them: for this is the law and the prophets." We should treat others in the way that we want to be treated. If we do good to others, it will come back to us and someone will be kind to us.

I once saw an ad for a particular airline on television. In this commercial, after the airplane arrived at the gate, a certain lady was having a hard time getting her carry-ons out of the overhead compartment because she couldn't reach it. A gentleman who was taller reached up and pulled the bag out for her. When she thanked him, he replied, "Oh, it is a pleasure." Then this man was shown picking up his baggage inside the airport. He had more suit cases than he could carry, but someone came up to him and offered to help him carry his bags. The message this commercial was trying to portray was that if we do good to others, someone will return the favor.

This "Golden Rule," as it is so called, should be the motto whereby we live the whole of our life. Love toward our neighbors is manifested in this way. We should always do good to others; for if we do, kindness will be shown to us in return.

Who is my neighbor?

Now we must consider the question of who our neighbor is. The Lord commanded us to love our neighbors, but how can we fulfill this commandment unless we comprehend whom we are to love? In Luke 10:25-29 we read: "And, behold, a certain lawyer stood up, and tempted [Jesus], saying, Master, what shall I do to inherit eternal life? He said unto him, What is written in the law? how readest thou? And he answering said, Thou shalt love the Lord thy God with all thy heart, and with all thy soul, and with all thy strength, and with all thy mind; and thy neighbour as thyself. And he said unto him, Thou hast answered right: this do, and thou shalt live. But he, willing to justify himself, said unto Jesus, And *who is my neighbour?*"

A certain lawyer asked the Lord what he had to do in order to inherit eternal life. Jesus answered his question by asking him a question. The lawyer then repeated the two greatest commandments of the law—to love God and to love our neighbor as ourselves. The lawyer wanted to justify himself, so he asked Jesus, "Who is my neighbor?"

The Lord replied in Luke 10:30-35 by giving the parable of the Good Samaritan. "A certain man went down from Jerusalem to Jericho, and fell among thieves, which stripped him of his raiment, and wounded him, and departed, leaving him half dead. And by chance there came down a certain priest that way: and when he saw him, he passed by on the other side. And likewise a Levite, when he was at the place, came and looked on him, and passed by on the other side. But a certain Samaritan, as he journeyed, came where he was: and when he saw him, he had compassion on him, And went to him, and bound up his wounds, pouring in oil and wine, and set him on his own beast, and brought him to an inn, and took care of him. And on the morrow when he departed, he took out two pence, and gave them to the host, and said unto him, Take care of him; and whatsoever thou spendest more, when I come again, I will repay thee."

In this parable, a man was beaten by bandits and left dying on the road from Jerusalem to Jericho. A priest and then a Levite came by and saw him lying there, but kept on going. However, a Samaritan passed by, stopped, and cared for him. He did for him as much as he could. This Samaritan did not even know this man, but had compassion on him and helped him in his hour of need.

Jesus then asked the lawyer: "Which now of these three, thinkest thou, was neighbour unto him that fell among the thieves?" The lawyer replied, "He that showed mercy on him." Then said Jesus to him, "Go, and do thou likewise." Therefore, our neighbor can be anyone. We should especially care for those who are in need and in distress.

God has a divine order for our lives. He must come first, and then our wife, if we are married. Next in priority are our parents and children. After that, we should minister to our brothers and sisters in Christ who are members of the family of God, and then care for the unsaved. This order must never be rearranged in any way. Our first duty is to love God before anyone else. He must come first and take priority before anyone else.

Jesus declared in John 10:14-15: "I am the good shepherd…and I lay down my life for the sheep." For whom did Christ lay down His life? The answer is found in Ephesians 5:25: "Husbands, love your wives, even as Christ also loved the church, and gave himself for it." Christ lived first and foremost for His Father, but He also gave His life for His Bride, the Church. In the same way, we should put the Lord first and then care for our wives.

We should also care for our parents and our children. Many Christians tend to fall into the same pit as the scribes and Pharisees. These men would find loopholes in the law and twist the Scriptures to free themselves from their responsibility to their parents and families. The Lord reproved them for this in Mark 7:9-12: "Full well ye reject the commandment of God, that ye may keep your own tradition. For Moses said, Honour thy father and thy mother; and, Whoso curseth father or mother, let him die the death: But ye say, If a man shall say to his father or mother, It is Corban, that is to say, a gift, by whatsoever thou mightest be profited by me; he shall be free. And ye suffer him no more to do ought for his father or his mother."

What Jesus is saying here is that in the Old Testament when an Israelite wanted to show his love and appreciation to the Lord, he would give an offering unto Him, and that offering became most holy. For example, if an Israelite gave a cup to the Lord, the scribes and Pharisees would say that this cup could no longer be used as a cup since it had been given to the Lord. They took this a step further and taught that since the Levites and Pharisees had given themselves to the Lord, they themselves were actually a Corban (or a gift). Thus, because of this status they reasoned that they were free of all their responsibilities and duties, such as caring for their parents and families.

Many Christians and ministers fall into this trap. They think that because they are in the ministry or Christian service, they are free from their responsibilities to their families. The Lord said that we must love our neighbor as ourselves. Surely, our nearest neighbor is our spouse and family. Therefore, our family is of utmost importance. We will make the Word of God of none effect as the Pharisees did if we do not care for our loved ones. The first thing we will be asked by the Lord when we get to heaven is how we cared for our families.

Christ said in John 15:13, "Greater love hath no man than this, that a man lay down his life for his friends." After the Lord, our wives, and our families, we have an obligation to love and care for the family of God, our brothers and sisters in the Lord, and our friends in the Lord.

As we have mentioned before, the classic example of friendship in Scripture is the relationship between David and Jonathan. Jonathan laid down his life for David on at least two notable occasions. On one occasion, he went out to warn David of his father Saul's intention to kill him, thus jeopardizing his own life for David. Then he surrendered his right to the throne because of his love for David. We also have a duty to help those in the world who have a need, even if we do not know them. Love manifests itself to our neighbors through longsuffering and acts of kindness.

The Love that Restores

We are called to restore those who have once known the Lord but have then forsaken Him. Some of the greatest stories in the Word of God are the stories concerning the love of God that restores those who have backslidden. I want to consider very briefly two notable stories in the Scriptures of people who crashed terribly, but were then restored by the love of God: King David and Gomer (Hosea's unfaithful wife). Both fell into the terrible pit of adultery. For King David, it was a very long way out of the pit.

The first step out of the pit is clearly laid out by Jeremiah, as he cries, "Only acknowledge thine iniquity" (Jer. 3:13). It is God who initiates restoration, but the backslider must acknowledge his iniquity and take steps of repentance in order to be restored. God's character is that He loves the backslider. The Lord says in Jeremiah 3:14, "Turn, O backsliding children, saith the Lord; for I am married unto you." God is "not willing that any should perish, but that all should come to repentance" (2 Pet. 3:9). King David was truly repentant, and he acknowledged his iniquity. He cried out in repentance and was assured of forgiveness, but there are others like Esau who never get back to the Lord. They are not found worthy of mercy because they have no desire to change.

Gomer was also restored to her husband the prophet Hosea. Hosea was told to take her back and love her after she had been so unfaithful to him with her many other lovers. The Lord said to Hosea, "Go yet, love a woman beloved of her friend, yet an adulteress, according to the love of the Lord toward the children of Israel, who look to other gods, and love flagons of wine" (Hos. 3:1). It was love that restored Gomer, and it is God's love that will restore our loved ones.

We need to have this ministry of restoration, but it is based upon divine love. We want to reach out to loved ones who once knew the way and then went back into the world, because if they continue in that path, they will not make it to heaven. We want to see them restored, and it is uncompromising love that draws them back.

3. LOVE FOR OUR ENEMIES

The third duty of love that God requires of us is to love our enemies. Love can only be perfected in our lives if we have love for our enemies. The Lord Jesus taught on this in His sermon on the Mount, which was *an upgrading* of the law (see Mt. 5:43-48). He said in Matthew 5:43-44: "Ye have heard that it hath been said [by the scribes and Pharisees], Thou shalt love thy neighbour, and hate thine enemy. But I say unto you, Love your enemies, bless them that curse you, do good to them that hate you, and pray for them which despitefully use you, and persecute you."

The Pharisees taught that one should love his friends, and hate his enemies. This teaching was totally unscriptural, because Leviticus 19:18 distinctly says, "Thou shalt not avenge, nor bear any grudge against the children of thy people, but thou shalt love thy neighbour as thyself: I am the Lord." Exodus 23:4-5 clearly instructs us: "If thou meet thine enemy's ox or his ass going astray, thou shalt surely bring it back to him again. If thou see the ass of him that hateth thee lying under his burden, and wouldest forbear to help him, thou shalt surely help with him." Thus, the Pharisees were corrupting the Word of God.

The Lord then said in Matthew 5:46-48: "For if ye love them which love you, what reward have ye? do not even the publicans the same? And if ye salute your brethren only, what do ye more than others? do not even the publicans so? Be ye therefore perfect, even as your Father which is in heaven is perfect." True love, therefore, is to do good to our enemies and not despise them in our hearts. This is the pathway to perfection and maturity.

There is also a note of warning here so that we may rightly divide the Word of God. We are instructed to love our enemies, to pray for them, bless them, and do them good. However, the Word of God also explicitly warns against being joined to them and making an alliance with them. Jehoshaphat was rebuked for making an alliance with the wicked king Ahab, who was also an Israelite. Therefore, from the Scriptures, we can confidently say that love for our enemies and unity with them are two totally different things. We can never be one with our enemies and those who have major false doctrines; but we should have compassion on them and pray for their eternal souls. Doing good for our brethren who are walking in the ways of God brings us tremendous joy, and we are united in spirit with them for the purposes of God. However, this is not so with our enemies. God never told us to join hands with our enemies.

Who Are Our Enemies?

Let us now consider who our enemies are. Micah 7:6 says, "A man's enemies are the men of his own house." The enemies of the Christian are basically those from his own house—those closest to him and those within the Church. David's enemies were basically from his own nation, his principal enemy being Saul. David said in Psalm 41:9 about one of his enemies: "Yea, mine own familiar friend, in whom I trusted, which did eat of my bread, hath lifted up his heel against me."

Then David said in Psalm 55:12-14: "For it was not an enemy that reproached me; then I could have borne it: neither was it he that hated me that did magnify himself against me; then I would have hid myself from him: But it was thou, a man mine equal, my guide, and mine acquaintance. We took sweet counsel together, and walked unto *the house of God* in company."

David's enemies were those in the household of faith, those who went into the temple of God and worshipped the Lord with him. It is the same for us as Christians. Our greatest betrayal and suffering will come from those closest to us, those in the Church who turn against us. This hurts more than if it were someone in the world whom we barely knew.

The man who betrayed Christ was Judas. Judas was one of the original twelve apostles those who had spent the most time with Him during His three and a half year ministry. The Lord was crucified by the whole nation of Israel. His own people rejected Him. Exodus 12:6 speaks prophetically of the slaughter of Jesus the Lamb of God when it says, "And ye shall keep [the lamb without blemish] up until the fourteenth day of the same month: and *the whole assembly of the congregation of Israel shall kill it in the evening*."

It was the whole nation of Israel that killed the Lamb of God. They urged Pilate to crucify Him. As we have mentioned before, when the Lord returns and the Jews ask Him about the wounds in His hands, He shall tell them that He received those wounds "in the house of His friends" (Zech. 13:6).

Why Do We Have Enemies?

The reason we have enemies is because the Lord wants to perfect love in us. However, the reason people rise up against us and become our enemies is because of jealousy and envy in their lives. There were two spirits that animated Saul against David, even causing him to attempt to kill David. It is jealousy and envy that also cause our enemies to attack us. The root reason for their jealousy and envy is because of disobedience to God. Because of Saul's continued life of disobedience to the Lord, envy and jealousy crept into his heart (see 1 Sam. 15). Remember, partial obedience is considered disobedience by the Lord.

When the spirits of envy and jealousy take over a person, that person begins to attack the anointed and those who are genuine and true, as Saul attacked David. This is why there is division in the Church today. Those who are not willing to pay the price oppose those who are wholehearted, because they are envious of them.

The Attitude We Should Have Toward Our Enemies

We must know what our attitude toward our enemies should be. It can be seen in David's attitude toward Saul. Firstly, David did not try to take vengeance into his own hands and attack Saul. On two occasions David had the opportunity to kill Saul, but he did not. Therefore, we must not try to defend ourselves either. There have been people over the years who have turned against me and attacked me publicly. And because I loved them dearly, it has broken my heart. Several of those who have remained loyal to me have said to me: "Why don't you defend yourself ? This person is lying about you." My reply is simple, "It is the Lord's prerogative to take vengeance, not mine. I must bless them and love them."

Secondly, we must speak well of our enemies and not lash out at them with our tongues. King David always spoke well of his enemies, including the wicked Saul. He mourned for Saul and Jonathan when they died, and said, "The beauty of Israel is slain upon thy high places: how are the mighty fallen!" (2 Sam. 1:19). David called Ishbosheth, the son of Saul, a righteous man (2 Sam. 4:11). When Judas betrayed the Lord Jesus, He addressed him as "friend."

Thirdly, we must forgive our enemies. Although Jesus was betrayed and crucified by His own people, He could say to His Father while hanging upon the cruel cross of Calvary, "Father, forgive them; for they know not what they do" (Lk. 23:34). The victory is in forgiving and loving our enemies. The one who does this has the victory.

There is a statue erected in London, England in memory of a great nurse named Edith Cavell. She was an English nurse who went to Belgium during World War I, and served at a hospital there helping prisoners to escape. When the Germans were informed of this, they ordered her to be executed. The night before her execution, she was allowed to be served communion by a chaplain. During that time she said to the chaplain, "I must have no bitterness in my heart against those who take my life." Consequently, when she went out to face the firing squad, she had peace, joy, love, and forgiveness in her heart. We must have this same love in our lives as well.

First Corinthians 13:5 says, "Love thinketh no evil." In the original Greek it reads, "Love does not store up offenses." Love and forgiveness are inseparable. To love our enemies, we must be able to forgive them. Forgiveness is rooted in forgetfulness—in not remembering the offense.

This is seen in the life of Joseph. He named his firstborn son Manasseh, which means "forgetfulness," saying, "God hath made me forget all my toil, and all my father's house" (Gen. 41:51). What was the secret to Joseph's strength, enabling him to love and forgive his brethren after they had sold him into slavery? He was able *to forget* the evil they had done to him. We must ask the Lord for holy forgetfulness when people have wronged us, and we must not constantly meditate on what they have done to us, so that we can continue to love them. I try to practice this immediately every time someone does something against me.

When I was pastoring a certain church years ago, several of the elders turned against me and really attacked me. Years later, one of these elders came up to me and said, "I am dying of cancer, and I only have a few months to live; but I cannot die until I ask you to forgive me for what I did to you." I could not even remember what he had done, therefore, it was very easy for me to forgive him. Forgiveness starts in our will. We say to ourselves: "I forgive this person. I love them. Lord, please bless them." As we continue to do this, our hearts are set free of any bitterness toward them and we are able to love them.

Let us remember that all our enemy can do to us is ultimately bless us. Our enemies cannot destroy us. What they actually do when they persecute us is add to our eternal reward in heaven. The Lord said in Matthew 5:10-12: "Blessed are they which are persecuted for righteousness' sake: for theirs is the kingdom of heaven. Blessed are ye, when men shall revile you, and persecute you, and shall say all manner of evil against you falsely, for my sake. Rejoice, and be exceeding glad: for great is your reward in heaven: for so persecuted they the prophets which were before you." We are told to rejoice when our enemies rise up against us and speak evil of us. No matter what they may do against us, if we love our enemies, we will have complete victory.

Let us close this section on love by saying again that God is love. That is what God is like. Therefore, if we sincerely desire to be like Him, we must allow Him to develop His love in our lives—first for Him, then for our neighbors, and then for our enemies. Love is the bond of perfection (Col. 3:14). It is the summary and fulfilling of the law and the whole Word of God (Rom. 13:8,10; Gal. 5:14).

2. JOY

The next fruit of the Spirit after love is joy. Joy is a state of bliss derived through union and communion with the Lord. There is "fullness of joy" in God's presence (see Psa. 16:11). The source of *true* joy is the Lord Himself. Happiness that is obtained from any other source is not true joy at all, but a momentary and passing emotion. As David said in Psalm 43:4, the Lord must be our "exceeding joy."

I want to emphasize that this fruit is absolutely divine. It is given by God Himself. First of all, I want to make a clear distinction between rejoicing and joy, because these two words have been greatly misunderstood by many. Rejoicing is an attitude. It is our responsibility to rejoice in all circumstances. We are commanded by the Lord to rejoice. Rejoicing leads us to joy, but rejoicing must not be mistaken for joy. Joy is a fruit of the Spirit. This is something we cannot produce. Only God can give it to us, because joy is divine. Joy is the reality that God wants us all to experience, and the way to joy is through rejoicing. Rejoicing is a state of mind; whereas joy is a state of being.

Ecclesiastes 2:26 says: "For God giveth to a man that is good in his sight wisdom, knowledge and joy." God gives us His joy when we obey His commandments and we choose to rejoice in spite of outward circumstances. Those who do not do those things that are pleasing to the Lord are deprived of the joy of the Lord.

From Psalm 45:7 we understand clearly that joy is founded upon righteousness: "Thou lovest righteousness, and hatest wickedness: therefore God, thy God, hath anointed thee with the oil of gladness [or joy] above thy fellows." God gives joy to the man or woman who is good in His sight. There came a time when David lost the joy of the Lord. God removed His joy from David's heart after he had fallen into the snare of adultery with Bathsheba, which later led to the murder of her husband. For months, David tried to conceal his sin. His "moisture had turned into the drought of summer" (Psa. 32:4). However, in Psalm 51:12 he prayed for a restoration of the joy of his salvation, which God abundantly granted.

Joy is rooted in righteousness, but also in sorrow. Sorrow carves out a deeper capacity in our being to contain God's joy. Joy is developed in our lives through contrast—the contrast of sorrow. In Isaiah 61:3 the Lord says that He will give to those who mourn in Zion "beauty for ashes and the oil of joy for mourning." Therefore, joy is associated with sorrow. How can that be? How can we rejoice in sorrow when it is impossible in the natural? Well, in the Word of God, joy is intrinsically linked with sorrow and mourning.

In my own experience, I have recently lost my wife. Many of you have probably been through the pain of bereavement too. At first, I was overwhelmed with grief and sorrow, but after the funeral service, God met me in an extraordinary way. As I felt the clothes of mourning fall off, they were replaced by an abundance of joy. Psalm 30:11-12 says: "Thou hast turned for me my mourning into dancing: thou hast put off my sackcloth, and girded me with gladness: To the end that my glory [or my soul] may sing praise to thee, and not be silent. O Lord my God, I will give thanks unto thee forever." The Lord put this song in my heart and I have been rejoicing in the Lord and literally dancing before Him every day since this experience.

The joy of the Lord is perfected in sorrow. We have to experience deep heartaches before the joy of the Lord can be perfected in our lives. To a certain extent, this is seen through the plant that epitomizes joy—*camphire*. The camphire leaves are dried (speaking of the drying up of the human spirit), and then they are crushed and pulverized. After this crushing and drying process, they are used to beautify the hair.

This is what we have just read in Isaiah 61:3. God will give us beauty for our ashes, and the oil of joy for mourning. Even when we are passing through times of intense sorrow, the joy of the Lord can well up within us. Nehemiah 8:10 says, "The joy of the Lord is our strength." Joy carries us through times of difficulty; when we are tired and worn out, the joy of the Lord strengthens us.

This is true even in the natural. Some rejoice perhaps in a football game or a baseball game, or some other kind of entertainment. However, this is human joy. The strength that *human* joy gives was demonstrated in a very poignant way for me a number of years ago.

When my wife and I visited my father and mother in London, the four of us went walking down Oxford Street. Those of you who have been to London know that Oxford Street is filled with some of the best stores in England. My father and I, somehow in a weak moment, agreed to go shopping with my mother and my wife. We went into store after store after store. Near the end of the day, my father and I were worn out, and even the ladies were too. But suddenly we came to a new store that the ladies had not been in. As soon as they entered the door, it was as though new strength came into them. As they rushed up the stairs, my father and I looked at one another, and in utter exhaustion we found two chairs to collapse in while the ladies had a renewal of strength.

Joy in the natural gives strength, but human joy, of course, cannot carry us through the trials of life. This requires the joy of the Lord. The joy of the Lord is our strength (Neh. 8:10). Christ Himself triumphed through joy. Hebrews 12:2 says, "Looking unto Jesus the author and finisher of our faith; who for the joy that was set before him endured the cross, despising the shame and is set down at the right hand of the throne of God." Joy gave Jesus the ability to endure the cross. I believe that the joy of the Lord can take us through every circumstance we encounter and give us supernatural strength.

When the subjects of a king are joyful, it honors him. Why? Because by their joy they are saying to the king, "Oh, it is so wonderful to be one of your subjects!" There is no joy in many countries. My wife and I have been to numerous countries around the world where girls have said to us: "Will you please take us back with you? We want to leave our country and go to where you live." When we asked them why they wanted to leave their countries, they replied, "Because we do not like our country." This kind of statement was not glorifying to the ruler of their country, was it? Therefore, we want to be filled with the joy of the Lord because joy honors the Lord. Remember, He is the King of Kings, and by our joy we are expressing to Him what a delight it is to be one of His subjects.

Joy is very attractive. We have a saying in the United States: "Laugh and the world laughs with you. Cry and you cry alone." Who wants to be with someone who is crying and mourning all the time? No one. Even a man backs off from his wife when she cries because it is very depressing to him. On the other hand, when his wife is joyful and happy, he becomes full of joy too. Joy is contagious and infectious. It is what makes us attractive to the Lord, just as it makes a wife attractive to her husband.

God wants to permeate us with joy; for that is what keeps us going. Psalm 30:5 says, "Anger endureth but a moment; in his favour is life: weeping may endure for a night, but joy cometh in the morning." There is such joy when the sun rises in the morning in the natural. It is a new day, and there are new expectations. May I say that joy is perfected in sorrow, even though joy is the opposite of sorrow. As love is perfected through hatred and being pierced, so joy is only truly developed in our lives through sorrow. True joy cannot be manifested unless it is cradled in sorrow. Paul said in Philippians 4:4, "Rejoice in the Lord, and again I say rejoice." Where was the Apostle Paul when he wrote this? In a dark prison cell in Rome, chained to a Roman soldier.

In Matthew 5:10-12 the Lord Jesus tells us to rejoice *in persecution*, and Romans 5:2 tells us to rejoice *in hope*. In reality, we are to rejoice all the time. So whatever situation we are in, we are to rejoice. We are to be a rejoicing people. Remember, the joy of the Lord is perfected in us as we rejoice.

3. PEACE

The third fruit of the Spirit is peace. This fruit is epitomized by spikenard. I would just like to comment a little about spikenard, because it gives us an understanding of peace. Spikenard is a very costly ointment. It is obtained virtually from only one place in the world, and that is in the Himalayan Mountains in India. Even today, the Himalayas are not very accessible. First of all, it is a hard and arduous journey to get to the Himalayas. Secondly, once you get there, it requires a lot of strength to climb the mountains. Yet, this is where this precious spikenard plant is found.

Thus, can you imagine how costly this ointment was in the Middle East in Bible times? It had to be transported all the way from the Himalayan Mountains in India, and there was no air travel in those days. In fact, to preserve the spikenard it had to be kept in an alabaster box. The price of spikenard was extraordinary.

Remember what Judas said when Mary's box of spikenard was poured upon the Lord Jesus? He said that this spikenard was worth *three hundred pence* (see Jn. 12:4-5). Three hundred pence was an extraordinary amount of money. In those days, one penny a day was the average wage of a laborer. Therefore, three hundred pence was almost worth a whole year's wages. So can you see how costly spikenard is?

After all, peace is one of the blessings that is desired throughout the world, and it is perhaps prized above everything else. Everyone wants peace. However, true peace comes from God alone. The Lord Jesus Christ said to His disciples, "My peace I give unto you, not as the world giveth, give I unto you" (Jn. 14:27). The world looks for peace in things that are extraneous, but in reality, how many people have real peace within their hearts?

So many people say, "If only I could get this job, or if I could have this house then I would be at peace and I would have what I want." However, when they get those things, they have no peace. Many religious leaders, when asked in private if they have peace, say they do not. They do many good and charitable works hoping to obtain peace, but they fail to realize that peace only comes from the Prince of Peace, the Lord Jesus Christ.

When I was a student in Bible School, the Lord gave me this word, "I will give you My peace." At that time I did not realize the value of this promise. I was concerned with the spiritual gifts and other more exciting things, but as I have grown older I have thanked God time and time again for giving me His peace.

In both the Hebrew and the Greek, peace signifies "wholeness" and "fullness of life." It can also mean bodily health and long life. Peace really means to be in harmony and unity with ourselves, God, and our neighbors. It is so wonderful to have the peace of God within our hearts.

What is the way to peace? Isaiah 26:3 declares, "Thou wilt keep him in perfect peace, whose mind is stayed on thee because he trusteth in thee." As our trust and confidence in God deepens, so does the peace of God deepen. If we learn to focus wholeheartedly on God instead of on our problems, the peace of God will increase in our hearts.

Isaiah 26:12 says, "Lord, thou wilt ordain peace for us: for thou also hast wrought all our works in us." When we allow God to work in us, He ordains peace for us. The Apostle Paul stated in Philippians 2:13, "For it is God which worketh in you both to will and to do of his good pleasure." We become recipients of God's peace as we yield to Him and allow Him to work in our lives those things that are well pleasing in His sight. Peace leaves when our will is in conflict with the will of God. When we can have a holy resignation to do the Lord's will, peace grows and matures within us until our hearts and minds are enveloped with peace.

As we have said, the fruits of the Spirit are developed through opposites. Peace is developed and comes to its fullness through times of confusion. One of the most beautiful accounts and illustrations of peace is in the Song of Songs. In making reference to the Bride of Christ, there is a beautiful description of her in Song of Songs 7:4: "Thine eyes are like the fishpools in Heshbon, by the gate of Bath-rabbim." *Bath-rabbim* means "a city of strife or confusion."

This city was full of shoutings, confusion, strife, and arguments just like any large city today, but just outside the gates of the city were the pools of Heshbon. These beautiful pools that Solomon dug were very deep, and the waters were extremely calm. The Bride of Christ is like this—she manifests the peace of the Lord. The eyes are really the doors of the soul. If we have the peace of God in our hearts and minds, then it will be reflected in our eyes. In this way, we portray peace.

The Lord said to His disciples, "And when ye come into an house...if the house be worthy, let your peace come upon it" (Mt. 10:12-13). We should let the peace of God that is within us flow out from us and envelop the home into which we come. After all, we can only give to others what we have. If we are in strife and torment with others or within ourselves, that is what we will impart to others. On the other hand, if we have the peace of God in our hearts and minds, then we can let our peace come upon any situation, especially where there is confusion and frustration.

Romans 16:20 says, "The God of Peace shall bruise Satan under thy feet shortly." How did Jesus quell the storm? He quelled it through saying, "Peace, be still." The peace of God that is within us can calm all the activities of Satan. May we allow God to develop this beautiful fruit of the Spirit in our lives.

4. LONGSUFFERING

Longsuffering literally means "to *suffer* for a very *long* time." We should understand more specifically what longsuffering means from the Greek. Longsuffering deals with people more than it does with situations. There is a difference between patience and longsuffering. Patience means "endurance in *trials* and *circumstances*." In contrast, longsuffering means "to suffer *with people* for a very, very long time."

The plant that exemplifies longsuffering is saffron. Saffron powder is used in perfumes and medicines. Do you know that it takes stigmas from about four thousand flowers to make one ounce of saffron powder? So we can see that it is also very costly. Longsuffering is a fruit that we must pay a big price to obtain.

Longsuffering speaks of a holy acceptance of sufferings that people bring into our lives. It is an essential fruit. In fact, it is one of the attributes of God that the Lord mentioned to Moses when He met him on the Mount. We read in Exodus 34:6, "And the Lord passed by before him, and proclaimed, The Lord, The Lord God, merciful and gracious, *longsuffering*, and abundant in goodness and truth." David said in Psalm 86:15, "Thou, O Lord, art a God full of compassion, and gracious, *longsuffering*, and plenteous in mercy and truth."

This is a fruit that was developed to a very high degree in the life of the Apostle Paul. Paul himself testified that God had made him a pattern of longsuffering in order to be a source of encouragement to all those who followed him. "Howbeit for this cause I obtained mercy, that in me first Jesus Christ might show forth all longsuffering, for a pattern to them which should hereafter believe on him to life everlasting" (1 Tim. 1:16).

Before Paul accepted the Lord Jesus as his personal Savior, he was a terrible persecutor of the Church. He beat, persecuted, and imprisoned many of the Christians, and was even responsible for the death of several. However, because of this, when Paul gave his heart to the Lord, he felt indebted to Him because of all he had done. This godly sorrow for his sin produced within Paul an extraordinary ability to endure suffering for a very long time. And my, how he suffered! Paul's life is an example to all of us of how we should endure suffering for the name and gospel of Christ.

Longsuffering is an all-conquering patience and endurance with respect to people, because longsuffering conquers a person's spirit. I would like to illustrate this from Proverbs 25:15. "By long forbearing is a prince persuaded." A woman's prince is her husband, but sometimes her husband is not right. Although, as men, we would like to believe that the husbands are always right, the fact is that we are not. How, then, can a woman persuade her husband? It surely is not through preaching at him, pointing the finger at him, and constantly nagging him.

It is the beautiful fruit of longsuffering that persuades people, especially husbands. If we are willing to endure perhaps a wrong attitude by others, and simply respond graciously with a smile, eventually our longsuffering will conquer their attitudes. Proverbs 25:15 goes on to say, "And a soft tongue breaketh the bone." Longsuffering has a very soft tongue. Longsuffering yields constantly.

Without longsuffering none of us would be here. It is the longsuffering of God that has enabled Him to endure all the heartaches that we have brought to Him. If it were not for the longsuffering of God, we would never repent, because it is the longsuffering of God that leads us to repentance (see Rom. 2:4). Second Peter 3:9 says, "The Lord is not slack concerning his promise, as some men count slackness;

but is *longsuffering* to us-ward, not willing that any should perish, but that all should come to repentance." The Lord waits for a very long time for us to turn around, because He is longsuffering with us. The longsuffering of God deferred wrath for one hundred and twenty years in the days of Noah (see 1 Pet. 3:20).

Consider for a moment Manasseh, King of Judah (see 2 Chron. 33:1-20). He was the most wicked king Judah ever had. He filled Jerusalem with bloodshed and profanity, and he was guilty of martyring the prophet Isaiah, who was one of the greatest prophets of all time. Manasseh filled the streets of Jerusalem with idols. He even put idols in the temple of God. The whole nation of Israel, both the northern tribes of Ephraim and the southern tribes of Judah, degenerated into a deplorable spiritual state during his reign. But what does God say in Hosea about the backslidden children of Ephraim and others in a similar state?

God says through the prophet Hosea in chapter 11:7, "And my people are bent to backsliding from me: though they called them to the most High, none at all would exalt him." Then He said in Hosea 11:8-9: "How shall I give thee up Ephraim? How shall I deliver thee Israel? How shall I make thee as Admah…and Zeboim? [two little towns destroyed along with Sodom and Gomorrah] Mine heart is turned within me, my repentings are kindled together. I will not execute the fierceness of mine anger, I will not return to destroy Ephraim: *for I am God and not man.*"

We would have given up hope on Ephraim and King Manasseh, but God did not. We need the fruit of longsuffering worked out in our lives because it is longsuffering that causes people to turn around. Longsuffering is a very costly fruit. There is a big price to pay to have this fruit developed in our lives. However, it is this fruit that eventually wins people to the Lord.

5. GENTLENESS

The fifth fruit of the Spirit is gentleness. The Greek word for gentleness, "chrestotes," portrays the thought of being *easy* and *mellow*. The ancient Greeks used this word for very good wine which was mellow and flowed down the throat very easily. Christ said, "Come unto me all ye that labor and are heavy laden, and I will give you rest . . . For my yoke is *easy* and my burden is light." In this passage He used the root word for gentleness, which is "chrestos," for the word *easy* (see Mt. 11:28-30). Therefore, gentleness refers to a Spirit-produced mellowness.

Gentleness in our lives puts people at ease when they come into our presence, and makes them feel comfortable. This is how we feel when we come into the presence of the Lord, because He is the epitome of gentleness. This brings to mind a story about President Franklin D. Roosevelt. I am by no means aligning this man with God, but this story helps to illustrate this thought that gentleness puts others at ease. President Roosevelt had a close friend in the White House named Harry Hopkins, who had a son who was serving in the armed forces. His son invited one of his friends on leave to go with him to see his father.

When they arrived, Harry Hopkins was with the President of the United States. Harry Hopkins' son felt perfectly free to go right in to see his father, even though he was with the President. On the other hand, his friend, who was a private in the army, trembled and quaked at the thought of coming into the presence of the Commander in Chief of the United States. Do you know what finally set him at ease? He just happened to look down at the sleeve of Roosevelt's shirt, and instead of seeing beautiful cuff links or pearl buttons as he expected to see, he saw a paper clip. Immediately, this put him at ease in the presence of the President. There was a wholesome simplicity about Roosevelt that made people feel comfortable in his presence.

Gentleness is frequently translated "lovingkindness." The Hebrew counterpart of the Greek word "chrestotes" is the word "checed." It is translated *kindness* and *lovingkindness*. This is one of the meanings of gentleness. God's lovingkindness (or gentleness) is so very wonderful. David said to the Lord, "Thy lovingkindness is better than life" (Psa. 63:3). The question arises: Who can be a recipient of God's lovingkindness? The key is found in Psalm 107:42-43: "The *righteous* shall see it, and rejoice: and all iniquity shall stop her mouth. Whoso is *wise*, and will observe these things, even they shall understand the *lovingkindness* of the Lord." Those who are righteous and wise receive God's lovingkindness, and it is worked out in their character too. In a very real way, all the fruits of the Spirit depend upon righteousness. The fruits of the Holy Spirit cannot be developed in the life of one who is walking in *unrighteousness*.

Gentleness also carries the thought of *sweetness*. This precious fruit means being "sweet to all." We have a beautiful illustration of this from Jotham's parable, the first parable in the Word of God, in Judges 9:7-15. In this parable Jotham is speaking of certain trees. In verses 10-11, he is speaking of the fig tree. In verse 11, he gives the attribute of *sweetness* to the fig tree.

Often in some of the large cities of France there would be branches of fig trees that grew over the walls that surrounded a person's home. And because France was under the Levitical law, strangers were permitted to pluck the fruit off any branch that extended over the wall. During the time of the first ripe fruit, which is the best fruit, the passer-by could lift up his hand and pluck one of those ripe, juicy figs from any branch that was hanging on the street side of the wall. I remember doing this myself at times when I lived in France.

The Lord began to speak to me about gentleness at this time. He said: "Fig trees do not lower their branches to offer their fruit to someone they like, and then lift up their branches from people they do not like so that they cannot partake of their fruit. The fig tree is sweet to all." God wants the fruit of gentleness to be developed in our lives so that we are sweet to everyone, not just to our close friends. This is the character of God Himself. The Lord Jesus testified that His Father causes His sun to rise on the evil and on the good (see Mt. 5:45). God is sweet to all. He is impartial.

We must understand that there is a great difference between meeting people's needs, and meeting their needs in a delightful and sweet manner. The spirit in which we do things is so important. For example, when you go to restaurants, some waitresses can be very rude. They throw your food down on the table and leave quickly. Yes, they brought what you ordered, but you are not happy because of the manner in which you were served. Likewise, we must not only do what the Lord requires of us, but we must do it with a gentle and sweet attitude.

I remember a time in my life when the Lord was dealing with me about gentleness. My wife and I were in the southern states of America. We had just finished some meetings at a certain church and I had been given invitations to speak in two or three other churches in the area. As I asking the Lord which invitation I should accept, the Lord spoke to me: "I do not want you to take any of them at the moment. I want to speak to you." I inquired of the Lord, "Well, what am I going to do?" He told me to stay in a hotel, and He most graciously directed me to the right one. As soon as we entered our hotel room, the presence of God came in an extraordinary way.

My wife and I knelt by our beds, and then in the Spirit I was caught up into heaven. As all those who have been to heaven know, there is a river that you must pass through before you can get to heaven which cleanses the saints. As I walked through this crystal clear river with an angel, the condition of my heart was openly revealed. I saw such hardness in my heart, and I was in terrible agony because I knew that I was going to meet the Lord on the other side of the river. So I said to the angel: "I cannot meet the Lord like this. I need to go back through the river again." The angel was very gracious and took me through again, and then the vision ceased.

The Holy Spirit started to speak to me that it is not only a matter of preaching the truth, but the spirit and attitude in which we present the truth is the all-important thing. We must not preach with condemnation or hardness. The Lord said, "I want to take the hardness out of your heart." Then He quickened to me Psalm 18:35, where King David said, "Thy gentleness hath made me great." We must be gentle in everything we do, especially in our presentation of the truth.

Another aspect of gentleness is seen in First Thessalonians 2:7, where Paul said, "We were gentle among you, even as a nurse cherisheth her children." The Apostle Paul said that he cared for those he was responsible for with great gentleness as a nurse does her children. In England there are nannies who take care of children, and they are very gentle with them. This is how the Lord wants us to treat others.

6. GOODNESS

Goodness is the sixth fruit of the Spirit. When a person is called good in the Scriptures it means that they are *morally good*. The Scriptural definition of God's goodness is "to be incapable of doing anything evil." Goodness is one of the key virtues of the Godhead, as revealed to Moses when the Lord passed by before him and proclaimed, "The Lord [is] abundant in goodness" (Ex. 34:6).

When Moses cried out to the Lord in Exodus 33:18, "I beseech thee, show me thy glory," He replied, "I will make all my goodness pass before thee." Therefore, the glory of God is clearly synonymous with the goodness of God. Goodness is an intrinsic part of the Lord's character. That is what God is like. He is good. I remember one time when the Lord appeared to me. He stretched His arm out to me and said, "Touch me, I am altogether good." By this I understood that there is nothing evil in Him; He is incapable of doing anything wrong. This is what He desires to impart to our lives too.

Goodness is the glory of God. The glory of God is actually His very character. The Apostle Paul stated that Christ is the brightness of the Father's glory in Hebrews 1:3. The word *brightness* means the very effulgence, or source, of glory. In other words, God is the very source of goodness and glory. Goodness emanates from Him as glory and light do.

Something we must understand and grasp is the distinct difference between goodness and gentleness (or lovingkindness). Gentleness is being kind and sweet to people, whereas goodness is doing what is best for them, including discipline and reproof if necessary. God's goodness is related to His holiness. Goodness is what separates Him from all evil. Therefore, there is clearly a difference between gentleness and goodness.

Luke 7:36-50 is a record of Jesus' lovingkindness and gentleness with the sinful woman who anointed Him while He was in the house of Simon. In total contrast to this, in Matthew 23:17 the Lord denounced the Pharisees for their wickedness; and in Matthew 21:12, He overturned the tables of the money changers and drove them out of the temple. These two acts in Matthew's Gospel were acts of goodness and holiness. What the Pharisees and money changers were doing was not right, and goodness addressed it. A good man does what is right, regardless of people's reactions. Therefore, we can see that gentleness cannot be equated with goodness. Goodness makes a distinction between the upright and the ungodly; the holy and the profane. It will not permit us to compromise in any area. Goodness signifies a separated walk. Gentleness is being kind to your enemy, but goodness is not tolerating the evil in your enemy. Goodness demanded a rejection of Saul on Samuel's part; and God told Samuel to stop weeping for him (see 1 Sam. 16:1). The Lord's gentleness puts us at ease in His presence and His goodness purifies us from all sin. The gentleness of Christ permits Him to touch us, to fondle us, and to embrace us, but His goodness causes Him to punish us, to discipline us, and to judge us when we are wrong. We want the fruit of His goodness to permeate every pore of our being so that we may be separated from all sin and evil.

7. FAITHFULNESS

The seventh fruit of the Spirit is faithfulness. The King James Version translates it as "faith." These two words are intrinsically linked. Faithfulness is a product of faith; and faith is trusting and believing in the faithfulness of God. For this particular study, we will look at this fruit from the aspect of faithfulness.

This fruit of the Spirit is actually one of the titles of the Lord Jesus Christ. He is called *Faithful and True* in Revelation 19:11: "And I saw heaven opened, and behold a white horse; and he that sat upon him was called Faithful and True, and in righteousness he doth judge and make war." This title reveals the character of the Lord. Hebrews 2:17 says, "Wherefore in all things it behooved [Christ] to be made like unto his brethren, that he might be a merciful and faithful high priest in things pertaining to God, to make reconciliation for the sins of the people." Jesus is a merciful and faithful high priest. He is faithful to the ministry His Father has given to Him.

Faithfulness means to be faithful to finish the task God has given to us. It means that we are true to our words and promises, and we are reliable, trustworthy, and steadfast. Someone who is faithful is one who can be counted upon because he has a track record of always doing everything he is asked to do. Anyone who has ever been in the position of giving orders to other people knows what a priceless treasure it is to have someone you can always count on to finish the job. It is such a blessing to know this one will work as hard when you are gone as when you are there watching. This is a description of a faithful man or woman of God.

Revelation 17:14 says, "They that are with [the Lamb] are called, and chosen, and [found] faithful." Those who are closest to the Lamb are those who have been called, chosen, and *found faithful*. Being called by the Lord has basically two connotations. Firstly, we are "called out of darkness into His marvelous light" when we accept Christ as our Savior (1 Pet. 2:9). Secondly, being called by the Lord refers to receiving a call to a specific ministry or task. It is wonderful to receive the call of God; however, Jesus Himself said that "many are called, but few are chosen" (Mt. 22:14). Therefore, being called is not enough. Receiving a call does not mean that we have arrived at our designed goal and end. It is only the beginning.

Between being called and being chosen there is a time of preparation. Many might be *selected* for training, but few actually *qualify* during training. Many start out, but few go on to be chosen for the ministry. After we are called, then we begin the process of being *chosen*. In Isaiah 48:10 the Lord says, "Behold, I have refined thee, but not with silver; I have *chosen* thee in the furnace of affliction." The Lord chooses us for service in times of testing and trials. Regrettably, the majority of God's people give up at this point. They make their own way out of their trials and refuse this purifying process of the Lord (see Isa. 50:10-11). As a result, they are never chosen by Him. Once we have been chosen by God, and we are placed in the ministry He has for us, we must be faithful. This is a place that very few attain unto. It is very difficult to find faithful men and women.

Let me illustrate these three stages of the Christian life of being called, chosen, and found faithful from the life of King David. Around the age of seventeen, he was anointed by Samuel to be the next king and replace the *unfaithful* Saul. However, simply because he was called did not mean that he automatically received the throne. There were about thirteen years of preparation that followed this call until the time he was chosen, then anointed king of Judah at Hebron when he was thirty years old. During those thirteen years, he endured many trials and tests—such as fleeing from Saul and the Israeli army, who were seeking to kill him, and losing everything at Ziklag. Afterwards, when he was found faithful as king over Judah for seven years, he was then anointed a third time to be king over all Israel.

Faithfulness is the hallmark of a true servant of the Lord. Abraham is spoken of as being faithful (Neh. 9:8). One of the greatest men of all times who was found faithful was Moses. As we mentioned at the beginning of this chapter, the fruits of the Spirit are developed through opposites. Faithfulness is really developed through betrayal, when other people are unfaithful to us. This creates within us a tremendous desire to be faithful.

For Moses to be made faithful, he had to experience betrayal. He had about three million people (including men, women, and children) constantly complaining and murmuring against him. Korah and his company even rebelled against him. His brother Aaron and sister Miriam began to criticize him as well. Moses had no one he could turn to except the Lord. Leadership is a very lonely walk.

However, because of this terrible betrayal by his people, and even his own brother and sister, he earned an eternal commendation and accolade by the Lord. The Lord said of him, "My servant Moses is *faithful* in all mine house" (Num.12:7). Among all these unstable, untrustworthy Israelites, God found a man whom He could count on—Moses.

It is interesting who betrays and criticizes those in leadership. The one who betrayed David was his son Absalom, the son who had committed murder. Judas was a thief for many years before he betrayed the Lord Jesus. There are always terrible flaws in the character of those who rebel and betray their leaders, because they have never allowed God to change these particular areas of their lives. Those who betrayed Moses were themselves unfaithful to the Lord. Just think of Aaron for a moment. He did not just turn on Moses overnight and begin to criticize him. There was a reason. This flaw had never been cleansed from his character. When Moses went up the Mount to meet with God for forty days, the hearts of the children of Israel soon grew cold toward the Lord. Pressured by the people, he succumbed to that pressure by making a golden calf, about which he said, "These be thy gods, O Israel, which have brought thee up out of the land of Egypt." Therefore, it is no surprise that he momentarily turned against Moses too.

All of this betrayal worked out for Moses' good and benefit. It is futile to ask the Lord to make us faithful, and then reject the means which He provides to make us faithful. God said of Moses that he was faithful in all of His house. Paul repeats this in Hebrews 3:2, where he compares Christ with Moses. "[Christ] was faithful to him that appointed him, as also Moses was faithful in all his house." He then says in Hebrews 3:5, "And Moses verily was faithful in all his house, as a servant, for a testimony of those things which were to be spoken after."

One particular aspect in which Moses was faithful was in the pattern of the Tabernacle. Moses was admonished of God when he was about to build the tabernacle to make all things according to the pattern shown to him in the mount (see Heb. 8:5). God gave the pattern of the Tabernacle to Moses because He knew he would be faithful to it, and not alter it in any way. He did everything just as God commanded him.

In the 1960's, the Lord spoke to various ministers to open up homes for former drug addicts to help them. Because they were very successful when they obeyed the Lord, others began to try to do the same thing, even though the Lord had not specifically told them to start similar programs. God spoke clearly to one minister who was also considering opening a Teen Challenge because it was the popular thing to do. "Do all things according to the pattern shown to *you*." The key to life is to do what God has told *us* to do personally, not to do something God has told someone else to do. There is no reward for doing someone else's job.

The Lord spoke many parables concerning His second coming. There is a constant theme that runs through many of these parables, and it is the necessity of faithfulness. The Lord Jesus said in Matthew 24:45-46: "Who then is a faithful and wise servant, whom his lord hath made ruler over his household, to give them meat in due season? Blessed is that servant, whom his lord when he cometh shall find so doing."

Martin Luther was asked once, "If you knew the Lord was coming this week, what would you do?" His simple, yet profound reply was this, "If God had given me the task of planting fruit trees, I trust that when He came He would find me planting fruit trees." We want to be faithful to do everything that the Lord has commissioned us to do whether it is great or small.

We must be faithful to use the talents and abilities the Lord gives us. The Lord said to the servant who was given five talents and gained five more, "Well done, thou good and faithful servant: thou hast been faithful over a few things, I will make thee ruler over many things: enter thou into the joy of thy lord" (Mt. 25:21).

God has given everyone talents and abilities. The question we should ask ourselves is: What has He given to me? We should maximize on our talents and use them for God's purposes and glory. Brother Lawrence was faithful as a dish washer because that is what God called him to do for that time in his life. Because of his faithfulness, God has given him an eternal name, and he is known by many even today.

Faithfulness is one of the primary qualifications for ministry and leadership. God removed Eli from the position of high priest because he was not faithful to execute God's judgments upon sin, especially in the lives of his own children. The Lord said in First Samuel 2:35, "And I will raise me up a faithful priest, that shall do according to that which is in mine heart and in my mind." This faithful priest was Samuel. Eli was *demoted* because of unfaithfulness and Samuel was *promoted* because of faithfulness.

Paul was chosen to be the teacher of the New Testament Church. He was the one who opened up the Old Covenant and set forth the majority of the New Testament doctrines. Without his accuracy when handling the Word of God, our theology would be unsound.

Why did God choose Paul for this special ministry? After all, before he met the Lord on the road to Damascus, he was one of the biggest violators of the truth. The reason is that in His foreknowledge, the Lord knew that Paul would be faithful to the ministry and to the vision after he was shown the truth. Paul testified in First Timothy

1:12, "And I thank Christ Jesus our Lord, who hath enabled me, for that he counted me faithful, putting me into the ministry." God knew that Paul would do everything precisely as He had told him.

Areas of Faithfulness

Now let us consider for a moment a few areas in which we must be faithful.

Faithful in that which is least. "He that is faithful in that which is least is faithful also in much: and he that is unjust in the least is unjust also in much" (Lk.16:10). Jesus clearly taught that if we are not faithful in the small, seemingly insignificant things of life, we will not be faithful with things that are important. Those who are promoted are the ones who are faithful in the little, mundane things, such as mopping the floors and washing the dishes.

Faithful in the things of this world, especially finances. "If therefore ye have not been faithful in the unrighteous mammon [or natural riches], who will commit to your trust the true riches?" (Lk.16:11). If we are not faithful with the things of this world and our finances, God will never commit unto us the true riches of His kingdom.

Faithful in that which is another man's. "And if ye have not been faithful in that which is another man's, who shall give you that which is your own?" (Lk.16:12). In order for the Lord to give us a ministry or position of our own, we must be faithful to those God places in authority over us, doing things their way. When we are placed in charge of a work, then we can run things the way we think they should be run.

Faithful as stewards in the mysteries of God. "Let a man so account of us, as of the ministers of Christ, and stewards of the mysteries of God. Moreover it is required in stewards, that a man be found faithful" (1 Cor. 4:1-2). We must also be faithful in the realm of doctrine and the Word of God, especially if we are teachers. There was a well-known minister in England many years ago who believed in a certain doctrine because that was the doctrine his denomination embraced. Every time he read a verse that contradicted this teaching, he would quickly turn the page in his Bible and not read that verse again. However, the Lord eventually convicted him of this, and he changed his doctrine. This is an area in which God holds ministers extremely responsible. We must be sure that what we believe and teach is what the Word of God really teaches.

Faithful in the realm of sexual purity. "Now concerning virgins I have no commandment of the Lord: yet I give my judgment, as one that hath obtained mercy of the Lord to be faithful" (1 Cor. 7:25). Paul said that the Lord had shown him mercy to remain faithful in the realm of being unmarried. At that time, Paul had probably been a widower for many years.

People say to me when they are struggling with temptation in this very area, "But you don't know the temptations I face, Pastor." However, Paul clearly says in First Corinthians 10:13, "There hath no temptation taken you but such as is *common* to man: but God is faithful, who will not suffer you to be tempted above that ye are able; but will with the temptation also make a way to escape, that ye may be able to bear it." Where sin or temptation abounds, grace can much more abound. By God's grace and mercy it is possible to be faithful in this area and keep ourselves pure.

It does not matter what stage of life we are in, we are commanded to be faithful. Wives are exhorted to be faithful in First Timothy 3:11: "Even so must their wives be grave, not slanderers, sober, faithful in all things." Children must also be faithful (Titus 1:6). Therefore, let us seek for this virtue to be fully developed in our lives so that we are faithful in the natural things and in spiritual things.

8. MEEKNESS

The eighth fruit of the Spirit is meekness. Meekness is an inwrought work of God's grace. This fruit makes us pleasing to the Lord, for it is highly treasured in His eyes. Peter tells us that "a meek and quiet spirit is of great price in the sight of God" (1 Pet. 3:4). Meekness is strength controlled. It is perhaps the virtue that epitomizes strength the most. This fruit of the Spirit is actually great strength and control of our spirit so that we do not respond or react when people oppose us and persecute us. Meekness is the strength of character that does not retaliate or defend itself. Instead, it enables us to see everything as coming from the Lord's hand. Make no mistake about it, meekness is not weakness. Jesus is the meekest man who ever lived, and He is also the strongest man who ever lived.

This fruit is the embracing of Romans 8:28, where Paul says, "And we know that all things work together for good to them that love God, to them who are the called according to his purpose." Those who possess this precious virtue have their eyes totally fixed upon the Lord, and they *accept* whatever He brings their way. Meekness could be defined as "a holy acceptance of one's circumstances with joy."

The fact is that everything that happens to us is ultimately permitted by the Lord. Therefore, if we seek to defend and justify ourselves, we are actually rejecting the Lord's purposes for our lives. For this reason, meekness deals with our relationship with the Lord more than it does with our relationship with others. For meekness to be developed in our lives toward others, it must first be worked out in our hearts toward the Lord.

The Greek word for meekness portrays the thought of an animal that has been *tamed*. For example, when a colt is young, it runs around totally unrestrained and unhindered. It is beautiful to watch colts run around in such a care-free manner. However, as this horse grows older, if it is to be of any use, its spirit and will must be broken so that it acknowledges its new master and obeys the slightest movement of the reins in his hands.

There is a beautiful illustration of meekness in the Song of Songs, when the Lord says to His Bride, "I have compared thee, O my love, to a company of horses in Pharaoh's chariots" (Song.1:9). In the days of King Solomon and at the time of the writing of the Song of Songs, the best horses in the world came from Egypt, and the finest horses would obviously have been used for Pharaoh's chariots. The thought expressed here is that of a company of horses standing motionless, waiting for the command of their master. These horses were known for their submissiveness, instantaneous obedience, and their broken wills which were totally submitted to their master. This is one of the most beautiful illustrations of meekness in the whole of the Word of God. This is an accurate description of a meek man or woman—their wills are submissive and obedient to the Lord Jesus.

Meekness is one of the chief virtues of the Lord Jesus Christ. He testified in Matthew 11:29 that He is "meek and lowly in heart." The first time my wife and I went to Israel, our tour group went to see the Garden Tomb of Jesus. Once we had seen it and come out, I went back in by myself. I took my shoes off, knelt down by the tomb, and said to the Lord, "Lord, what are You like?" Then written across the tomb I saw the word "meekness." This is the quality by which the Lord wants to be known. I realized after this experience that I had another inclination He wanted to circumcise from my life so that He could replace it with His meekness.

The animal that best portrays the fruit of meekness is the lamb. Lambs are harmless. The nature of Christ the Lamb of God is revealed in Isaiah 53:7: "He was oppressed, and he was afflicted, yet he opened not his mouth: he is brought as a lamb to the slaughter, and as a sheep before her shearers is dumb, so he openeth not his mouth." The Lord Jesus epitomized the character of meekness when He stood silent before Pilate during His mock trial, and did not defend Himself against the false accusations that were brought up against Him. As a lamb does not respond when it is sheared of all that it possesses, so Christ did not react when He was stripped of His robes, dignity, honor, and life by the Jews. Even Pilate marveled at the great control Jesus had of His spirit as he was able to refrain from defending Himself.

The fruit that parallels meekness is myrrh. Myrrh was the embalming fluid in Bible times. Therefore, myrrh represents death. This is also true of meekness, for meekness is a complete separation from self and our personal feelings. A truly meek person is not occupied with self and overly concerned about his rights being vindicated. When we have meekness worked out in our lives, we see everything from God's point of view. This enables us to overcome injustices and offenses.

Meekness is such a rare virtue. Few people ever bring this fruit to maturity in their lives. There are only two people in the whole of Scripture who are called meek—the Lord Jesus and Moses. After Christ, Moses was the meekest man who ever lived. God's testimony of Moses was this: "Now the man Moses was very meek, above all the men which were upon the face of the earth" (Num.12:3). From the life of Moses, we can see how meekness is developed. As with all the fruits, meekness is produced through its opposite, which is anger. It is only in an atmosphere of anger that meekness can truly be developed in our lives. This is the way it was worked out in the lives of Moses and Christ, and it is the way it will be worked out in our lives too. Moses constantly had forces opposing him and trying to provoke his spirit. As Moses yielded to the workings of the Lord in his life, he was eventually made meek.

As we have already said, those who have meekness do not seek their own revenge, but they allow the Lord to fight for them. King David was such a man. He had a broken and contrite heart. However, he obtained this fruit at a very costly price. On one occasion, a man named Shimei of the house of Saul cursed David.

"And when king David came to Bahurim, behold, thence came out a man of the family of the house of Saul, whose name was Shimei, the son of Gera: he came forth, and cursed still as he came. And he cast stones at David, and at all the servants of king David: and all the people and all the mighty men were on his right hand and on his left. And thus said Shimei when he cursed, Come out, come out, thou bloody man, and thou man of Belial: The Lord hath returned upon thee all the blood of the house of Saul, in whose stead thou hast reigned; and the Lord hath delivered the kingdom into the hand of Absalom thy son: and, behold, thou art taken in thy mischief, because thou art a bloody man" (2 Sam.16:5-8).

Some of David's men wanted to kill Shimei for treating the king like this. David's reply to this request was: "What have I to do with you, ye sons of Zeruiah? so let him curse, because the Lord hath said unto him, Curse David. Who shall then say, Wherefore hast thou done so? And David said to Abishai, and to all his servants, Behold, my son, which came forth of my bowels, seeketh my life: how much more now may this Benjamite do it? let him alone, and let him curse; for the Lord hath bidden him. It may be that the Lord will look on mine affliction, and that the Lord will requite me good for his cursing this day" (2 Sam.16:10-12).

What a beautiful attitude David had. This is a true picture of meekness. David *accepted* this mistreatment by Shimei because he realized that God was in control of everything, and recognized that this had been sent from the Lord.

We must be careful of *false* meekness in our pursuit of *true* meekness. As we said in the introduction, there is a counterfeit to every fruit of the Spirit. Revelation 13:11 describes the false prophet, who will arise in the last days with the Antichrist, as having "two horns like a lamb, but he spoke like a dragon." He will have the outward appearance of meekness like a lamb, but inwardly he will be full of the devil. Christ also warned of false prophets who come in sheep's clothing, but are wolves inwardly (see Mt. 7:15). There is a false meekness that is only outward. It is passive and it compromises God's standards in order not to offend others. This is not true meekness.

Righteousness is the foundation for meekness, as it is for all of the fruits of the Spirit. Those who are not walking uprightly always seek to defend themselves and justify their ways in the eyes of man because deep down in their hearts they know that God's approval is not upon their lives. By the same token, those who are righteous do not feel a need to vindicate themselves because they know they have done nothing wrong, and they know that God will eventually make it clear who is right.

Righteousness and meekness are linked together in Zephaniah 2:1-3. "Gather yourselves together, yea, gather together, O nation not desired; Before the decree bring forth, before the day pass as the chaff, before the fierce anger of the Lord come upon you, before the day of the Lord's anger come upon you. Seek ye the Lord, all ye meek of the earth, which have wrought his judgment; seek righteousness, seek meekness: it may be ye shall be hid in the day of the

Lord's anger." There is an exhortation by the prophet Zephaniah to seek righteousness and meekness so that we may be hidden and protected in the day when God's judgments are poured out upon the earth.

One of the primary messages of the last day Church will be restoration. For us to have a part in this glorious ministry of restoration, we must have the fruit of meekness developed in our lives, as set forth by the Apostle Paul in Galatians 6:1. "Brethren, if a man be overtaken in a fault, ye which are spiritual restore such an one in the spirit of *meekness,* considering thyself lest thou also be tempted." We must treat backsliders with great kindness and gentleness, making them feel accepted, and yet at the same time we must not compromise God's standards. This difficult task is accomplished through the spirit of meekness.

There is an admonition by Paul in Second Timothy 2:24 to teachers to instruct in meekness. "And the servant of the Lord must not strive; but be gentle unto all men, apt to teach, patient." Without this precious ingredient in our teaching, all we will do is offend people, rather than win them to the Lord. I cannot stress enough the importance of this. We must not preach and teach in a legalistic manner, but in the spirit of meekness.

Blessings of Meekness

Now let us consider briefly a few of the blessings that come upon those who allow the Lord to work out the fruit of meekness in their lives.

The meek inherit the earth. Quoting Psalm 37:11, the Lord Jesus said in Matthew 5:5, "Blessed are the meek: for they shall inherit the earth." This is a very important truth. Meekness is necessary for us to obtain our inheritance, spiritual or natural. I am reminded of a certain missionary I was talking to some time ago. At the time of our conversation, he was having an altercation with the director of the mission field where he was ministering, and he could not get along with him. This man refused to submit to the director of this work. He even told me, "I am not in submission to him," and then asked for my counsel.

After I prayed, I felt led by the Lord to say to him, "That which will save your ministry and give you an inheritance in the land of your calling is meekness. Unless you become submissive to your director and accept the orders of those in authority over you, you will not remain in your inheritance." Unfortunately, this man did not heed this word from the Lord. As a result, today he is not enjoying the inheritance God had prepared for him.

The meek are taught God's ways and guided by Him. Psalm 25:9 says, "The meek will he guide in judgment: and the meek will he teach his way." To know God's ways and be guided in judgment by Him, we must have meekness worked out in our lives. Psalm 103:7 states that Moses knew God's *ways*, but the children of Israel only saw His *acts*. Moses knew what God did and why He did it. He understood His ways; whereas the children of Israel only saw His acts. The reason for this is that Moses was meek and the Israelites were not.

The meek increase their joy in the Lord. Joy is one of the fruits of meekness. Isaiah 29:19 says, "The meek also shall increase their joy in the Lord." One of the fruits of meekness is joy. The meek increase their joy in the Lord because they realize that everything is working out for their good. In closing, may I just encourage you to allow the Lord to develop the precious fruit of meekness in your life, for it is so essential to our eternal inheritance.

9. TEMPERANCE

The ninth fruit of the Spirit is temperance. Temperance in the original Greek language means to have the mastery over our desires and the love of pleasures. This applies to every area of our lives, not just liquor and food. For this reason, without temperance we will not succeed in the Christian life.

This fruit could also be translated "self-control" or "Spirit-controlled." I want to emphasize that temperance is a fruit *of the Spirit*. It is not something we can produce by our own efforts. Many people practice forms of self-denial that are very grievous and harmful to the human body. This must never be mistaken for the fruit of temperance. Remember, however, that although temperance is a divine work of the Spirit, there is our part too. We are the ones who have to exercise self-control, but we do it through the help of the Holy Spirit.

Paul gives us a very good illustration of self-control in First Corinthians 9:24-27: "Know ye not that they which run in a race run all, but one receiveth the prize? So run, that ye may obtain. And every man that striveth for the mastery is temperate in all things. Now they do it to obtain a corruptible crown; but we an incorruptible. I therefore so run, not as uncertainly; so fight I, not as one that beateth the air: But I keep under my body, and bring it into subjection: lest that by any means, when I have preached to others, I myself should be a castaway."

Here Paul uses the natural illustration of an athlete to describe temperance. Athletes have one goal and desire in life—to win the prize and to win the particular event in which they participate. Athletes must be very disciplined and have tremendous self-control. A true athlete is one who is an athlete twenty-four hours a day. Paul tells us that if we are not temperate, we could end up being castaways and be rejected by the Lord.

When I played soccer while I was in the Royal Air Force in England, there was a very famous soccer player, also in the Air Force, who gave me some very wise counsel that I have remembered all of my life. He said to me: "To be a good soccer player, you must stay away from wine, women, and pleasures. You must dedicate yourself completely to soccer." In the very same way, to win God's best in the Christian life we must have self-control, and we must dedicate ourselves completely to the Lord and to the Gospel.

Proverbs 21:17 gives us a very serious warning: "He that loveth pleasure [or sport] shall be a poor man: he that loveth wine and oil shall not be rich." We must be careful what we give ourselves and our time to. Temperance really means that we have everything in our lives in its proper place and perspective, so that nothing in our lives is over-prioritized or under-prioritized.

For example, it is good to relax and rest at times. Someone saw the Apostle John feeding some fish one day. Surprised, they asked him, "How is it possible for an apostle of the Lamb to be spending time feeding fish?" John replied: "A bow must not be taut all the time. It must be released occasionally so that it can straighten out." It is good to relax at times to get our minds off our pressures and to be refreshed. However, if that is all we ever do, we will never accomplish anything in life. Temperance enables us to have a proper balance in our lives.

Many years ago I was preaching on the subject of temperance in the northeastern United States. As I was speaking, I asked the Lord to give me an illustration to make my point very clear. Then I saw a coffee pot before me. I said to the congregation, "If a person wants to drink coffee, that is perfectly fine, but you must not be bound by coffee." I thought this was a good illustration, and I thought that surely it would not apply to anyone there.

However, after the service a lady came up to me and said: "The Lord gave you the illustration of the coffee pot for me. My husband was offered a promotion by his boss to go to a certain country, but I told him that we could not go there because they did not know how to make good coffee in that country. I am completely bound by coffee. I must have it in the morning, at noon, and in the evening, and many times in between. Will you please pray for me to get deliverance from this bondage?" We prayed with her, and I trust that she has freedom in this area today. I hope you can see how important it is for us to have self-control in every area of our lives, even in things which are seemingly insignificant.

There are certain things that are bad for us and wrong for us to do because they can easily lead us away from the Lord. These things we must avoid all together. However, there are other things that are not technically wrong for us, and even good in themselves, but in excess they are bad. We must be careful that we do not allow pleasures, hobbies, and sports to govern our lives. We must always have the control over everything in our lives and not be bound by anything. In First Corinthians 7:9 Paul speaks of having control over our sexual desires. "But if they cannot contain [or control themselves], let them marry: for it is better to marry than to burn." Paul uses the same Greek word here for "contain" that he does for "temperate" in First Corinthians 9:25. This is an area in which we must absolutely have self-control. A lack of moral temperance could result in one's eternal destruction.

We also must have control over our tongue. James 3:2 says: "For in many things we offend all. If any man offend not in word, the same is a perfect man, and able also to bridle [or control] the whole body." The tongue is the most difficult member of our body to tame and control. The words we speak come from the very depths of our hearts (see Mt. 12:34). If you want to know what kind of a person you are, just listen to yourself speak for a while. It will reveal your spiritual condition.

Perfection involves having our tongues submitted to the Spirit of God. May we pray with David, "Set a watch, O Lord, before my mouth; keep the door of my lips" (Psa.141:3). We need to have self-control over our body, our mind, our emotions, our tongue and our spirit. Let us seek the Lord and ask Him to develop this fruit in our lives so that it spares us from becoming *castaways* because of something in our life that is out of order that can eventually lead us away from the Lord.

Conclusion

The fruits of the Spirit, which are an extension of love, may be understood from Paul's first epistle to the Corinthians, chapter 13. Here Paul enunciates the qualities of love by saying that love bears with people for a very long time, and is sweet at all times with the most trying and difficult dispositions. But in order that the fruits of the Spirit may come to perfection, such maladies as envy, rashness, pride, and behavior unbecoming to a Christian must be extirpated out of our lives.

Also, self-seeking motives cannot dwell with love. An attitude that is easily offended or meditates and stores up evil against other people cannot dwell with a loving spirit. Certainly, any kind of pleasure in sinful practices would be like a little fox that spoils the fruit of the Spirit in our hearts. Love, however, desires truth and supports with much graciousness and kindness those who are battling against and trying to overcome sinful areas in their lives. Love believes, hopes and encourages, and is willing to endure the shortcomings of others but never fails them in their hour of need. Beloved, may these characteristics which come about through the development of the fruits of the Spirit be manifested in our lives. In so doing we shall become more and more like our blessed Lord Jesus.

Part Seven

THE SPIRIT-FILLED AND SPIRIT-LED LIFE

THE SPIRIT-FILLED LIFE

Being filled with the Spirit is a blessing that is available to all of the Lord's people who will obey him (Acts 5:32). It is essential to be baptized in the Holy Spirit with the initial evidence of speaking in other tongues (Acts 2:1-4). Although this experience is a one time event, we need renewals of the Holy Spirit, as evidenced in Acts 4:31. "And when they had prayed, the place was shaken where they were assembled together; and they were all filled [again] with the Holy Ghost, and they spake the word of God with boldness." The same disciples who had been initially baptized in the Holy Spirit on the day of Pentecost were filled again with more of the Holy Spirit in this prayer meeting.

Paul gives the Church instructions from Ephesians 5:18-19 concerning the Spirit-filled life. He gives us many keys to having a free flow of the Spirit in our lives. He begins in verse 18 by exhorting each believer to be filled (*present tense*, continuous action) with the Holy Spirit. There must be a constant, progressive enlargement of our spiritual capacity to receive more and more of the Holy Spirit. How are we filled with more of the Holy Spirit?

The Apostle Paul explains in Ephesians 5:19 how to achieve this continuous infilling: "Speaking to yourselves in psalms and hymns and spiritual songs, singing and making melody in your heart to the Lord." We have a ministry to ourselves. Christians are instructed to speak to themselves in the Holy Ghost. I would now like to illustrate this from several scriptures.

Psalm 43 was written while King David was fleeing from his son Absalom. David was greatly outnumbered; yet his greatest problem was not from outside, but from within. His soul was in a deep pit of depression. In verse 5, he addressed his soul and said: "Why art thou cast down, O my soul? and why art thou disquieted within me? hope in God: for I shall yet praise him, who is the health of my countenance, and my God."

David spoke to his discouraged soul and commanded it to hope in God; he took the ascendancy over his soul and emotions, which were running wild. We do not have to be soulish and allow our emotions to rule us, nor should we. This only leads to turmoil and disaster. We can overcome our soulish nature through the continual infilling of the Holy Spirit.

Many people have said to me, "But you don't understand, Pastor, I am an emotional person, and I always have been." Well, that may be true, but is that how you want to remain for the rest of your life? We all have a soul and emotions. They are a very real part of our makeup. But do you want to live the whole of your life governed by your emotions? Soulish people are very moody. They are happy when things are going well, but discouraged when things do not go the way they wanted them to. Is that the kind of person you want to be? Or do you want to be a spiritual person, with your emotions subjugated to the anointing of the Holy Spirit? Of course, the answer is that we want to be Spirit-controlled, not controlled by our soul. However, we can only truly be *controlled* by the Spirit if we are *filled* with the Spirit.

King David spoke to his soul because his soul was cast down. Do you know what the phrase "cast down" means? It is an old English expression used of a sheep who has rolled over on its back. When a sheep is rolled over on its back, it will normally stay there until it dies because it cannot lift itself up, and it gives up trying. This was how David's soul was feeling. He was thinking to himself, "I am lost. There is no hope. Absalom is going to take my life." But then David rose up and said to his soul, "Why have you given up?" He was a very spiritual man. The decision to be soulish or spiritual is ours. Are we going to be emotional or spiritual? The key to being spiritual is to take the ascendancy over our emotions by speaking to our soul and allowing the life of the Spirit to flow through us.

In John 4:14, the Lord Jesus said to the woman at the well, "Whosoever drinketh of the water that I shall give him shall never thirst; but the water that I shall give him shall be in him a well of water springing up into everlasting life." This is what God does for us when we come to Him and receive Him as our Savior. He puts within us a well of bubbling water, which is the Holy Spirit.

This work of the Holy Spirit in our lives can be seen symbolically in the Old Testament when God promised the children of Israel that He would give them water in the wilderness (Num. 21:16). "Then Israel sang this song, Spring up, O well; sing ye unto it" (Num. 21:17). In other words, we have to sing unto the well that is within us, and as we sing our well bubbles up.

It is one thing to have this well of the Holy Spirit within our hearts; however, it is another thing to keep this well from becoming blocked. Isaac cleared out the wells which his father Abraham had dug, because the Philistines had stopped them up with earth (Gen. 26:15). The Philistines are representative of envy.

We must be very careful that envy does not take root within us because it can be a boulder that stops up the well in our lives. Later on there were other problems that he had, and we find that strife and hatred also stopped up his wells (see Gen. 26:20-21). These enemies of the Spirit in our lives, and any other of the works of the flesh can block the well within us (Gal. 5:19-21).

How do we get our spiritual wells free if they have been stopped up by one of the sins mentioned above? We are given the key in Numbers 21:18. "The princes digged the well, the nobles of the people digged it, by the direction of the lawgiver, with their staves." This is not recorded in Holy Scripture just for a historical fact. It was included for the purpose of instructing us. You will notice that it was the *princes* that digged these wells.

In actuality, it is to show us that if the wells of our heart get stopped up, we must go to the princes (our pastors and leaders) to receive the remedy to our problem. God-appointed leaders have the Spirit of counsel upon them to discern what is blocking our well. The princes or leaders built these wells under the direction of Moses, the one in supreme authority. Therefore, under the direction of the Holy Spirit, the ministers of God should have the ability to show people how to get freedom in their lives.

With all of this said, we should understand that the baptism of the Holy Spirit is not necessarily a sign that someone is mature. As a matter of fact, it is given to those who are babes in Christ. This thought-provoking fact is clearly seen in Hebrews 6:2, which speaks of the doctrine of baptisms as being one of the elementary principles of Christ. Sometimes the Lord will save and baptize believers with the Holy Ghost all in one day. Nevertheless, it is important to constantly be filled with His Spirit, irrespective of our level of maturity.

THE SPIRIT-LED LIFE

Flowing out from the Spirit-filled life is the truth of being led by the Spirit. Those who are continuously seeking the Lord for more of His Spirit, and are following the steps mentioned above, become eligible to experience the Spirit-led life. While it is true that we do not have to be filled with the Spirit to experience His leading on an *elementary* level, if we are going to experience the *fullness* of being sovereignly guided by the Spirit, we must be baptized in the Holy Spirit.

In contrast to the baptism of the Holy Spirit, the *Spirit-led life* is something quite different. It is experienced by those who are mature in Christ. Paul makes this clear in Romans 8:14, where he said, "For as many as are led by the Spirit of God, they are the [mature] sons of God." The term "sons of God" refers to *mature sons* of God in the original Greek, not *babes* in Christ.

Paul says in Galatians 5:25, "If we live in the Spirit, let us also walk in the Spirit." In other words, the Lord wants all of our steps to be directed by Him because He has a plan for our lives. He has preplanned our lives before the foundation of the world for His divine purposes. Jeremiah said, "O Lord, I know that the way of man is not in himself: it is not in man that walketh to direct his steps" (Jer. 10:23). We cannot direct our lives by our own mind because our lives have been preordained. Therefore, we need to be led by the Holy Spirit so that we fulfill God's plan for our lives.

One of the promises for the Church Age (and for Israel in the Millennium) is seen in Ezekiel 36:27: "And I will put my spirit within you, and cause you to walk in my statutes, and ye shall keep my judgments, and do them." In this verse, the Lord is saying to us, "I am going to ensure that you fulfill My purposes through the Holy

Spirit who will cause you to walk in My ways." Let us now consider several examples of being led by the Spirit in the Scriptures, and then we will see how to achieve this glorious spiritual state.

OLD TESTAMENT EXAMPLES OF THE SPIRIT-LED LIFE

In choosing a bride: Eliezer, the servant of Abraham, was led by the Spirit in the matter of selecting a bride for Isaac. He confessed, "I being in the way the Lord led me" (Gen. 24:27). In effect, he was saying, "By staying on God's path, God has brought me to the right person." As he searched for a bride for Isaac, Eliezer requested a sign from God, and because Rebekah fulfilled that sign, she was chosen to be Isaac's bride.

Direction: The guidance of the Holy Spirit is seen in the whole journey of the children of Israel. Moment by moment, throughout their wilderness journey, the Israelites were led by the cloud and the pillar of fire (Ex. 13:21). The Spirit led them into tests, but also into many victories. Ultimately, the Spirit brought them into the land of promise, into God's purposes for their lives.

Confirmation and assurance: We can also see in the life of Gideon how he received the Spirit's assurance that God was with him when he placed a fleece before the Lord (Judg. 6:36-40). The Lord further encouraged Gideon by giving him a dream that assured him of victory (Judg. 7:12-15).

Receiving the battle plan: King David experienced the leading of the Holy Spirit on numerous occasions. However, in this section we are only going to mention just two of them to help illustrate that the Old Testament saints experienced precise guidance by the Spirit. When David was threatened by the Philistines after his third anointing at Hebron, he inquired of the Lord what he should do. Through the agency of the Holy Spirit, the Lord gave him the battle plan. We read of this account in Second Samuel 5:19: "David inquired of the Lord, saying, Shall I go up to the Philistines? wilt thou deliver them into mine hand? And the Lord said unto David, Go up: for I will doubtless deliver the Philistines into thine hand."

After this battle, the Philistines came up against David again. David took nothing for granted. Again he sought the Lord for His direction. This time the battle plan was different, even though the circumstances were the same. "And the Philistines came up yet again, and spread themselves in the valley of Rephaim. And when David inquired of the Lord, he said, Thou shalt not go up; but fetch a compass behind them, and come upon them over against the mulberry trees. And let it be, when thou hearest the sound of [a going in the tops of] the mulberry trees, that then thou shalt bestir thyself: for then shall the Lord go out before thee, to smite the host of the Philistines. And David did so, as the Lord had commanded him; and smote the Philistines from Geba until thou come to Gazer" (2 Sam. 5:22-25).

Provision: The prophet Elijah was directed by the Spirit when he was commanded to hide by the brook Cherith. It was here that God brought provision. Later, when the brook dried up, the Spirit further directed him to a widow's house. Here again the prophet was sustained because he obeyed the voice of the Spirit (see 1 Kings 17:2-8).

Instruction: "Arise, and go down to the potter's house, and there I will cause thee to hear my words" (Jer. 18:2). Jeremiah was told to go to a particular place, and *there* God would cause him to hear His words. Sometimes God sends us to special places where He can speak something fresh and new to our hearts. Jeremiah needed a tangible object lesson, so the Spirit sent him to the potter's house. He saw a marred vessel in the hands of the potter, and that same vessel was remolded by the potter into a good one.

"Then the word of the Lord came to me, saying, O house of Israel, cannot I do with you as this potter? saith the Lord. Behold, as the clay is in the potter's hand, so are ye in mine hand, O house of Israel" (Jer. 18:5-6). After watching the potter, Jeremiah returned to the congregation with a new message. He declared that God was able to totally remake lives that have been warped and marred by sin, thus bringing hope to fallen humanity.

NEW TESTAMENT EXAMPLES OF THE SPIRIT-LED LIFE

The Life of Jesus

Throughout the earthly life of the Lord Jesus Christ, not only was He directed by the Holy Spirit, but others who were involved at major junctures of His life were directed as well. For example, at His birth, the wise men experienced guidance through the means of a star, as recorded in Matthew 2:1-2. "Now when Jesus was born in Bethlehem of Judea in the days of Herod the king, behold, there came wise men from the east to Jerusalem, Saying, Where is he that is born King of the Jews? for we have seen his star in the east, and are come to worship him." These men were supernaturally led right to the birth place of Jesus (Mt. 2:9-10).

Then a few days later in the temple, a godly man named Simeon was led by the Spirit to the baby Jesus. "And, behold, there was a man in Jerusalem, whose name was Simeon; and the same man was just and devout, waiting for the consolation of Israel: and the Holy Ghost was upon him. And it was revealed unto him by the Holy Ghost, that he should not see death, before he had seen the Lord's Christ. And he came by the Spirit into the temple: and when the parents brought in the child Jesus, to do for him after the custom of the law, Then took he him up in his arms, and blessed God…" (Lk. 2:25-28). At the same moment, the Holy Spirit guided the prophetess Anna to Jesus (Lk. 2:36-38).

In reality, the whole life of Jesus was Spirit-controlled and Spirit-guided. We will now examine four occasions in His life to illustrate this truth.

Morning by morning: "The Lord God hath given me the tongue of the learned, that I should know how to speak a word in season to him that is weary: he wakeneth morning by morning, he wakeneth mine ear to hear as the learned" (Isa. 50:4). The Lord's testimony was that at the beginning of each day, as He spent time in prayer and waiting upon His Father, the Holy Spirit would unfold to Him the plan of God for that day. This prepared Him for the discourses He would have to give on that particular day, and also gave Him a sense of direction as to which cities and localities He should go.

Led into the wilderness: Immediately after His baptism by John, the Lord was led of the Spirit into the wilderness to be tested for forty days by the devil (Mt. 4:1). Mark 1:12 tells us that the Spirit "driveth Him into the wilderness." It is also the Spirit of God that leads us into the wilderness experiences of our Christian walk where we are tested. However, we can be assured that just as the Spirit leads us into the wilderness, He will lead us out victoriously as He did the Lord Jesus.

Led to a particular city and to a particular woman: As the Lord was departing from Judea for Galilee, He felt urged in His spirit and constrained to go through the town of Samaria. "And he must needs go through Samaria" (Jn. 4:4). The Spirit of God was directing Him to Samaria for a distinct purpose, that He might come in contact with a certain woman who would evangelize a whole city and reap a mighty harvest for the Lord after she herself drank of the Fountain of Living Waters (Jn. 4:39).

A little experience that my wife and I had might help to illustrate the necessity of being in a certain place appointed by God. We did not want to go to a particular town because there was a church in that town which I knew we would have to attend if we passed through. We were hesitant to go there because the pastor's wife had a very sharp tongue. Unfortunately, she was in the habit of verbally lashing out at those who were not in good standing with her, or those who had sought to correct her spiritually; which, in all honesty, she needed! Therefore, I determined to take another route.

However, about three o'clock in the morning of our departure, the Lord woke me up abruptly. I went into another room and knelt down by a chair. At this moment, I received a vision of the bleeding face of Christ. The scripture that came to me was Isaiah 50:6: "I gave my back to the smiters, and my cheeks to them that plucked off the hair: I hid not my face from shame and spitting." From this verse, I knew that we would have to go through that town and go to that church. As we expected, the pastor's wife sought us out at the end of the service, and verbally abused us until we felt as though the skin of our cheeks had been ripped off. However, after that experience we felt great joy because of our obedience. To some small degree, we felt like the disciples who rejoiced to have been counted worthy to partake of the fellowship of Christ's sufferings (see Acts 5:41).

Led to the Cross: In the culmination of Christ's mission and work upon earth, which was to offer Himself upon the cross, He was led and enabled by the Spirit to fulfill His commission from His Father. Paul says in Hebrews 9:14, "How much more shall the blood of Christ, who through the eternal Spirit offered himself without spot to God, purge your conscience from dead works to serve the living God?" Thus, it was through the dealings of the Holy Spirit in His life that Christ was enabled to be that Lamb of God without spot or blemish. Likewise, it is only through the agency of the Holy Spirit that we can be presented spotless before His Presence with great joy (Jude 1:24). It is also by the Spirit that we mortify the deeds of the flesh (Rom. 8:13).

Philip the Evangelist

One of the most unusual and extraordinary leadings of the Holy Spirit in the life of a believer was surely in the ministry of Philip. He was responsible for a city-wide revival in Samaria. Acts 8:5-8 records this wonderful move of God. "Then Philip went down to the city of Samaria, and preached Christ unto them. And the people with one accord gave heed unto those things which Philip spake, hearing and seeing the miracles which he did. For unclean spirits, crying with loud voice, came out of many that were possessed with them: and many taken with palsies, and that were lame, were healed. And there was great joy in that city."

However, in the midst of this tremendous outpouring of the Spirit of God, the Holy Spirit directed Philip to leave and go toward Gaza in the wilderness (Acts 8:26). To the natural mind, this would seem like a relatively fruitless endeavor compared to the revival he left behind in Samaria. Yet in the economy of God, the Lord wanted Philip to minister to just one man in the desert. This man was an Ethiopian eunuch, and he was the treasurer of the Queen of Ethiopia. By virtue of his position, he was a man of great authority and influence.

As he sat in his chariot reading the book of Isaiah, without understanding what he was reading, the Spirit told Philip to go up to him (Acts 8:29). By the Spirit, Philip opened up this man's understanding of the Scriptures and preached Jesus unto him. As a result of this man's conversion to Christ, the church in Ethiopia was founded. Thank God for the obedience of Philip to the leading of the Holy Spirit in his life.

After Philip baptized this man, the Spirit of the Lord caught away Philip, and he was supernaturally transported to the town of Azotus, where he continued to preach the gospel of Christ (Acts 8:39-40). As we have already said, this act of being transported by the Spirit will be a feature of the last day revival to enable the gospel to be preached in many inaccessible places.

The Apostle Peter

Peter was the apostle to the circumcised (Gal. 2:8), yet the Lord chose him in a very singular way to open up the gospel to the Gentiles. The Holy Spirit gave Peter a vision to assure him of God's acceptance of the Gentiles (Acts 10:9-16). At the same time the Lord was preparing the vessel who would take the gospel to the Gentiles, He was also preparing the recipients. In this case, God chose the house of Cornelius, who was a Roman centurion. In a vision, the Lord told Cornelius to call for Peter (Acts 10:1-5). While Peter was meditating upon the vision he had received, the Spirit said unto him, "Behold, three men seek thee. Arise therefore, and get thee down, and go with them, doubting nothing: for I have sent them" (Acts 10:19-20). Cornelius had sent a few of his servants to invite Peter to come preach to him and his household. Thus, Peter, the devout Jew who for many years would not even eat with Gentiles, was commanded by the Holy Spirit to minister to them.

I cannot claim an experience of this magnitude, but a similar situation arose when the Holy Spirit led me to preach in a denomination that was different than my own. In the beautiful garden nation of Singapore, I had the privilege for several years of ministering, whenever I was in that part of the world, in a certain main-line Pentecostal denomination. However, on one trip we had sent a letter as usual to the pastor, but the letter did not arrive.

I said to my wife in our hotel room, "Well, dear, it looks like we will just have to rest for a few days before we continue on to our next scheduled country." As soon as I had said these words, I saw the word "purpose" in a vision. It was only a half an hour later that we met a delightful vicar of the Anglican church, who later introduced us to a wonderful Christian who was the Bishop of Singapore at that time. He invited us to preach the truth of the baptism of the Holy Spirit in his churches, resulting in many coming into the Pentecostal blessing.

It is so important for us to be like Peter and realize that the Lord does not want us to be limited to our own denominational family and fellowship. The Lord wants our bough to go over the wall as Joseph's did (see Gen. 49:22). We must not be exclusive. Rather, we should be open to receive from and minister to every member of the Body of Christ.

The Apostle Paul

His selection for missionary service: "As they ministered to the Lord, and fasted, the Holy Ghost said, Separate me Barnabas and Saul for the work whereunto I have called them. And when they had fasted and prayed, and laid their hands on them, they sent them away. So they, being sent forth by the Holy Ghost, departed unto Seleucia; and from thence they sailed to Cyprus" (Acts 13:2-4).

The Holy Spirit made His will known for Paul to be sent out as a missionary. Not only was Paul sent out by the Spirit, he was constantly led and guided by the Spirit in all of his missionary journeys and travels. The Holy Spirit was very active in the early Church. Through prophecy the Holy Spirit revealed whom He had chosen for certain ministries. We are also experiencing this in our days, as the Lord confirms His callings through the prophetic gifts and through the laying on of hands.

His second missionary journey: The Holy Spirit directed the paths of Paul and his traveling companions in a very precise manner during his second missionary journey. "Now when they had gone throughout Phrygia and the region of Galatia, and were forbidden of the Holy Ghost to preach the word in Asia" (Acts 16:6). The Holy Spirit was leading Paul in a very unique fashion. There obviously must have been a very strong presence of the Spirit with him. The Holy Spirit, at this particular time, was actually forbidding them to tarry in Asia to preach the Word of God there, because the Lord had another place in mind.

At this juncture, the apostles could have been tempted to give up and return to Antioch, the place from where they had originally departed. Instead, they practiced what we call "guidance in motion." They kept going until they received precise instruction from the Holy Spirit to change their course.

This truth was made very real to my wife and me when we were in the Cameroons a number of years ago. We had felt that we were to leave the Cameroons and go on to Zaire, and we had written to a Christian guest house in the capital city. However, we did not realize that Kinshasa had over two million inhabitants, and we had addressed the letter to this particular guest house in Kinshasa without giving a street address.

When we did not receive a reply from the guest house, we began to wonder what we should do. Well, one afternoon as I was lying down on my bed for a much needed rest, I watched a colony of ants moving on the wall opposite my bed. Those who are acquainted with the maneuvers of these hardy and industrious little creatures know that they first send out little "spies" who determine the path for the rest of the ants.

As I watched these little forerunners go across the wall, I noticed that there was a certain portion of the wall stained with kerosene. This kerosene caused the ants to lose their scent, and therefore they could not pick up the trail of the previous ant. I watched intently as some, in bewilderment, turned back and did not get to the desired goal. Others, however, kept plodding on, and after they went through the kerosene barrier, they picked up their scent and guidance again.

That demonstration, of course, was a sign to me. I knew the Lord was telling me to keep going forward with my plans to go to Kinshasa. He was assuring me that as I did I would pick up my course again, even though I had not received a response to my letter. We boarded the plane at Douala in the Cameroons, and we arrived very early the next morning in Zaire. For the whole duration of the flight, the Holy Spirit was speaking to me, "My angel will be there when you arrive."

However, I was not feeling very victorious at that time in the morning, so I said to my wife, "We might as well wait for the others to get off the plane first." When we finally disembarked, we saw a dear Christian brother whom we had never met holding up a sign with our names in bold print. He was the angel the Lord had promised. What had happened is that our letter had been received, but their reply did not reach us before we left.

The Apostle Paul kept on going forward until the Spirit revealed something different to him. "After they were come to Mysia, they assayed to go into Bithynia: but the Spirit suffered them not. And they passing by Mysia came down to Troas. And a vision appeared to Paul in the night; There stood a man of Macedonia, and prayed him, saying, Come over into Macedonia, and help us. And after he had seen the vision, immediately we endeavoured to go into Macedonia, assuredly gathering that the Lord had called us for to preach the gospel unto them" (Acts 16:7-10).

Again the Holy Spirit changed their direction. He would not allow them to go to Bithynia. The Spirit of God was leading and directing the lives of the apostles in a very forcible manner. After this they went to Troas, and during the night, the Apostle Paul received a vision from the Lord in which he received a call to Macedonia.

Finally, after being blocked twice by the Holy Spirit, the Spirit guided Paul and his companions to the place He had in store for them. Later, they came back to Asia at the appointed time, led of the Spirit, and Paul remained in Ephesus for about two or three years. The whole of the province of Asia heard the gospel through the preaching of Paul at this time, but it was in the timing of God. If we will yield to the Holy Spirit and begin walking in the Spirit, we will feel His gentle promptings and leadings.

A Canadian pastor friend and myself had the reverse experience of Paul's Macedonian call. Many years ago we were in Berlin ministering to a delightful German congregation. As we were seeking the Lord about where we should go next, He spoke to us to go to Greece. We returned for a few days to Switzerland. Then, taking the Orient express, we went to Italy and then down to Brindisi. We crossed by ship over the Adriatic Sea through the Corinth canal to Pireaus, where we were met by a dear Greek pastor. He most graciously escorted us to his home and we stayed there for a while and ministered to his congregation.

However, we did not feel that we were completely fulfilling our call to Greece. So, later we journeyed by train to a little town in the shadow of Mount Olympus. Here we were warmly received by a pastor who had been alerted of our coming by the pastor in Athens, and we ministered in his church. After the first service, the pastor told us this story.

Several weeks before, while we were still in Berlin and we were praying for guidance, the Holy Spirit had given a vision to a very spiritual lady in this particular assembly. In this vision, she saw that the church had mud on the interior walls. Then she saw two light-complexioned men enter and start to clean the walls. The Holy Spirit then said to her, "Tell the pastor to pray for God to send these men to the church to clean it and make it a fit dwelling place for the Lord." The first night of meetings she recognized us as the two men that she had seen in the vision. Truly, we praise the Lord for the way the Holy Spirit leads and guides God's people!

His final journey to Jerusalem: After Paul left Ephesus, he was warned repeatedly by the Holy Spirit concerning the bonds and imprisonments that awaited him in Jerusalem. Paul himself testified in Acts 20:22-23: "And now, behold, I go bound in the spirit unto Jerusalem, not knowing the things that shall befall me there: Save that the Holy Ghost witnesseth in every city, saying that bonds and afflictions abide me." This warning was repeated at Tyre. "Now when we had discovered Cyprus, we left it on the left hand, and sailed into Syria, and landed at Tyre: for there the ship was to unlade her burden. And finding disciples, we tarried there seven days: who said to Paul through the Spirit, that he should not go up to Jerusalem" (Acts 21:3-4).

Much has been written on whether Paul was going against the Holy Spirit's guidance at this moment in his life. I personally feel that he was wrong in continuing his journey to Jerusalem. However, the Lord is able to turn around all of our well-intentioned mistakes and bring us back on course again. The following is my personal testimony of the Lord's graciousness in my own life.

Many years ago while my wife and I were visiting a certain Bible School, we were invited to minister there. However, things were not well spiritually at this place and God showed me in a vision that this college was a *Sardis* type fellowship—having a name that they were alive and yet in reality they were spiritually dead (cf. Rev. 3:1).

Because of this revelation of the terrible spiritual state of the school, I was determined to leave. Yet just before I left, I received an invitation to be on the faculty. I should also say that before this invitation had been given, the Lord told me to listen to what the president of the school had to say to me. I was so absorbed with the vision, however, that I did not listen, and I left that place.

One year later, after a very fruitless detour, the Lord most graciously brought me back to the school, and I remained there on the faculty for several years. A number of the students I taught there have been with me for almost thirty years now, and they themselves have risen to the status of international ministers of repute. The Lord has truly been very merciful to me over the years, in spite of misinterpreting at times the leadings of the Holy Spirit.

CONCLUSION

As you have been musing over these chapters concerning the Person and ministry of the blessed Holy Spirit, you may have felt that this intimacy with the third Person of the Holy Trinity is not possible for you. This is quite untrue. He longs for you to be filled with His power and anointings, and He wants you to come into that place of knowing His continual leadings and guidance in your life. It is, therefore, with this thought in mind that I would like to conclude with these little thoughts and examples that I trust will be a source of help and encouragement to you.

Two very godly Canadian ministers, who were certainly experiencing God's blessings upon their lives and ministries, had covenanted in desperation to meet together for prayer. They resolved not to leave the room until they had received a special visitation in the area of guidance from the Holy Spirit. They began to pray at eight o'clock that particular morning and by three o'clock in the afternoon they had still not received a word from the Holy Spirit. Then the Spirit spoke to them, "Do according to the wisdom you have been given." They were perplexed.

Later that afternoon I arrived and they asked me my feelings on the matter. I clearly felt that they were already on the path the Lord had for them, and that they did not need any particular guidance from the Holy Spirit at that time. Thus, I told them just to continue in the direction they were already going.

The illustration that I gave them was of being on a road to a certain town. If you are on the right path you do not need signposts telling you that you are going in the right direction. It is only when you leave that path that you need signposts to inform you that you are off the path and to direct you back on the path again.

For example, if you are traveling from New York City to Buffalo, you would get on the four lane highway in New York City and stay on it the whole time until you arrive in Buffalo. You do not need signs along the way to tell you to keep on going, because you are on the right path. However, if you get off this road and get lost, you would need signs to lead you back to the freeway. This is true concerning walking in the Spirit.

The scripture that came to my mind while I was speaking with these two ministers was from Isaiah 30:21: "And thine ears shall hear a word behind thee, saying, This is the way [the path you were on and then turned from], walk ye in it, when ye turn to the right hand, and when ye turn to the left." Through the prophet Isaiah the Lord promises to warn us and lead us back to the right way when we get off it and begin to go in a way contrary to the Lord's will for our lives.

At that moment, these godly ministers felt a real peace from the Holy Spirit. So you see, in the Spirit-led life we do not necessarily hear the Spirit of God speaking to us moment by moment. Guidance often means walking in the wisdom that the Lord has already given to us.

Peace is one of the greatest keys to the Spirit-led life, because the Apostle Paul tells us that peace is our *umpire*. The Greek word for "rule" in Colossians 3:15 literally means "an umpire." Peace lets us know how we are doing spiritually. The indwelling peace of God will bear witness with our hearts if we are making the right choices. However, if we leave the path of God, then the peace of God will lift from our hearts and we will begin to feel the convicting work of the Holy Spirit telling us that we are making a mistake.

Whenever I have to counsel people, I check my spirit to see whether I feel peace about what I want to say to them. When we feel the peace of God leave us, we should immediately stop and inquire of the Lord where we missed His leading. Of course, when we have major decisions to make, we must always ask counsel of the Lord. At all times, we should seek to be sensitive to that small voice within.

I would like to conclude our message on the Holy Spirit with two little examples that were so precious to me at the time of their occurrence. Both happened around the time I was writing this chapter, and they both involve elevator rides in hotels in which I was staying. The first one was while I was in India with a group of ministers. We were conducting a teaching seminar for ministers. On one particular day, I did not have to speak until later in the morning, so I had planned to have breakfast at eight o'clock. I got in the elevator and pressed the button for the ground floor where the restaurant was located.

However, the elevator stopped at the second floor because someone had already summoned the elevator to that floor. When the elevator doors opened, I felt the Holy Spirit speak to me to get out on that floor. After I got out of the elevator, not really knowing what I was going to do next, I saw a sign pointing to a hair salon. The Spirit then directed me with His gentle promptings to get a haircut. I desperately needed a haircut so this did not bother me at all. I was also happy to see that I was the first customer, so I did not have to wait in line. Naturally, I thought that the Holy Spirit was being very kind to me.

After my haircut, I went to the restaurant which by this time was emptying fast. As I was quickly seated, I sat in a comfortable chair contemplating the goodness of the Lord. After I finished my bowl of oatmeal, which I eat for breakfast whenever I can throughout the world, a young man approached me. He appeared quite agitated, but very relieved to see me. He had a problem that was very pressing, and he needed an immediate solution, and the Holy Spirit most graciously gave me the answer for him. I then realized that if I had not obeyed the Holy Spirit's promptings, I would have missed a very important appointment in the plan of God for this young man.

Another time I was staying on the eighteenth floor of a hotel in the state of New Mexico. The pastor had arranged to pick me up for the evening service at 7:20 p.m. But at seven o'clock the Spirit told me to go to the elevator. So I packed my briefcase, went to the elevator and pressed the button to summon it. However, no elevator came. I waited about ten minutes and then the Spirit told me to walk down the stairs.

When I arrived at the first floor, I discovered that the elevators were out of service. It was then that I began to understand that the Holy Spirit had actually caused me to wait ten minutes so I would know He was with me and guiding me with precision. I am happy to say that I reached the lobby at the very moment the pastor arrived. It was such a joy to feel the Holy Spirit leading me so gently. If I had left my room at the usual time I would have been late, and I would not have had the beautiful comfort of knowing that the Holy Spirit was constantly watching over me and directing everything I did. I might also add that we had a glorious service that night, as the Holy Spirit took me away from my notes and ministered as only He can to the needs of the congregation.

Let me finish by quoting again Ezekiel 36:27 where God promises to pour His Holy Spirit upon us and cause us to walk in His ways. "And I will put my Spirit within you, and cause you to walk in my statues, and ye shall keep my judgments, and do them." This is that which God desires to do for His children, that we might all be filled with and led by the beloved Holy Spirit to fulfill all the good works that God has ordained for us to do in our own individual lives. Beloved, the Holy Spirit truly is the Comforter sent forth by the Father and the Son to tenderly care for us. May we all come to know Him more and more intimately, day by day. Amen.

EPILOGUE

We trust that this little book on the beloved Comforter has been a blessing to you! We have sought to present the third Person of the Godhead in a way that you might desire to know Him more intimately, even as you know our beloved Savior, the Lord Jesus Christ, the One whom the Holy Spirit has been sent to exalt.

In these pages we have set forth the qualities of the life and ministry of the Holy Spirit, showing the diverse aspects of His ministry to the body of believers who form the Church of Jesus Christ. In particular, we have endeavoured to show the difference between the anointings of the seven Spirits of the Lord, contrasting them with the nine spiritual gifts, which are manifested as a result of the baptism in the Holy Spirit. Then we encouraged balance in the life of the believer with an exhortation to major in the fruits of the Spirit.

The concluding chapter shows believers how to live a life that is filled and led by the Holy Spirit so that we might fulfill Paul's admonition: "Walk in the Spirit and ye shall not fulfill the lusts of the flesh." The Spirit-filled and Spirit-led life should be our goal and desire, for they enable us to fulfill the righteousness of God in our own lives. In so doing, we shall see at the end of our lives the beautiful face of our Savior and hear those lovely words from His lips: "Well done thou good and faithful servant, enter thou into the joy of thy Lord." May this be so for each one of us.

It was through the Holy Spirit that the Lord Himself fulfilled His calling upon earth. The Holy Comforter has been sent by the Father and the Son to encourage and strengthen us so that we also fulfill our course triumphantly. Seek to know Him, beloved, and in so doing you will feel His presence walking alongside you throughout your journey from earth to heaven.

OTHER BOOKS AVAILABLE BY DR. BRIAN J. BAILEY

Studies in the Lives of David and Solomon

The Three Houses of Esther

Ruth (The Gentile Bride of Christ)

The Bride

The Journey of Israel

Daniel

Romans (More Than Conquerors)

Isaiah

Colossians and Philemon

Pillars of Faith

Hebrews (Within the Veil)